ZAGATSURVEY.

2003
LONDON RESTAURANTS

Edited and coordinated by
Sholto Douglas-Home, Susan Kessler
and Randi Gollin

Published and distributed by
ZAGAT SURVEY, LLC
4 Columbus Circle
New York, New York 10019
Tel: 212 977 6000
E-mail: london@zagat.com
Web site: www.zagat.com

Acknowledgments

We thank Lisa Bauer, Deborah Bennett, Sarah Bluet, Karen Bonham, Caroline Clegg, Ricki Conway, Alex, Louis and Tallulah Douglas-Home, Ray Fine, Amanda Fox, Sandra and Michael Howard, Barbara Illias, Larry Kessler, Le Cordon Bleu, Pamela and Michael Lester, Margaret Levin, Jenny Linford, Ben and Sheila Miller, Zoë Miller, Jean Oddy, Taryn Pember, Zoë Price, Natasha Robinson, Molly Rouse, Anne Semmes, Clare Sievers, Alexandra Spezzotti, Peter Vogl, Susan and Jeffrey Weingarten and Vanessa Whicker.

This guide would not have been possible without the hard work of our staff, especially Betsy Andrews, Reni Chin, Anna Chlumsky, Larry Cohn, Carol Diuguid, Jessica Gonzalez, Katherine Harris, Diane Karlin, Natalie Lebert, Mike Liao, Dave Makulec, Laura Mitchell, Rob Poole, Robert Seixas, Daniel Simmons and Sharon Yates.

The reviews published in this guide are based on public opinion surveys, with numerical ratings reflecting the average scores given by all survey participants who voted on each establishment and text based on direct quotes from, or fair paraphrasings of, participants' comments. Phone numbers, addresses and other factual information were correct to the best of our knowledge when published in this guide; any subsequent changes may not be reflected.

© 2002 Zagat Survey, LLC
ISBN 1-57006-395-8
Printed in the United States of America

Contents

What's New....................................	5
About This Survey	6
Key to Ratings & Symbols	7
Most Popular Places	9
TOP RATINGS	
By Food; Cuisines, Features, Locations	10
By Decor; Outdoors, Romance, Rooms, Views	15
By Service	16
Best Buys..................................	17
RESTAURANT DIRECTORY	
Names, Addresses, Phone & Fax Numbers,	
Ratings and Reviews....................	19
INDEXES	
Cuisines	172
Locations	182
Special Features	192
All-Day Dining	192
Breakfast/Brunch	193
Business Dining.......................	193
BYO...................................	194
Celebrity Chefs........................	195
Cheeseboards	195
Child-Friendly.........................	196
Critic-Proof	197
Dancing/Entertainment................	197
Delivery/Takeaway	198
Dining Alone	199
Fireplaces	199
Game in Season	200
Historic Places	201
Hotel Dining	201
"In" Places	202
Late Dining...........................	203
No Smoking Sections	203
Noteworthy Newcomers...............	204
Offbeat	205
Outdoor Dining	205
People-Watching	206
Power Scenes	207
Pre-Theatre Menus	207
Private Rooms	208
Pubs/Microbreweries	210
Pudding Specialists...................	210
Quiet Conversation	210
Romantic Places	211
Senior Appeal	211
Set-Price Menus.......................	212

Singles Scenes........................213
Sleepers 214
Smoking Prohibited...................214
Special Occasions 215
Sunday Dining 215
Tea Service...........................217
Visitors on Expense Account 218
Water Views..........................219
Winning Wine Lists 219

Wine Chart............................220

What's New

No matter the economic climate, London's appetite for lively dining destinations continues unabated, inspiring ever-bolder ventures. For every notable closing (cheznico, Neat Restaurant, Oak Room Marco Pierre White, to name a few), there's another restaurateur waiting in the wings, often joined by an expensive team of architects and designers.

High Stakes: In recent months alone, several multimillion-pound hot spots have opened around town. The gigantic Café Grand Prix, a £5 million development, zoomed into Mayfair, and so did the sleek Sumosan, an offshoot of a Moscow-based chain, which cost almost half as much. Zuma, another rumoured £2 million investment, debuted in Knightsbridge and is generating a major buzz. Much like trailblazer Nobu (voted this *Survey*'s Most Popular), Sumosan and Zuma serve sexy, fashionable Japanese food in equally dazzling settings.

Signature Style: Some of the city's most revered chefs have also borne offspring, many in classy hotels. Albert Roux unveiled Brasserie Roux in the Sofitel St. James London, whilst Gordon Ramsay added Claridge's and the revamped Connaught (with several restaurants due to open this autumn) to his string of accomplishments and Giorgio Locatelli brought Locanda Locatelli to the Churchill Inter-Continental. Meanwhile, Nico Ladenis opened Deca in Mayfair, and Marco Pierre White refurbished the venerable Wheeler's in St. James's.

Plucky Places: Smart spots are ever in demand, still, there's always room for spirited newcomers like The Electric, a brasserie in Portobello Road; La Trompette, a New French yearling in Chiswick; and Timo, a Modern Italian Zafferano sibling.

Crystal Ball: Whatever the future holds, restaurateurs are hell-bent on lining up more tempting ventures. As we go to press, Cru, a trendy restaurant/bar, is due to open in a Hoxton warehouse, and Edera, another Italian undertaking from A to Z, in Holland Park Avenue. Also in the works: Hospi+al, a multimillion-pound food, music and arts complex, backed by Eurythmics star Dave Stewart (reportedly involving American chef Charlie Trotter), who is also re-launching the Islington rock club Marquee with a top-notch restaurant boasting chef Garry Hollihead; and Sketch, a lavish Conduit Street venture from French chef Pierre Gagnaire and Momo's Mourad Mazouz.

Price Point: There's every reason to believe that our vibrant restaurant scene will continue to thrive. In the past year, the average price for a meal in London has risen over 4 percent, to £32.15, a relative bargain compared to Tokyo (£38.72), but not quite the deal found in New York City (£23.82) or Paris (£29.96).

Wimbledon, London
13 September, 2002

Sholto Douglas-Home

About This Survey

For 24 years, Zagat Survey has reported on the shared experiences of diners like you. Here are the results of our *2003 London Restaurant Survey,* covering some 957 restaurants. This marks the seventh year we have covered restaurants in London.

By regularly surveying large numbers of avid local restaurant-goers about their collective dining experiences, we hope to have achieved a uniquely current and reliable guide. For this book, nearly 3,700 people participated by paper ballot and another 1,800 registered their opinions via the Internet. Since the participants dined out an average of 2.4 times per week, this *Survey* is based on over 500,000 meals annually.

The real authors of this guide are the surveyors, 42% of whom are women, 58% men; the breakdown by age is 22% in their 20s, 36% in their 30s, 17% in their 40s, 15% in their 50s and 10% in their 60s or above. The one thing this diverse group has in common is a love of food. To produce the reviews in this guide, our editors synopsized these surveyors' opinions, with their exact comments shown in quotation marks.

Of course, we are especially grateful to our editor/coordinators: Sholto Douglas-Home, a London restaurant critic for 16 years, and Susan Kessler, cookbook author and consultant for lifestyle publications in the U.K. and U.S.

To help guide our readers to London's best meals and best buys, we have prepared a number of lists. See Most Popular (page 9), Top Ratings (pages 10–16) and Best Buys (page 17). To assist the user in finding just the right restaurant for any occasion, without wasting time, we have also provided 42 handy indexes and have tried to be concise.

As companions to this guide, we also publish the upcoming *London Nightlife, Europe's Top Restaurants* and *Top International Hotels,* as well as *Zagat Surveys* and Maps to more than 70 other markets around the world. For more information, go to **www.zagat.com**, where you can also vote and shop.

To join our **London Survey** or any of our other upcoming *Surveys*, you can request a ballot by registering at zagat.com and then selecting the *Survey* in which you'd like to participate. Each participant will receive a free copy of the resulting guide when it is published.

Your comments, suggestions and even criticisms of this *Survey* are also solicited. There is always room for improvement with your help. You can contact us at london@zagat.com or by mail at Zagat Survey, 4 Columbus Circle, New York, NY 10019. We look forward to hearing from you.

New York, NY
13 September, 2002

Nina and Tim Zagat

Key to Ratings/Symbols

Name, Address, Tube Stop, Phone* & Fax

Hours & Credit Cards

Zagat Ratings

F	D	S	C
▽ 23	5	9	£9

Tim & Nina's Fish Bar ◐ S ⌀

Exeter St., WC2 (Covent Garden), 020-7123 4567; fax 020-7123 4567

◪ Open seven days a week, 24 hours a day (some say that's "168 hours too much"), this "cheerful" and "chaotic" Covent Garden stalwart serving "cheap, no-nonsense" fish 'n' chips is an "ideal, dingy spot" for a "quick grease fix"; no one's impressed by the "tired, tatty decor" or "patchy service", but judging from its "perpetual queues", the food's worth it.

Review, with surveyors' comments in quotes

Restaurants with the highest overall ratings and greatest popularity and importance are printed in CAPITAL LETTERS.

Before each review a symbol indicates whether responses were uniform ■ or mixed ◪.

Hours: ◐ serves after 11 PM
S open on Sunday

Credit Cards: ⌀ no credit cards accepted

Ratings: Food, Decor and Service are rated on a scale of **0** to **30**. The Cost (C) column reflects our surveyors' estimate of the price of dinner including one drink and service.

F	Food	D	Decor	S	Service	C	Cost
23		5		9		£9	

0–9 poor to fair   **20–25** very good to excellent
10–15 fair to good   **26–30** extraordinary to perfection
16–19 good to very good   ▽ low response/less reliable

A place listed without ratings is either an important **newcomer** or a popular **write-in**. For such places, the estimated cost is indicated by the following symbols.

I	£15 and below	**E**	£26 to £35
M	£16 to £25	**VE**	£36 or more

* When calling from outside the U.K., dial international code + 44, then omit the first zero of the number.

www.zagat.com

Most Popular

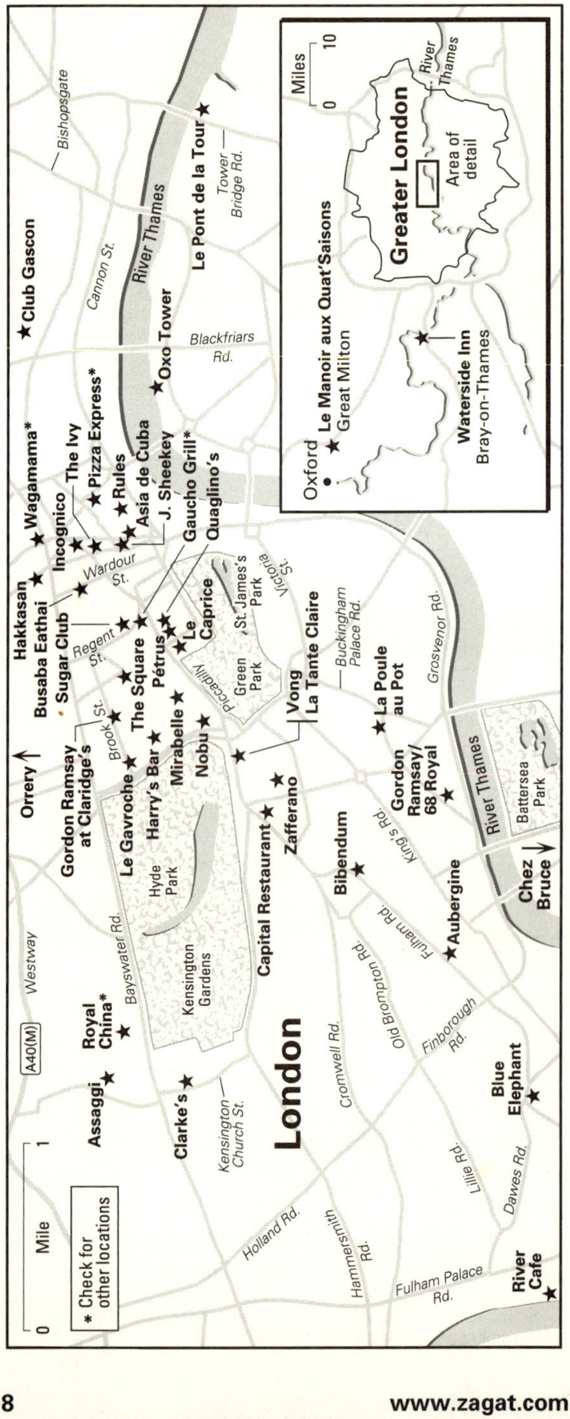

Greater London

- Le Manoir aux Quat'Saisons — Great Milton
- Waterside Inn — Bray-on-Thames
- Oxford

London

- Club Gascon
- Le Pont de la Tour
- Oxo Tower
- Wagamama*
- Incognico
- The Ivy
- Pizza Express*
- Rules
- Asia de Cuba
- J. Sheekey
- Gaucho Grill*
- Quaglino's
- Hakkasan
- Busaba Eathai
- Sugar Club
- Le Caprice
- The Square
- Pétrus
- Orrery
- Gordon Ramsay at Claridge's
- Le Gavroche
- Harry's Bar
- Mirabelle
- Nobu
- Vong
- La Tante Claire
- La Poule au Pot
- Zafferano
- Gordon Ramsay/68 Royal
- Capital Restaurant
- Bibendum
- Aubergine
- Chez Bruce
- Royal China*
- Assaggi
- Clarke's
- Blue Elephant
- River Cafe

*Check for other locations

8   www.zagat.com

Most Popular

Each of our reviewers has been asked to name his or her five favourite restaurants. The places most frequently named, in order of their popularity, are:

1. Nobu
2. Ivy, The
3. Gordon Ramsay/68 Royal
4. Le Caprice
5. Square, The
6. Le Gavroche
7. Zafferano
8. Mirabelle
9. River Cafe
10. Gordon Ramsay at Claridge's
11. J. Sheekey
12. Asia de Cuba
13. Bibendum*
14. Le Manoir/Quat'Saisons†
15. Royal China
16. Blue Elephant
17. Pétrus
18. Club Gascon
19. Sugar Club
20. Pizza Express
21. Assaggi
22. Wagamama
23. Chez Bruce
24. Oxo Tower
25. Hakkasan
26. La Tante Claire
27. Clarke's
28. Rules
29. Waterside Inn†
30. Aubergine
31. Gaucho Grill*
32. Busaba Eathai
33. Le Pont de la Tour
34. Capital Rest.
35. Quaglino's
36. Orrery
37. La Poule au Pot
38. Incognico
39. Harry's Bar (club)
40. Vong

It's obvious that many of the restaurants on the above list are among the most expensive, but if popularity were calibrated to price, we suspect that a number of other restaurants would join the above ranks. Given the fact that both our surveyors and readers love to discover dining bargains, we have added a list of 80 Best Buys on page 17. These are restaurants that give especially high quality at extremely reasonable prices.

---

* Tied with restaurant directly above it
† Outside London

www.zagat.com

Top Ratings

Top lists exclude restaurants with low voting.

Top 40 Food Rankings

- **28** Gordon Ramsay/68 Royal
- **27** Le Gavroche
  La Trompette
  Nobu
  Le Manoir aux Quat'Saisons †
  Pétrus
  Gordon Ramsay at Claridge's
- **26** Chez Bruce
  Waterside Inn †
  Ubon
  Square, The
  Richard Corrigan
  Monsieur Max
  La Tante Claire
  Capital Rest.
  Club Gascon
  Mosimann's (club)
- **25** Clarke's
  Pied à Terre
  Vama

  Zafferano
  Foliage
  J. Sheekey
  Tatsuso
  L'Oranger
  River Cafe
  Ishbilia
  Aubergine
- **24** Assaggi
  Le Soufflé
  French Horn †
  Roussillon
  Jin Kichi
  Mju
  Four Seasons, Quadrato
  Tentazioni
  Mark's Club (club)
  L'Escargot
  Gravetye Manor †
  Le Caprice

Top Food by Cuisine

British (Modern)
- **26** Chez Bruce
  Richard Corrigan
- **25** Clarke's
- **24** Gravetye Manor †
  City Rhodes

British (Traditional)
- **24** French Horn †
  Mark's Club (club)
  Dorchester, Grill Room
- **23** Savoy Grill
  Wilton's

Chinese
- **24** Kai
- **23** Mandarin Kitchen
  Royal China
  Hunan
  Dorchester, Oriental

Chophouses
- **23** Rib Room & Oyster Bar
- **22** Smiths of Smithfield-Top Fl.
- **21** Rules
- **20** Gaucho Grill
  Quality Chop House

Eclectic/International
- **26** Mosimann's (club)
- **23** Blakes Hotel
  Four Seasons, Lanes
- **22** Providores Rest./Tapa Room
  Archipelago

Fish 'n' Chips
- **22** Sweetings
- **21** Two Brothers Fish
  Nautilus Fish
- **18** Rudland Stubbs
  Livebait

French (Bistro)
- **26** Monsieur Max
- **22** Incognico
  Le Café du Marché
- **21** La Poule au Pot
  L'Aventure

French (Classic)
- **27** Le Gavroche
- **26** Waterside Inn †
  La Tante Claire
- **25** Foliage
- **24** L'Escargot

† Outside London

Top Food

French (New)
- *28* Gordon Ramsay/68 Royal
- *27* La Trompette
- Le Manoir/Quat'Saisons †
- Pétrus
- Gordon Ramsay at Claridge's

Greek
- *22* Real Greek
- *20* Halepi
- *19* Daphne
- *18* Lemonia
- *16* Beoty's

Indian
- *25* Vama
- *24* Sarkhel's
- *23* Tamarind
- Zaika
- Rasa

Italian
- *25* Zafferano
- River Cafe
- *24* Assaggi
- Four Seasons, Quadrato
- Tentazioni

Japanese
- *27* Nobu
- *26* Ubon
- *25* Tatsuso
- *24* Jin Kichi
- Cafe Japan

Mediterranean
- *22* Moro
- Eagle, The
- *21* Nicole's
- *19* Rocket
- *18* Oxo Tower Brasserie

Mexican/Tex-Mex/SW
- *18* Montana
- *17* La Perla Bar & Grill
- Canyon
- Dakota
- *15* Cafe Pacifico

Middle Eastern
- *25* Ishbilia
- *23* Noura
- *21* Maroush
- Fairuz
- *20* Al Sultan

Modern European
- *25* J. Sheekey
- *24* Le Caprice
- *23* Ivy, The
- *22* Brown's Hotel, Rest. 1837
- *21* Le Pont de la Tour

North American
- *20* Prospect Grill
- *19* Christopher's American Grill
- *16* PJ's Grill
- Joe Allen
- Arkansas Cafe

Pacific Rim
- *23* Blakes Hotel
- Sugar Club
- *20* I-Thai
- Polygon Bar & Grill
- *18* Oxo Tower Brasserie

Pizza
- *24* Pizza Metro
- *21* Pizzeria Castello
- *20* Red Pepper
- West Street
- *19* Friends

Seafood
- *25* J. Sheekey
- *23* Poissonnerie de l'Avenue
- Wilton's
- *22* One-O-One
- Creelers

Spanish
- *24* Eyre Brothers
- *22* Moro
- *21* Cambio de Tercio
- *20* Gaudí
- Cigala

Thai
- *23* Vong
- *22* Busaba Eathai
- Mango Tree
- *21* Blue Elephant
- Patara

Vegetarian
- *24* Roussillon
- *23* Rasa
- Blah! Blah! Blah!
- *21* Gate, The
- Food for Thought

---

† Outside London

www.zagat.com

Top Food
Top Food by Special Feature

Breakfast*
- 23 Cinnamon Club
- 19 Patisserie Valerie
- Tom's Deli
- 18 Simpson's/Strand/Grand Divan
- Bank Aldwych

Brunch
- 25 Clarke's
- 24 Le Caprice
- 22 Providores Rest./Tapa Room
- Smiths of Smithfield-Top Fl.
- 19 Villandry

Cafes
- 21 Truc Vert
- Bibendum Oyster Bar
- 19 Patisserie Valerie
- Tom's Deli
- Carluccio's Caffe

Cheeseboards
- 28 Gordon Ramsay/68 Royal
- 27 Le Gavroche
- Pétrus
- 26 Square, The
- 25 Pied à Terre

Child-Friendly
- 24 Pizza Metro
- 21 Blue Elephant
- 20 La Famiglia
- 16 Fifth Floor Cafe
- 14 Sticky Fingers

Hotel Dining (London)
- 27 Nobu
  - Metropolitan
- Gordon Ramsay at Claridge's
  - Claridge's Hotel
- 26 La Tante Claire
  - Berkeley Hotel
- Capital Rest.
  - Capital, The
- 25 Foliage
  - Mandarin Oriental

In-Store Eating
- 22 Books for Cooks
- 21 Nicole's
- 19 Fifth Floor
- Carluccio's Caffe (Fenwick)
- 17 Cafe at Sotheby's

* Other than hotels

Lunch
- 27 Nobu
- 26 Club Gascon
- 23 Ivy, The
- 20 Monte's
- Drones

Meet for a Drink
- 23 Cinnamon Club
- 21 E&O
- Cecconi's
- 20 Smiths of Smithfield-Din. Rm.
- 18 Avenue

Newcomers/Rated
- 24 Eyre Brothers
- 22 Providores Rest./Tapa Room
- Almeida Rest.
- Mango Tree
- 21 E&O

Newcomers/Unrated
- Deca
- Locanda Locatelli
- Racine
- Timo
- Zuma

Offbeat
- 26 Club Gascon
- 22 Providores Rest./Tapa Room
- Archipelago
- Books for Cooks
- 20 Asia de Cuba

Olde England
- 24 Ritz (1906)
- 23 Wilton's (1742)
- 22 Sweetings (1889)
- 21 Rules (1798)
- 19 Simpson's/Strand/Simply (1828)

Outdoor
- 25 River Cafe
- 22 Smiths of Smithfield-Top Fl.
- 21 La Poule au Pot
- Le Pont de la Tour
- 20 Belvedere, The

People-Watching
- 27 Nobu
- 23 Ivy, The
- 22 Hakkasan
- 20 Drones
- 19 San Lorenzo

Top Food

Private Clubs – Members Only
- 26 Mosimann's
- 24 Mark's Club
- 23 Harry's Bar
- 21 George
- 19 Annabel's

Private Rooms
- 27 Nobu
- Gordon Ramsay at Claridge's
- 26 Square, The
- 23 Mirabelle
- Dorchester, Oriental

Pub Dining
- 22 Eagle, The
- 21 Havelock Tavern
- Churchill Arms
- 20 Chiswick, The
- Duke of Cambridge

Rooms with a View
- 27 Nobu
- 25 Foliage
- 22 Putney Bridge
- Smiths of Smithfield-Top Fl.
- 21 Le Pont de la Tour

Sunday Lunch/Town
- 25 Zafferano
- River Cafe
- 24 Orrery
- 23 Wilton's
- 20 Belvedere, The

Sunday Lunch/Country
- 27 Le Manoir aux Quat'Saisons
- 26 Waterside Inn
- 24 French Horn
- Gravetye Manor
- Fat Duck

Tasting Menus
- 28 Gordon Ramsay/68 Royal
- 27 Nobu
- 26 Square, The
- La Tante Claire
- Capital Rest.

Tea Service
- Brown's Hotel
- Connaught Hotel, The
- Lanesborough, The
- Ritz Hotel
- St. Martin's Ln./Tuscan Steak

Theatre District
- 26 Richard Corrigan
- 25 J. Sheekey
- 23 Ivy, The
- 22 Incognico
- 20 West Street

Wine Bars
- 22 Cellar Gascon
- L'Estaminet
- 21 Bleeding Heart
- 16 Ebury Wine Bar
- 15 Le Metro

Top Food by Location

Belgravia/Knightsbridge
- 26 La Tante Claire
- Capital Rest.
- 25 Zafferano
- Foliage
- Ishbilia

Bloomsbury
- 25 Pied à Terre
- 23 Rasa
- 22 Hakkasan
- Passione
- Le Cabanon

Canary Wharf
- 26 Ubon
- 24 Four Seasons, Quadrato
- 23 Royal China
- 20 Gaucho Grill
- Wapping Food

Chelsea
- 28 Gordon Ramsay/68 Royal
- 25 Vama
- Aubergine
- 23 Poissonnerie de l'Avenue
- 22 Creelers

City
- 25 Tatsuso
- 24 City Rhodes
- 23 Lahore Kebab House
- City Miyama
- Don, The

Clerkenwell/Smithfield
- 26 Club Gascon
- 22 Cellar Gascon
- Maison Novelli
- Moro
- Smiths of Smithfield-Top Fl.

www.zagat.com

Top Food

Covent Garden/Soho
- *26* Richard Corrigan
- *25* J. Sheekey
- *24* L'Escargot
- *23* Ivy, The
  Savoy Grill

Hampstead
- *24* Jin Kichi
- *21* Nautilus Fish
  Gate, The
- *20* Singapore Garden
  Gaucho Grill

Islington
- *22* Almeida Rest.
- *20* Frederick's
  Metrogusto
  Duke of Cambridge
- *19* Granita

Kensington
- *25* Clarke's
- *23* Zaika
  Koi
- *22* Launceston Place
  Memories of China

Marylebone
- *24* Orrery
  John Burton-Race
- *23* Royal China
  Defune
- *22* Providores Rest./Tapa Room

Mayfair
- *27* Le Gavroche
  Nobu
  Gordon Ramsay at Claridge's
- *26* Square, The
- *24* Le Soufflé

Notting Hill
- *24* Assaggi
- *22* Books for Cooks
  Chez Moi
- *21* E&O
  Osteria Basilico

South Kensington
- *23* Blakes Hotel
  Bibendum
- *21* Patara
  Lundum's
  Bibendum Oyster Bar

St. James's
- *27* Pétrus
- *25* L'Oranger
- *24* Le Caprice
  Ritz
  Suntory

In the Country
- *27* Le Manoir aux Quat'Saisons
- *26* Waterside Inn
- *24* French Horn
  Gravetye Manor
  Fat Duck

Top 40 Decor Rankings

27 Ritz
26 Les Trois Garcons
   Hakkasan
25 Le Manoir aux Quat'Saisons †
   Momo
   Waterside Inn †
   Criterion Grill
   Mosimann's (club)
   Gravetye Manor †
   Mark's Club (club)
24 Hartwell House †
   Gordon Ramsay at Claridge's
   Cliveden Hotel, Waldo's †
   Blakes Hotel
   Savoy River Rest.
   Lanesborough Conservatory
   Archipelago
   La Porte des Indes
   Four Seasons, Lanes
23 Blue Elephant
   Cinnamon Club
   Gordon Ramsay/68 Royal
   Home House (club)
   Belvedere, The
   French Horn †
   I-Thai
   Oxo Tower
   Dorchester, Grill Room
   Souk
   Bam-Bou
22 Harry's Bar (club)
   Wapping Food
   Le Gavroche
   Putney Bridge
   Sir Charles Napier †*
   Asia de Cuba
   Rules
   Bibendum
   Vineyard at Stockcross †
   Square, The

Outdoors

Belvedere, The
Coq d'Argent
Dan's
La Famiglia
La Poule au Pot
Le Colombier
Le Pont de la Tour
Oxo Tower
Ransome's Dock
Ritz
River Cafe
Rosmarino
Smiths of Smithfield-Top Fl.
Spoon+ at Sanderson

Romance

Andrew Edmunds
Blakes Hotel
Club Gascon
Criterion Grill
Gordon Ramsay/68 Royal
Julie's
La Poule au Pot
Launceston Place
Lundum's
Mirabelle
Momo
Odin's
Richard Corrigan
Ritz

Rooms

Asia de Cuba
Aurora
Cecconi's
Cinnamon Club
Criterion Grill
Drones
Hakkasan
Les Trois Garcons
Locanda Locatelli
Momo
Prism
Ritz
Square, The
Zuma

Views

Belair House
Blue Print Cafe
Cafe, Level Seven
Coq d'Argent
Foliage
Le Pont de la Tour
Nobu
Oxo Tower
People's Palace
Putney Bridge
Smiths of Smithfield-Top Fl.
Thai on the River
Ubon
Waterside Inn †

† Outside London
* Tied with the restaurant listed directly above it

www.zagat.com

Top 40 Service Rankings

27 Gordon Ramsay/68 Royal
26 Le Gavroche
 Mark's Club (club)
 Le Manoir aux Quat'Saisons †
 Waterside Inn †
25 Ritz
 Mosimann's (club)
 Monsieur Max
 Capital Rest.
 Dorchester, Grill Room
24 La Tante Claire
 Square, The
 Four Seasons, Lanes
 Le Soufflé
 Gravetye Manor †
 Goring Dining Room
 Gordon Ramsay at Claridge's
23 Oslo Court
 John Burton-Race
 Pétrus
 Four Seasons, Quadrato
 Mju
 Chez Bruce
 Savoy Grill
 La Trompette
 Foliage
 Richard Corrigan
 Savoy River Rest.
 Clarke's
 Vineyard at Stockcross †
 Tatsuso
 J. Sheekey
 Cliveden Hotel, Waldo's †
22 Orrery
 George (club)
 Dorchester, Oriental
 Chez Moi
 Pied à Terre
 Ivy, The
 Archipelago

---

† Outside London

Best Buys

Top 40 Bangs for the Buck

List derived by dividing the cost of a meal into its ratings.

1. Food for Thought
2. Troubadour, The
3. Busaba Eathai
4. Churchill Arms
5. Place Below
6. Little Bay
7. Lucky Seven
8. Books for Cooks
9. Ed's Easy Diner
10. La Porchetta Pizzeria
11. Patisserie Valerie
12. Wagamama
13. Buona Sera at the Jam
14. Chutney's
15. Chelsea Bun
16. Eco
17. Pepper Tree
18. Lahore Kebab House
19. Mildreds
20. Mandalay
21. Tartuf
22. Blah! Blah! Blah!
23. Masala Zone
24. Prince Bonaparte
25. Tom's Deli
26. Tas
27. Mandola
28. Tokyo Diner
29. Pizza Express
30. Nautilus Fish
31. Arkansas Cafe
32. Cafe, Level Seven
33. New Culture Revolution
34. Viet Hoa
35. Ask Pizza
36. Pizzeria Castello
37. Kulu Kulu Sushi
38. Black & Blue
39. Souk
40. Satsuma

Other Good Values

Alounak
Anglesea Arms
Aperitivo
Bangkok Rest.
Bombay Bicycle Club
Cafe at Sotheby's
Cafe Japan
Carluccio's Caffe
Cellar Gascon
Chiang Mai
Cicada
Eagle, The
Efes Kebab House
Engineer, The
Esarn Kheaw
Fairuz
Four Seasons Chinese
Galicia
Gate, The
Golden Dragon
Havelock Tavern
Ifield, The
itsu
Iznik
Kalamaras Taverna
Khan's
Made in Italy
Malabar Junction
Maroush
Noto
Pizza Metro
Pizza on the Park
Rasa
Red Pepper
Rocket
Royal China
Spiga
Truc Vert
Two Brothers Fish
Zaika Bazaar

Restaurant Directory

| F | D | S | C |

Abingdon, The 🆂   17 | 16 | 16 | £29
54 Abingdon Rd., W8 (High St. Kensington), 020-7937 3339; fax 020-7795 6388

◪ Offering a "decent take on the gastro-pub", this family-run "neighbourhood haunt" in Kensington draws locals with its "reliably good" Modern European fare, "eager to please" service and "comfy" seating; but snipers deride it as a "noisy", "not that special" spot, cautioning "bring a gas mask", as it can get "smoky near the bar"; N.B. at press time the bar was slated for renovation, complete with ventilators.

Adam Street 🌗   ▽ 20 | 21 | 20 | £31
Private club; inquiries: 020-7379 8000

◼ What a "brilliant, cheeky restoration of a period building" declare devotees "lucky enough to be members or get invited" to this private club in Covent Garden, an "excellent newcomer" serving Traditional British "comfort food done well" in a "posh", vaulted 18th-century setting beneath the Strand; the "beautifully diverse wine list" and "enthusiastic young staff" also "deserve accolades"; N.B. open to non-members for lunch.

Admiral Codrington, The 🆂   17 | 16 | 16 | £27
17 Mossop St., SW3 (South Kensington), 020-7581 0005; fax 020-7589 2452

◪ The "poseurs have gone", but this "smart boozer" in Chelsea, with a "surprisingly good" Modern European menu is still a "lively canteen and watering hole", attracting a "chic local crowd"; sceptics shrink at the "loud", "braying voices", suggesting it's become "a bit complacent", but even they appreciate the "sliding glass roof" for summer dining.

Admiralty, The 🌗🆂   18 | 18 | 15 | £40
Somerset House, The Strand, WC2 (Temple), 020-7845 4646; fax 020-7845 4647

◪ When you want to "linger over a lovely lunch" of "stylish, tasty" New French fare complete with "sophisticated surroundings", a "superb", Thames-side terrace and "unhurried" service, steer over to Oliver Peyton's place in The Strand's historic Somerset House; critics carp that the "so-so food" and "gloomy" "decor are not up to the splendid setting", plus staff are so "aloof" you "could run a mile between courses"; N.B. the restaurant was sold post-*Survey*, but Peyton will still act as creative advisor.

Alastair Little   22 | 15 | 19 | £39
49 Frith St., W1 (Leicester Sq./Tottenham Court Rd.), 020-7734 5183; fax 020-7734 5206

◪ It "still performs for a night out" applaud admirers of this "legendary Soho spot" where "imaginative" yet "unfussy" Modern British dishes are served in a "simple", but "comfortable" setting; it's not everyone's "cup of tea", however – snipers sniff that it "feels like a hairdresser's salon", but even they admit the "unimpressive decor

| F | D | S | C |

is offset" by its "cosy", "informal style", concluding it's a "real London experience."

Alastair Little at Lancaster Rd. S   21 | 14 | 18 | £36
136A Lancaster Rd., W11 (Ladbroke Grove), 020-7243 2220; fax 020-7792 4535

☑ "Interesting combinations with a Modern British twist" make Alastair Little's Notting Hill sibling a "great place for foodies"; cynics complain about "cramped" quarters ("we enjoyed our neighbours' conversation more than the food") and decor that "needs tarting up."

Alba   19 | 12 | 16 | £28
107 Whitecross St., EC1 (Barbican/Moorgate), 020-7588 1798; fax 020-7638 5793

■ Popular with the "Barbican's post-concert crowd", this "little diamond in the rough", in an "out-of-the-way location" on the "City fringes" lures patrons with its "reliable, cheap" Modern Italian food and "efficient" staff; N.B. a post-*Survey* refurbishment may impact the above Decor score.

Al Bustan S   – | – | – | M
68 Old Brompton Rd., SW7 (South Kensington), 020-7584 5805

Formerly located on Motcomb Street, this relaxed, midpriced Lebanese eaterie has resurfaced in South Kensington in the premises once occupied by Hilaire; customers dine on Middle Eastern specialties in the small, well-lit dining room on the ground floor, or graze on mezze in the downstairs bar and grill; pavement seating is available in warm weather.

Al Duca   20 | 16 | 17 | £33
4-5 Duke of York St., SW1 (Green Park/Piccadilly Circus), 020-7839 3090; fax 020-7839 4050

■ A "great formula" of "sleek surroundings and somewhat sleek" Modern Italian fare makes this "well-oiled machine" in "handy St. James's" an "upmarket experience at middle-market prices"; some squawk that the "tables are too close", but, it's a "favourite for pre-theatre dining" and "good for business lunches", plus it's "reasonable for the location."

Al Hamra ●S   20 | 13 | 15 | £30
31-33 Shepherd Mkt., W1 (Green Park), 020-7493 1954; fax 020-7493 1044

☑ When in need of a "Middle Eastern fix", make the trek to this Shepherd Market Lebanese where "superb veggie dishes" and "awesome mezze" are "consistently well prepared"; the "service is friendly and caring", and what's more, it's "superb to sit outside in the summer"; cynics scoff that it's "pretty average for the price."

Alloro   21 | 17 | 17 | £40
19-20 Dover St., W1 (Green Park), 020-7495 4768; fax 020-7629 5348

■ Exuding an "understated elegance" that compensates for its "odd", narrow shape, this "friendly", "trendy, Milano-

www.zagat.com

style" cousin of Zafferano "exceeds expectations" with its "imaginative", "well-executed" Modern Italian cooking and "amazing wine list"; a few gripe that the "staff are sometimes charming but disorganised" and advise that the *vino* selection "needs some cheaper options."

Almeida Restaurant S   22 | 19 | 21 | £36
30 Almeida St., N1 (Angel/Highbury & Islington), 020-7354 4777
■ "A new high for Islington" enthuse surveyors smitten by the "spot-on" Classic French fare, "superb execution of brasserie favourites" and "retro trolleys of pâtés and desserts" at this "excellent addition" to the Conran Group; "smart" surroundings and "attentive service" seal the deal – this "great newcomer" "deserves to do well."

Alounak ●S   20 | 9 | 12 | £18
10 Russell Gardens, W14 (Olympia), 020-7603 1130
44 Westbourne Grove, W2 (Bayswater/Queensway), 020-7229 4158; fax 020-7792 1219
◪ "Don't go for the decor, go for the delicious food" suggest fans of this "deservedly popular" Persian pair in Olympia and Westbourne Grove "buzzing with Iranian families" and "lots of locals", where it's a "pleasure to eat the kebabs" and the "fabulous bread", all offered at "great value"; detractors declare it's "way too cramped for a good time", plus the "dour" service "wants you out fast!"

Al San Vincenzo   23 | 15 | 18 | £39
30 Connaught St., W2 (Marble Arch), 020-7262 9623
■ "We just dropped by" this petite, "cosy", family-run Bayswater eatery and "it turned into a wonderful evening" fawn fans won over by the "excellent" Modern Italian fare, "very good wines" and welcoming staff; even first-timers say they're "planning a second, third and fourth visit."

Al Sultan ●S   20 | 13 | 17 | £29
51-52 Hertford St., W1 (Green Park), 020-7408 1155; fax 020-7408 1113
■ "Consistently good" with "surprisingly friendly service", this Middle Eastern Shepherd Market spot next to the Curzon cinema is "helpful to those unfamiliar" with its "very tasty" Southern Lebanese dishes; whilst a minority feel the fare is "not exciting", a loyal majority bow to the "great selection" and "reasonable prices."

Al Waha ●S   ▽ 19 | 14 | 19 | £27
75 Westbourne Grove, W2 (Bayswater/Queensway), 020-7229 0806; fax 020-7229 0806
◪ Though little known, this "brilliant Bayswater Lebanese" pleases its core customers with "good and filling" dishes and "great mezze", all at "tasty prices"; "friendly, efficient staff" help make this diminutive spot a "real pleasure to visit", nevertheless a few "disappointed" diners pout "we were expecting more."

| F | D | S | C |

Andrew Edmunds ⑤   20 | 17 | 18 | £28
46 Lexington St., W1 (Oxford Circus/Piccadilly Circus), 020-7437 5708

■ "Great for seductions", "making up with your partner" or a "girlie chat", this "intimate", "candlelit" Soho "bolt-hole", bolstered by "varied", "innovative" Modern European cuisine, "never fails to charm"; it's a "low-cost, high-taste venue" ("dirt cheap" for the locale) and especially "nice for an informal night out"; whilst a "claustrophobic" handful complain about "tables barely inches apart", the faithful retort it's "cosy for canoodling."

Anglesea Arms ⑤   18 | 14 | 12 | £19
35 Wingate Rd., W6 (Ravenscourt Park), 020-8749 1291; fax 020-8749 1254

◪ "If only more gastro-pubs were like it" say devotees of this "excellent neighbourhood hangout" in Shepherd's Bush where the "exemplary" Modern British "blackboard specials" change twice daily and are offered at the "right price"; the "relaxed setting", particularly the "wonderful outdoor terrace", and "affable staff" make it a "favourite", although cynics harrumph that it "could do better", citing "disinterested service" and a "smoky" atmosphere.

Annabel's ◐   19 | 21 | 22 | £56
Private club; inquiries: 020-7629 1096

◪ "For a certain group of people" this "chic" private club in Mayfair is still a "scene", indeed the "only place to go" for "dancing, drinking and people-watching"; even those who "don't come for the food" say the "consistent" Modern European fare is "better than you would think", plus the "service is impeccable"; detractors dismiss it as "tired", declaring it's "not what it was in the '60s and '70s."

Aperitivo   20 | 16 | 19 | £22
41 Beak St., W1 (Oxford Circus/Piccadilly Circus), 020-7287 2057; fax 020-7287 1767

■ "Delight" in "a bit o' this, a bit o' that" at this "great Italian tapas" yearling off Regent Street, an "ideal" place for a pre- or post-theatre meal, the "stylish", "interesting dishes" are "great for sharing" and "knowledgeable and helpful" staff help grazers navigate the "outstanding range" of "tasty menu" options.

Arancia ⑤   ▽ 21 | 14 | 21 | £24
52 Southwark Park Rd., SE16 (Bermondsey), 020-7394 1751; fax 020-7394 1044

■ The "fresh", "interesting" Modern Italian fare is "worth the hike" proclaim patrons who pack this "unpretentious" spot in an "offbeat" Bermondsey location; inside awaits "quality cooking" dished out in a "pleasantly surprising", "warm", "cheerful" atmosphere by staff that make you "feel special"; at the meal's end, the "miniscule bill leaves you with an uplifted feeling."

www.zagat.com

| F | D | S | C |

Archipelago
22 | 24 | 22 | £41

110 Whitfield St., W1 (Goodge St./Warren St.), 020-7383 3346; fax 020-7383 7181

■ "Locusts, anyone?" – that's "just one of the intriguing menu items" that make this "cool" Eclectic Soho eaterie a "truly incredible" "dining experience"; it's a "fun night out" announce adventurers who deem the "exotic fare" as "stimulating" as the "bohemian, out-of-this-world" decor; P.S. the "downstairs lounge is supreme for a chatty evening."

Ark S
15 | 15 | 15 | £31

122 Palace Gardens Terrace, W8 (Notting Hill Gate), 020-7229 4024; fax 020-7792 8787

☑ "Generally a winner" proclaim surveyors who set sail for this "friendly" little Modern Italian "neighbourhood hangout" off Notting Hill Gate; the "deliciously inventive" dishes offer "good value", and it's "particularly enjoyable" to eat on the "patio in the summertime"; but naysayers claim the "food is average", the "room is uncomfortable" and this Ark "should ask Noah how to improve the service."

Arkansas Cafe S
16 | 8 | 15 | £15

107B Commercial St., Old Spitalfields Mkt., E1 (Liverpool St.), 020-7377 6999; fax 020-7377 6999

☑ "Mouthwatering, meaty cooking" and an all-American "no-frills", "down-home feel" are what customers count on at Bubba Helberg's "authentic BBQ" dining concept near Spitalfields Market; whilst critics squawk it's "nothing brilliant" – the food is "bland" and the "decor dreadful" – "homesick Americans" insist you'll find the "best beef brisket outside Texas" here; N.B. now open for dinner Wednesday–Friday; closed Saturday lunch.

Aroma Chinese S
18 | 11 | 14 | £21

11 Gerrard St., W1 (Leicester Sq.), 020-7439 2720; fax 020-7437 0377 ◐
39 Gerrard St., W1 (Leicester Sq.), 020-7439 0534
118 Shaftesbury Ave., W1 (Leicester Sq.), 020-7437 0377; fax 020-7437 0377 ◐

■ A "cut above normal Chinatown fare", the "daunting spread" at Kitty Lee's Theatreland trio includes "no-fuss noodles", "good, authentic" Asian specialties and "some strange dishes" for "those brave enough" to "try something adventurous"; the "austere surroundings" are "nothing special", yet few seem to mind, since it's "reliable" "pre-cinema" and "good value for a group outing."

Artigiano S
18 | 17 | 16 | £34

12A Belsize Terrace, NW3 (Belsize Park/Swiss Cottage), 020-7794 4288; fax 020-7435 2048

☑ "An oasis in a desert", this "stylish", "friendly" Belsize Park neighbourhood "classic" draws fans with Modern Italian "food that's artful and tasty", a "hand-picked wine list" and "super-smart decor", including multi-coloured lights that shine through the glass canopies; sceptics sulk that this "likable local has become too pricey lately" and caution "service can be slow at peak times"; N.B. Artigiano is Italian for 'the craftsman.'

ASIA DE CUBA ●S 20 | 22 | 17 | £43
St. Martin's Lane Hotel, 45 St. Martin's Ln., WC2 (Leicester Sq.), 020-7300 5588; fax 020-7300 5540

☑ "Ohhh myyy gawwwdd, the noise" is "overbearing", but that's just part of the "buzzy atmosphere" at Ian Schrager's Asian-Cuban "cosmopolitan treat" in the St. Martin's Lane Hotel; "go with a group and play guess the ingredients" say insiders who "love the amalgam" of "sumptuous" flavours, "stylish with a capital S" surroundings and "eye-candy" crowd; this is "expense-account country" gripe grumblers who find it "too cool to relax in" and denounce the "fusion confusion" fare and "smug" service.

Ask Pizza S 14 | 14 | 14 | £16
145 Notting Hill Gate, W11 (Notting Hill Gate), 020-7792 9942 ●
222 Kensington High St., W8 (High St. Kensington), 020-7937 5540; fax 020-7937 5540
219-221 Chiswick High Rd., W4 (Turnham Green), 020-8742 1323 ●
121-125 Park St., W1 (Marble Arch), 020-7495 7760; fax 020-7495 7760 ●
48 Grafton Way, W1 (Warren St.), 020-7388 8108; fax 020-7388 8112 ●
1 Gloucester Arcade, SW7 (Gloucester Rd.), 020-7835 0840 ●
345 Fulham Palace Rd., SW6 (Hammersmith/Putney Bridge), 020-7371 0392 ●
300 King's Rd., SW3 (Sloane Sq.), 020-7349 9123 ●
160-162 Victoria St., SW1 (St. James's Park/Victoria), 020-7630 8228; fax 020-7630 8228
216 Haverstock Hill, NW3 (Belsize Park/Chalk Farm), 020-7433 3896; fax 020-7435 6490 ●
Additional locations throughout London

■ "You get exactly what you expect" at this "casual", "child-friendly", "firm favourite" Italian chain: "fresh, crispy pizza and nice, saucy pasta" plus "cheery service" and "very reasonable prices"; a few find it "a bit formulaic" and "ho-hum in every way – but reliably so."

ASSAGGI 24 | 17 | 21 | £43
39 Chepstow Pl., W2 (Notting Hill Gate), 020-7792 5501; fax 020-7792 9033

☑ "It's been discovered by the world, so book weeks ahead" advise admirers of this "festive" Italian destination above a Notting Hill pub; the "brilliant food" is worth "savouring", and the "spacious, tranquil room" exudes just the "right mix of casual and hip"; it "isn't all it's hyped up to be" moan a minority who object to the "upscale prices", but for most, this "jewel" has "all-round star quality"; P.S. "lunch is easier" to reserve.

| F | D | S | C |

Atlantic Bar & Grill ◐ S
14 | 19 | 13 | £36

20 Glasshouse St., W1 (Piccadilly Circus), 020-7734 4888; fax 020-7734 5400

◪ "The impressive decor", "excellent cocktails" and "better than expected" Modern British menu (thanks to new chef Stephen Carter) add up to a "fun night out" at Oliver Peyton's large "lively" underground restaurant/bar in Piccadilly; it's "so '90s", plus "staff are arrogant" carp critics, contending this "complacent" "yobbo's heaven" has "lost its sparkle."

AUBERGINE
25 | 19 | 22 | £54

11 Park Walk, SW10 (Gloucester Rd./South Kensington), 020-7352 3449; fax 020-7351 1770

◪ "Classy in every respect" say loyalists about this "small, sophisticated" Chelsea venue where "service is as it should be" and chef William Drabble's "immaculately presented" New French cooking is "as good as when Gordon Ramsay" was there; still, critics counter "nothing wrong, nothing memorable", citing sometimes "snooty staff" and "out-of-sight prices"; N.B. a new bar and glass-fronted wine-cooling room were recently added.

Aurora
20 | 19 | 19 | £38

Great Eastern Hotel, 40 Liverpool St., EC2 (Liverpool St.), 020-7618 7000; fax 020-7618 7001

◪ Offering "luxury without arrogance" and "thoroughly enjoyable" Modern European fare that's "ideal for a business lunch", Sir Terence Conran's "stylish" stained-glass-domed "romantic location" in the Great Eastern Hotel makes diners "feel special"; whilst faultfinders pout this "soul-less" setting is "not for the truly hungry", most agree it's "great if you're on an expense account"; N.B. the post-*Survey* arrival of chef Warren Geraghty from Cannes may impact the above Food score.

Avenue ◐ S
18 | 18 | 17 | £38

7-9 St. James's St., SW1 (Green Park), 020-7321 2111; fax 020-7321 2500

◪ Whilst "not as fashionable as it once was", this "sleek", "minimalist" "Manhattan-style" "barn" in St. James's "still holds its own" with Modern European "food that continues to surprise and delight"; service varies from "very good" to "distracted" and "rushed" ("so rapid it's unnerving"), which may be why some prefer to "impress" a date at the "fashionable bar", where "terrific cocktails" and a "relaxed attitude" are de rigueur.

Axis ◐
21 | 19 | 19 | £41

One Aldwych Hotel, 1 Aldwych, WC2 (Charing Cross/Covent Garden), 020-7300 0300; fax 020-7300 0301

◪ "Unremittingly cool, with stylish" Modern British–Eclectic food that "ranges from traditional to imaginative", this "beautiful culinary and aesthetic experience" within the One Aldwych Hotel is "good for entertaining clients" or a

| F | D | S | C |

pre- or post-theatre dinner (look for "some great [prix fixe] deals"); whilst many give "professional" service a pat on the back, dissenters say it's "attitude-laden" and "almost so smart it's intimidating."

Aykoku-Kaku 21 | 10 | 18 | £34
Bucklersbury House, 9 Walbrook, EC4 (Bank), 020-7236 9020; fax 020-7489 8040
■ It looks "a little dated" and "in need of refurbishment", but this "handy" City stalwart remains a "reliable" option for a "quick lunch" of "excellent" Japanese fare, including "good tempura" and "pleasant sushi"; wallet-watchers warn "expensive" prices can rankle.

Ayoush S 13 | 19 | 12 | £24
58 James St., W1 (Bond St.), 020-7935 9839; fax 020-7935 1708
◪ Though set in Mayfair, this "fun", "friendly" North African spot, boasting hookah pipes, belly dancers (on Friday and Saturday nights) and a casbah-inspired setting, "feels like the real thing"; it's "ok for a change" say fence-sitters, but the "inconsistent" "food could be better"; P.S. the private members club "downstairs in the cave" has a "great" "funky" atmosphere.

Babylon 16 | 21 | 15 | £38
The Roof Gardens, 99 Kensington High St., W8 (High St. Kensington), 020-7368 3993
■ Perched on top of The Roof Gardens in Kensington, Sir Richard Branson's new, "undeniably attractive", "funky environment" lives up to its name, with an outdoor terrace and "stunning views" of the "absolutely exquisite" greenery and London itself; after dining on "good" Modern European fare, the "trendy" set "work off the calories on the dance floor in the nightclub below."

Balans ●S 14 | 13 | 15 | £21
187 Kensington High St., W8 (High St. Kensington), 020-7376 0115; fax 020-7938 4653
60 Old Compton St., W1 (Leicester Sq./Piccadilly Circus), 020-7439 2183; fax 020-7734 2665
◪ Aficionados "love the buzz of a gay-straight crowd" and the "great camp waiters" at this "lively" Modern British cafe chain; the "unpretentious" "American-style breakfasts" and other "reasonably priced" fare are served into the "wee hours" (with a 5 AM license, the Soho branch is "more nightclub than restaurant, so dress appropriately"); bashers blast that it's "average everything"; N.B. the Knightsbridge branch has closed.

Baltic ●S 20 | 20 | 16 | £32
74 Blackfriars Rd., SE1 (Southwark), 020-7928 1111; fax 020-7928 8487
◪ "Very cool, very delicious" exult enthusiasts who contend the Eastern European "food is fabulous" and the "beautifully

| F | D | S | C |

contemporary dining room" (formerly a coachbuilders) makes a "striking backdrop" at this "still undiscovered" Wòdka sibling in "out of the way Southwark"; whilst some items "may not sound tempting", the results are "better than expected" and "make an interesting change"; the "chic bar" with a long vodka list is "a great place to hang out."

Bam-Bou ⏺ 19 | 23 | 16 | £34
1 Percy St., W1 (Tottenham Court Rd.), 020-7323 9130; fax 020-7323 9140

◪ "Carries it off" opine supporters "seduced" by the "slightly louche atmosphere", "mouthwatering" French-Vietnamese fare and "ace cocktails" at this "lovely", "out-of-the-ordinary" Fitzrovian townhouse; "more style than substance" blast bashers convinced the "ambience distracts you from the child-size portions"; P.S. there's a "lovely" private members club on the upper two floors.

Bangkok Restaurant 20 | 11 | 16 | £23
9 Bute St., SW7 (South Kensington), 020-7584 8529

◪ The "excellent quality", "reasonably priced" "food is the thing, not the atmosphere" at this Thai stalwart that looks like a "cafe, not a restaurant"; whilst some maintain it's been a "favourite" since opening in 1967, nonplussed patrons claim it's "nothing special", offering "no charm" and "cramped" quarters.

Bank Aldwych ⏺ S 18 | 17 | 16 | £35
1 Kingsway, WC2 (Holborn), 020-7379 9797; fax 020-7240 7001

◪ A "jolly restaurant for meetings", this "noisy", "bustling", "streamlined operation" in Aldwych has the "wonderful ability to make you feel welcome" with "very skillful" Modern European cooking and "top cabin" service; it's "banking on its past glory" as an "'80s power dinner" venue, sniff snipers who deride the "braying" wheelers and dealers, "inconsistent" food and "snooty" staff.

Bankside 18 | 18 | 17 | £26
32 Southwark Bridge Rd., SE1 (London Bridge), 020-7633 0011; fax 020-7633 0011

◪ Art and commerce collide in this new L-shaped basement spot in Southwark where works from local galleries add to the "lively atmosphere" and the daily changing Eclectic-International menu "exceeds expectations"; foes feel "let down by the cold decor" and complain about "erratic service"; N.B. it's located near the Tate Modern.

Bank Westminster & 17 | 19 | 17 | £34
Zander Bar ⏺ S
45 Buckingham Gate, SW1 (St. James's Park), 020-7379 9797; fax 020-7240 7001

◾ The "cool, trendy bar" (at 48 metres, the longest in Europe) plying "fabulous cocktails" and the "glossy, chic" restaurant, serving "simple, effective" Modern European

| F | D | S | C |

fare, "make a smart couple" in an "otherwise dull area" near Victoria Street; the glass-enclosed conservatory is "nice, especially in the summertime"; N.B. there's also a DJ several nights a week and on Saturdays.

Bayee House S ▽ 17 | 14 | 15 | £32
24 High St., SW19 (Wimbledon), 020-8947 3533; fax 020-8944 8392
100 Upper Richmond Rd., SW15 (East Putney), 020-8789 3161; fax 020-8780 5638
■ Surveyors in Putney and Wimbledon depend on this Chinese pair for "swift service" and "decent", "value"-oriented Szechuan/Peking dishes that are "always good"; the "atmosphere is so-so" and "the menu is limited" (expect "no surprises"), but most say they're "great for locals."

Beiteddine ● S ▽ 18 | 11 | 16 | £27
8 Harriet St., SW1 (Knightsbridge/Sloane Sq.), 020-7235 3969; fax 020-7245 6335
■ "High-quality, fresh ingredients abound" at this "friendly", "authentic" Middle Eastern eatery in Knightsbridge, where the Lebanese "food is as good as in Beirut" and "nothing is too much trouble for the consistently excellent staff"; N.B. unlike the 19th-century palace it's named after, this setting is far from royal, but behold, takeaway is available.

Belair House S 17 | 19 | 17 | £38
Gallery Rd., Dulwich Village, SE21 (West Dulwich B.R.), 020-8299 9788; fax 020-8299 6793
■ "Smart, but unstuffy" enthuse "romantics" who revel in the "perfect for Valentine's Day" decor at this Georgian Grade II–listed establishment near the Dulwich Picture Gallery, overlooking Belair Park, where the "very good" New French dishes and "lively" atmosphere make "special events" all the more so; there's "beauty everywhere, but not in the food" gripe a few who find it "sometimes inconsistent."

Belgo Centraal ● S 15 | 15 | 14 | £22
50 Earlham St., WC2 (Covent Garden), 020-7813 2233; fax 020-7209 3212
◪ The "best thing to come out of Belgium since the waffle" wax "mussel-lovers" who delight in the "gimmicky, cheap" eats, "delicious beers" and friar-attired servers at this "industrial"-looking "trappist treat" in Covent Garden; the "long queues" are worth enduring for a "rowdy night out with friends" set in a scene "straight out of *Blade Runner*"; it's "crowded and noisy" contend critics, plus the "monks are not as cheerful as they used to be."

Belgo Noord ● S 16 | 16 | 16 | £21
72 Chalk Farm Rd., NW1 (Camden Town/Chalk Farm), 020-7267 0718; fax 020-7916 8036
■ When in need of a "Belgian beer fix" and some of the "best *moules-frites* this side of the Channel" head to this Chalk Farm Belgo original considered by many to be "more

| F | D | S | C |

pleasant than its Covent Garden counterpart"; a few feel that the "food often disappoints" and can do without the "stag nights" and "office parties."

Belgo Zuid ⓢ   14 | 17 | 15 | £21
124 Ladbroke Grove, W10 (Ladbroke Grove), 020-8982 8400; fax 020-8982 8401

■ "Stunning design" and a "very good" selection of beers ("try the mango" brew) are the hallmarks of this "cool" Belgian Belgo outpost in Ladbroke Grove, where believers say it's "perfect for a light, casual dinner", indeed, "faultless for the money", a handful scoff it's "average" at best.

Belvedere, The ⓢ   20 | 23 | 18 | £42
Holland Park, off Abbotsbury Rd., W8 (Holland Park), 020-7602 1238; fax 020-7601 4382

■ Marco Pierre White's "accessibly posh", "well-oiled machine" in the "splendid grounds" of Holland Park is "one of the most beautiful" in London, where the smitten savour "excellent" New French–Modern British "food that matches" the "sumptuous" setting; the "discreet service" makes it a "place to impress", with a dining terrace that's "paradise" for a "sunny lunch"; still, a critical few counter the "food needs more zip" and say staff are "cavalier."

Bengal Clipper ◐ⓢ   21 | 18 | 17 | £27
Shad Thames, 11-12 Cardamom Bldg., Shad Thames, SE1 (London Bridge/Tower Hill), 020-7357 9001; fax 020-7357 9002

■ When you're in the mood to "eat an enjoyable curry and listen to the piano" in a "dreamy" setting, steer over to this Butlers Wharf venue near Tower Bridge; the "very tempting menu" of "unusual" Indian-Bangladeshi dishes "consistently fails to disappoint."

Benihana ⓢ   18 | 15 | 18 | £33
37 Sackville St., W1 (Green Park/Piccadilly Circus), 020-7494 2525; fax 020-7494 1456
77 King's Rd., SW3 (Sloane Sq.), 020-7376 7799; fax 020-7376 7377
100 Avenue Rd., NW3 (Swiss Cottage), 020-7586 9508; fax 020-7586 6740

◪ "You pay for the entertainment as much as the food, and both are worth it" fawn fans of this "efficiently run" Japanese trio where teppanyaki chefs "cook at your table"; "lots of sizzle, not much steak" grouch gripers who conclude this "concept is really for the kids, but the prices aren't"; P.S. "lunchtime specials are great value."

Ben's Thai   18 | 11 | 15 | £18
48 Red Lion St., WC1 (Holborn), 020-7404 9991
93 Warrington Crescent, W9 (Maida Vale/Warwick Ave.), 020-7266 3134; fax 020-7221 8799 ⓢ
283 Ballards Ln., N3 (Finchley Central), 020-8492 0201 ⓢ

■ "Who wants the bells and whistles anyway" chorus supporters of this "friendly", "no-fuss" Thai trio where the "delicious", "stellar" cooking is "reasonably priced"; whilst "erratic service" and "smoky rooms" let the side down, the fact that each location is "always busy" speaks volumes; P.S. the Maida Vale site above the Warrington Castle pub is "great with kids."

Bentley's ◐S   19 | 17 | 17 | £38

11-15 Swallow St., W1 (Piccadilly Circus), 020-7734 4756; fax 020-7287 2972

◪ Exuding "old-world charm" and "traditional comfort", this "typical English", "reliable as ever" seafooder off Regent Street is a "London treasure"; dissenters declare that it "used to be a great standby" but, alas, nowadays it's "coasting on its reputation", and what's more, it's "expensive for what you get."

Beoty's ◐   16 | 14 | 20 | £33

79 St. Martin's Ln., WC2 (Leicester Sq.), 020-7836 8768; fax 020-7497 0355

◪ "They don't make them like this anymore" announce admirers of this "comfortable", "clubby" French-Greek Theatreland stalwart where the "lovely old-fashioned service" "makes you feel special"; the less forgiving dismiss this "time warp" as "rather shabby", but even critics concede that it's "convenient for the West End theatres" and "very useful for the ENO."

Bertorelli   17 | 15 | 15 | £29

44A Floral St., WC2 (Covent Garden), 020-7836 3969; fax 020-7836 1868 ◐
11-13 Frith St., W1 (Leicester Sq./Tottenham Court Rd.), 020-7494 3491; fax 020-7439 9431 ◐S
19-23 Charlotte St., W1 (Goodge St./Tottenham Court Rd.), 020-7636 4174; fax 020-7467 8902

◪ Opinions on this "casual", "no nonsense" Italian bistro trio in Soho, Covent Garden (the popular original) and Fitzrovia are polarised: fans say the "consistent", "tasty" fare and "speedy service" make it an "old reliable in the theatre district" and a "great place to while away a lunch hour", but sceptics claim the "unexciting menu" has a "formula feel" and believe "quality wobbles"; N.B. now part of Groupe Chez Gerard.

BIBENDUM ◐S   23 | 22 | 20 | £48

Michelin House, 81 Fulham Rd., SW3 (South Kensington), 020-7581 5817; fax 020-7823 7925

◪ "As good as it gets" gush gaggles of gastronomes of this "superlative" Brompton Cross New French "institution" set in the "swish" Michelin landmark; chef Matthew Harris' "fantastic, faultless food" ("excellent" "for all occasions") is "professionally" served, making this "classic" "exciting to entertain in"; disenchanted diners, however, insist it's "not up to the hoopla" and call "service a bit of a shambles."

| F | D | S | C |

Bibendum Oyster Bar S
21 | 18 | 17 | £30

Michelin House, 81 Fulham Rd., SW3 (South Kensington), 020-7589 1480; fax 020-7823 7925

■ It's "ideal for a light meal" of "deliciously fresh" seafood and a "good glass of wine" say shellfish seekers who find "fortification for a shopping spree" at this "friendly" Brompton Cross bistro in the Michelin building downstairs from the Bibendum; "service is quick and competent", and the "very French" "setting is civilised"; N.B. it can get quite crowded, so expect to queue or make use of the takeaway service.

Bice
19 | 16 | 18 | £38

13 Albemarle St., W1 (Green Park/Piccadilly Circus), 020-7409 1011; fax 020-7493 0081

◪ "Stunning food whichever Bice in the world you eat in" fawn the faithful who head to this offshoot of the venerable Milanese chain, "hidden away in a basement" location off Piccadilly; the "elegant, excellent dishes" are made with "fine ingredients" – add "friendly staff" and it amounts to an "always fun" evening; "it's interesting, but a little expensive" baulk naysayers, who suggest the "old-fashioned decor" could do with "some changes."

Bierodrome
14 | 14 | 13 | £19

67 Kingsway, WC2 (Charing Cross/Holborn), 020-7242 7469; fax 020-7242 7493
678-680 Fulham Rd., SW6 (Parsons Green), 020-7751 0789; fax 020-7751 0678 S
44-48 Clapham High St., SW4 (Clapham North), 020-7720 1118; fax 020-7720 0288 ●S
173-174 Upper St., N1 (Highbury & Islington), 020-7226 5835; fax 020-7704 0632 S
71 St. John St., EC1 (Farringdon), 020-7608 0033; fax 020-7608 0003 S

◪ Customers craving a "super selection of beers and hearty", "reasonably priced" Belgian fare head to Belgo's expanding chain of "cheerful" restaurants, where an "interesting menu" is on offer (in addition to the trademark "lovely fries and mussels"); it should be called the "bore-odrome" gripe grouchers who find the "service poor" and the "unexciting food" "distinctly average", advising stick to the "damn fine ale."

Big Easy S
14 | 13 | 15 | £21

332-334 King's Rd., SW3 (Sloane Sq.), 020-7352 4071

■ It's a "lovely place to stuff your face", especially when you need a "taste of 'N'awlins'" crow admirers of this "big American dining" experience in King's Road; it's "lively, loud and lots of fun", with "friendly, accommodating service" that can handle "lots of kids"; whilst a handful wish it would "sink back into the swamp", most say "you can always be assured of a good night out"; N.B. a popular guitar duo plays live every night.

| F | D | S | C |

Bistrot 190 ◐S   16 | 16 | 16 | £30
Gore Hotel, 190 Queen's Gate, SW7 (Gloucester Rd./ South Kensington), 020-7581 5666; fax 020-7581 5872

✍ "Still a great place to dine after all these years" proclaim fans of this "perennial favourite" Modern British bistro/bar in South Kensington's Gore Hotel; the "good looking" room exudes "lots of character" and "service is pleasant", plus you can hop next door to Bar 190 for a drink, making it a "full evening out"; doubters pronounce it "predictable", but even they accede that it's a "useful location before and after Albert Hall"; N.B. last orders are taken at midnight.

Black & Blue S   18 | 18 | 19 | £22
215-217 Kensington Church St., W8 (Notting Hill Gate), 020-7727 0004; fax 020-7229 9359

■ "For the price, you can't go wrong" at this "surprisingly good" "Houston-like" steakhouse in Kensington, where carnivores dig into "lovely, well-cooked comfort food" in a "funky", "ultra-modern" setting that's a "great atmosphere for couples or dining alone" and "good for a casual meal with old friends"; a few snipers fire back "mediocre" and "noisy"; N.B. at press time, a Gloucester Road branch and a Chiswick High Road branch were slated to open in late summer and winter respectively.

Black Truffle   20 | 16 | 17 | £34
40 Chalcot Rd., NW1 (Chalk Farm/Primrose Hill B.R.), 020-7483 0077; fax 020-7483 0088

✍ "Terrific Italian cooking", "smart surroundings" and "attentive service" make this "cosy" "fave neighbourhood spot" in Primrose Hill worthy of "repeat visits"; there's more "style than substance" to be had counter critics, who also lament that service is "uneven and slow."

Blah! Blah! Blah! S⌽   23 | 12 | 17 | £19
78 Goldhawk Rd., W12 (Goldhawk Rd.), 020-8746 1337

■ "Amazingly good for a Vegetarian restaurant" chorus fans who gather at this "chilled-out" Shepherd's Bush "hole-in-the-wall" for "creative" "comfort food" so "fantastic" "even carnivorous friends" are sated; the "excellent" dishes offer "good value", giving boosters pause to wonder "how do they do it for the price?"; the "bring a bottle" policy also finds unanimous favour.

Blakes Hotel ◐S   23 | 24 | 21 | £53
Blakes Hotel, 33 Roland Gardens, SW7 (Gloucester Rd./ South Kensington), 020-7370 6701; fax 020-7373 0442

■ "Chic" and "fabulous", Lady Weinberg's "magical" hotel "dining experience" in South Kensington "makes you feel like a VIP"; chef Neville Campbell's "interesting and creative" Pacific Rim–influenced Eclectic cooking is decidedly "delicious" and the "superb" setting affords "peace, bliss and privacy" at what's not only an "impressive business venue", it's also a "super-romantic" spot that

www.zagat.com

| F | D | S | C |

"makes you want to stay on" (ahem, the "people next to us needed their hotel room").

Blandford Street ▽ | 19 | 16 | 16 | £42 |
5-7 Blandford St., W1 (Bond St.), 020-7486 9696; fax 020-7486 5067
The "fresh" Modern European fare, "pleasant" room and "efficient service" seem "up to Stephen Bull's standards" say fans familiar with the previous incarnation of this Marylebone eaterie now run by Nick Lambert; a few feel it's not "worth the price", as the "decor lacks something"; N.B. Stephen Bull left to run a Herefordshire pub.

Bleeding Heart Restaurant | 21 | 19 | 19 | £35 |
Bleeding Heart Yard, off Greville St., EC1 (Farringdon), 020-7242 8238; fax 020-7831 1402
Bleeding Heart Tavern
19 Greville St., EC1 (Farringdon), 020-7404 0333; fax 020-7404 2727
"An absolute star for supper", this "good all-rounder" "off-the-beaten-track" in a Holborn courtyard is "worth finding" for "excellent" New French cooking; the ground-floor bistro with outside tables is "tight on space", but makes "an excellent business-lunch destination", whilst the "romantic" cellar offers "charming alcoves"; N.B. the Tavern sibling serves spit-roasted Traditional British fare.

Bloom's S | 15 | 8 | 10 | £20 |
130 Golders Green Rd., NW11 (Golders Green), 020-8455 1338; fax 020-8455 3033
"The waiters make you finish your dinner like your mother would" at this "kosher equivalent of a greasy spoon" in Golders Green that feels like it's been "transplanted from another era" – as in, the "good old days"; most give the "tasty", "substantial" portions of "traditional Jewish" "nosh" the thumbs-up, though a minority caution "this is not your New York deli, so don't ask for the corned beef."

Bluebird S | 17 | 18 | 15 | £36 |
350 King's Rd., SW3 (Sloane Sq.), 020-7559 1000; fax 020-7559 1115
"Formulaic, but the formula works" opine loyalists of Sir Terence Conran's King's Road venue, an "impressive" Modern European–seafooder with a downstairs cafe that "feels like a page out of *Vogue* on weekdays"; the "delicious" dishes and "smart staff" make a meal in the "casual, but classy" dining room a "fantastic treat"; still, critics decry the "sterile atmosphere" and "lacklustre service"; P.S. it's "fun to visit" the food and flower shops plus the newly expanded bar within the same complex.

BLUE ELEPHANT ●S | 21 | 23 | 19 | £36 |
3-6 Fulham Broadway, SW6 (Fulham Broadway), 020-7385 6595; fax 020-7386 7665
"For an authentic taste of Thailand in the heart of Fulham", make a "great escape" to this "fantasy-like",

34 www.zagat.com

| F | D | S | C |

"lush" pond-and-"jungle"-themed eaterie, a "transporting" "dining experience not to be missed"; "everything, as expected, is exotic", including the "fab food" and "staff that make you feel like you're in Asia"; it's "tacky" and "too touristy" the less-tempted tut, as well as a "trifle pricey."

Blue Jade ▽ | 21 | 16 | 19 | £25 |
44 Hugh St., SW1 (Pimlico/Victoria), 020-7828 0321; fax 020-7630 9272
■ "Reliable food" and "attentive" "staff offering excellent service" are appreciated at this sweet and "traditional Thai" stalwart in Pimlico, filling a need as a "useful local restaurant", especially for "dinner à deux."

Blue Print Cafe S | 19 | 19 | 17 | £35 |
Design Museum, Butlers Wharf, 28 Shad Thames, SE1 (London Bridge/Tower Hill), 020-7378 7031; fax 020-7357 8810
◪ "Get a table by the window" and enjoy the "unparalleled view" of Tower Bridge along with the "fresh, subtle" Modern European fare at Sir Terence Conran's Design Museum destination; "it's the kind of place to go for lively but relaxing weekend meals" "with friends", especially "Sunday lunch" or when you want to "watch the sunset"; claims that the "food is perfunctory" suggest all is not rosy, but even foes admit it's "saved" by its "beautiful location on the Thames."

Boisdale | 19 | 18 | 16 | £36 |
15 Eccleston St., SW1 (Victoria), 020-7730 6922; fax 020-7730 0548 ●
202 Bishopsgate, EC2 (Liverpool St.), 020-7283 1763
■ "Essential for cigars, whisky and haggis", this "find" near Victoria Station also wins over fans with its "Hibernian decor" and "rich, meaty" Scottish–Traditional British dishes; it's "time warped, but enjoyable", with live jazz, "must-try cocktails" and enough amber-coloured potables "to turn a teetotaller into a single-malt fanatic"; "prices are hard to justify" at this "pin-striped" "male preserve" huff a handful; N.B. the City branch opened post-*Survey*.

Bombay Bicycle Club | 21 | 16 | 18 | £24 |
95 Nightingale Ln., SW12 (Clapham South), 020-8673 6217; fax 020-8673 9100
■ "Rajasthan meets Clapham" at this "unusual, individual" "local", the "smartest Indian adventure" around thanks to its "consistently appetising" menu, "welcoming" staff and "funky" British Colonial–style decor; it's "good for casual dining with a group of friends" and "excellent for takeaway if you fancy a night in."

Bombay Brasserie ●S | 19 | 19 | 18 | £34 |
Courtfield Rd., SW7 (Gloucester Rd.), 020-7370 4040; fax 020-7835 1669
◪ "Hot means really hot" at this "spacious", "upmarket Indian" stalwart in South Kensington where the "fantastic

www.zagat.com

array of flavours" and "old-time colonial feeling" add up to a "superb all-around" "event dining" experience; fans adore the "elaborate decor" and "professional service", but cynics retort it's "lost the edge."

Books for Cooks   22 | 14 | 16 | £17
4 Blenheim Crescent, W11 (Ladbroke Grove/Notting Hill Gate), 020-7221 1992; fax 020-7221 1517
■ "Bravo for creativity" chorus customers who "love the staff and concept" at this "very tiny" bookshop near Portobello Road where the recipe test kitchen offers Eclectic dishes whipped up "from a different cookbook and cook each time"; "now that it's been revamped it seems much more ordinary" gripe a rare few, but fans insist it's "still great for lunching and browsing" and, take note, it's "bloody hard to get a table."

Brackenbury, The S   20 | 15 | 17 | £31
129-131 Brackenbury Rd., W6 (Goldhawk Rd./Hammersmith), 020-8748 0107; fax 020-8741 0905
■ "Wish my neighbourhood had a place like this" gush admirers who lean on this "immensely reliable" Shepherd's Bush venue for "good-value" Modern European tucker; the "charming menu" and "friendly staff" bolster its status as a "great local" that's "worth the effort to get to"; our "high expectations were brought to earth with a bump" pout a few "let down by inattentive service" and "uninspired cooking."

Bradley's S   22 | 16 | 19 | £35
25 Winchester Rd., NW3 (Swiss Cottage), 020-7722 3457; fax 020-7435 1392
■ A "top dining experience in an out-of-the-way" Swiss Cottage location, this "small but perfectly formed" Modern British eaterie brings a bit of the "West End to the suburbs"; the "imaginative, consistently well-cooked food" turned out by the "proprietor who's the chef", along with the "very good wine list" and "excellent service", all set a "high standard."

Brasserie Les Sans Culottes   – | – | – | E
27-29 Endell St., WC2 (Long Acre), 020-7379 8500; fax 020-7836 4540
"Take a good appetite" to this Covent Garden newcomer, a "well-decorated", brightly lit French brasserie with gold-hued banquettes and tasteful artwork; the "authentic, simple country fare" features traditional dishes such as cassoulet and raclette, offset by an interesting wine list; a gleaming micro-brewery on-site adds to its appeal; N.B. a new chef was slated to start at press time.

Brasserie Roux ●S   – | – | – | E
Sofitel St. James London, 8 Pall Mall, SW1 (Covent Garden), 020-7968 2900; fax 020-7747 2242
Set on the site of a former bank in Pall Mall, the new Sofitel St. James hotel boasts a handsome, stylish brasserie with

| F | D | S | C |

high ceilings, a fireplace and its own entrance; the trump card is a daily changing, reasonably priced Classic French menu created by consultant Albert Roux, featuring a selection of the celebrated chef's signature dishes, as well as special menus for children and theatregoers.

Brasserie St. Quentin S | 18 | 15 | 16 | £32 |
243 Brompton Rd., SW3 (Knightsbridge), 020-7589 8005; fax 020-7584 6064
◪ At *Survey* time, original owner Hugh O'Neill bought back this "delightful" "standby" in Knightsbridge from Groupe Chez Gerard and renovated the premises; a competitively priced Classic French menu of "no-nonsense" cooking is now offered, including "reliable" prix fixe options; P.S. it's "close to Harrods."

Brinkley's S | 16 | 14 | 15 | £27 |
47 Hollywood Rd., SW10 (Earl's Court), 020-7351 1683; fax 020-7376 5083
■ "Relaxed" and "noisy", this "wonderful" Chelsea spot is "at its best" when you're dining on the Modern British fare "with a large-ish group" that likes to "hit the wine list hard" (not surprising, given the "great prices"); yes, the "food also passes muster", but sensitive types take heed: this place is "not for those who mind public-school high jinks"; N.B. there's a covered garden at the rear.

Brown's Hotel, Restaurant 1837 S | 22 | 21 | 22 | £44 |
Brown's Hotel, 32 Albemarle St., W1 (Green Park), 020-7408 1837; fax 020-7518 4099
■ "Oozing ambience" reminiscent of a "country mansion", this "formal but modern" Edwardian/Jacobean hotel restaurant in Mayfair also "charms" visitors with "lovely" Modern European fare from "genius" chef Andrew Turner; the "food is delightful to the palate" (the "tasting menu is supreme"), the "excellent wine list" boasts 300 by-the-glass options and the "friendly, but not intrusive staff" are a "joy" to behold; N.B. not to be confused with the adjacent Library, where traditional English tea is served.

Browns Restaurant | 15 | 16 | 15 | £23 |
82-84 St. Martin's Ln., WC2 (Leicester Sq.), 020-7497 5050; fax 020-7497 5005 ● S
47 Maddox St., W1 (Bond St./Oxford Circus), 020-7491 4565; fax 020-7497 4564 S
201 Castelnau Row, SW13 (Hammersmith), 020-8748 4486; fax 020-8563 8601 S
9 Islington Green, Islington, N12 (Angel), 020-7226 2555; fax 020-7359 7306 ● S
8 Old Jewry, EC2 (Bank), 020-7606 6677; fax 020-7600 5359 Hertsmere Rd., E14 (Canary Wharf/West India Quay), 020-7987 9777; fax 020-7537 1341 S
◪ "Ideal when not sure what you want or haven't got a booking" sums up supporters' views of this "upbeat" chain

www.zagat.com

where you're "guaranteed a good feed" on "generally tasty" British comfort food in "relaxing" surroundings; cynics say the "bland" tucker is "nothing to write home about" and put the "bored staff" on the same "substandard" par; P.S. the West End sites are "great pre-theatre."

Bug-Bar, Restaurant & Lounge S | – | – | – | M |

The Crypt, St. Matthews Church, SW2 (Brixton), 020-7738 3366; fax 020-7738 3345

There might be even more reason to believe in this "gothic" crypt beneath Brixton's St. Matthews Church now that it's converted its name from Bah Humbug, modernised its ecclesiastically themed look with luxurious banquettes and introduced a revamped International menu that now offers a few meat dishes as well as selections "good for fish-eating vegetarians"; there are a new private dining room and stylish lounge, whilst the cocktail bar, offering DJs and dancing, remains a refuge for "lots of hip young things."

Builders Arms S | 16 | 16 | 14 | £20 |

13 Britten St., SW3 (Sloane Sq./South Kensington), 020-7349 9040; fax 020-7351 3181

■ Expect a "young, moneyed crowd" at this "fun", "friendly addition to Chelsea", a "laid-back" Modern British gastro-pub that's "just right, given the location", especially for a "quiet, casual evening"; find a "cosy alcove to sit in" and enjoy the "decent portions" of "simple, yet tasty food"; P.S. the "smoke can be an issue" for some.

Buona Sera ●S | 18 | 13 | 15 | £19 |

22-26 Northcote Rd., SW11 (Clapham Junction B.R.), 020-7924 1666; fax 020-7228 1114

■ A "buzzy atmosphere" and "lovely, hearty, filling" Italian food including "good pizza" make this "child-friendly" Battersea "favourite" an "excellent party venue"; "families and groups" settle into the "tightly packed tables" and tuck into the "huge portions" of "cheap", traditional fare that offers a "good take for the money"; N.B. there's a new layout with open bar.

Buona Sera at the Jam ●S | 16 | 18 | 16 | £18 |

289A King's Rd., SW3 (Sloane Sq.), 020-7352 8827; fax 020-7352 8827

■ Both adults and "kids love" this "cosy, small" King's Road Buona Sera sib as much for "climbing the ladders" up to the "fun" bunk-bed tables as for the "good", "authentic" Modern Italian cooking; P.S. the "tree-house atmosphere is great for a date!"

BUSABA EATHAI S | 22 | 20 | 16 | £17 |

106-110 Wardour St., W1 (Piccadilly Circus/Tottenham Court Rd.), 020-7255 8686; fax 020-7255 8688

◪ Thai-food lovers "wish" this "hip", "achingly minimalist" "gobble-and-go-type place" with "large communal tables"

| F | D | S | C |

"was undiscovered", but alas, the constant "queue outside proves it's not"; "be careful not to savour" each bite of the "outstanding food", as "they pride themselves on quick service" (some say they "rush you out") – but that's just as well, since it's a "groovy" spot to "kick off a night in Soho."

Busabong Too S | 20 | 15 | 18 | £28 |
1A Langton St., SW10 (Fulham Broadway/Sloane Sq.), 020-7352 7414; fax 020-7352 7534

■ Set in an elegant World's End townhouse, this two-floor eaterie offers "superb" Thai fare that's "good value for the money", plus service that's "nice and friendly"; when dining in the private room upstairs, "leave your shoes at the door" before easing into the low tables with cushion seating.

Bush Bar & Grill ●S | 16 | 17 | 15 | £29 |
45A Goldhawk Rd., W12 (Goldhawk Rd./Shepherd's Bush), 020-8746 2111; fax 020-8746 1331

◪ It's "nice to find" "lovely", "understated" New French fare on the "increasingly trendy Goldhawk Road" crows the "fun, young crowd" that flocks to this "loud, lively", "barn-like" restaurant, set in a former dairy; dissenters "disappointed" by the "bland food" claim "the only reason to venture into the Bush" is the "cool", "bustling bar"; N.B. opened by former staff from Woody's, The Groucho Club and 192.

Butlers Wharf Chop House S | 19 | 17 | 17 | £33 |
Butlers Wharf, 36E Shad Thames, SE1 (London Bridge/Tower Hill), 020-7403 3403; fax 020-7403 3414

■ With "plenty" of "delicious, hearty" Traditional British "choices from the old world as well as the new", "great views of the Tower Bridge" and "swift service", Sir Terence Conran's "lively" "riverside haunt" not only "lives up to expectations", it's a "favourite spot" of many; expect to compete for the "brilliant alfresco" tables – that's the "place to be on a warm summer's day."

Byron's S | ▽ 20 | 21 | 20 | £32 |
3A Downshire Hill, NW3 (Hampstead), 020-7435 3544; fax 020-7431 3544

■ "Quiet and romantic", so it's actually "possible to talk" whilst dining on "tasty", "innovative" Modern European fare exult a few admirers who've made their way to this "special" Regency townhouse in Hampstead; the "interesting choices are cooked really well" and served by "friendly" staff; P.S. "good-value set menu" for lunch is also offered.

Cactus Blue ●S | 14 | 16 | 14 | £26 |
86 Fulham Rd., SW3 (South Kensington), 020-7823 7858; fax 020-7823 8577

◪ "Giddyup, cowboy", bring on the "transporting drinks" and the "pickup lines, not the food" yee-haws the "young, hip crowd" who hangs at the "great bar" of this "fun", "funky" Southwestern cantina in Chelsea; whilst it "tries

---

www.zagat.com 39

| F | D | S | C |

to be authentic", the borderline eats are sometimes "hit or miss" (it's "shameful to call this Mexican" food), though it's "popular with homesick U.S. expats."

Cafe at Sotheby's ⓓ 17 | 16 | 16 | £24
Sotheby's Auction House, 34 New Bond St., W1 (Bond St.), 020-7293 5077

■ "They have the right formula" at this "clubby" dining room within the famous Mayfair auctioneers say the bidding bunch who vote it an "ideal" spot for a "quick", "pleasant, light lunch" of "good quality" Modern British fare; the "menu is limited", but the food is "well-presented", plus there's the added perk of "good people-watching"; N.B. open for breakfast and tea, but closed for dinner.

Café Boheme ⓓ S 15 | 15 | 14 | £23
13-17 Old Compton St., W1 (Leicester Sq.), 020-7734 0623; fax 020-7434 3775

■ "Convenient to Soho theatres", this "lively yet intimate" French bistro/bar is a "terrific spot" for dinner with friends; the "atmosphere is lovely", "low-key" and "comfortable" and it's "reasonably priced", which may explain why it's usually "bustling" at night (and around the clock on the weekends) and regulars "keep coming back"; N.B. Boheme Kitchen next door serves casual meals.

Café des Amis du Vin ⓓ 16 | 14 | 15 | £27
11-14 Hanover Pl., WC2 (Covent Garden), 020-7379 3444; fax 020-7379 9124

■ Set on a "quiet Covent Garden side street", this "classic French cafe" is a "great place to escape the crowds"; the "predictable, but acceptable bistro" fare includes "good value" prix fixe theatre options, plus the popular bar downstairs is "nice" for cheese and "wine lovers."

Cafe Fish ⓓ S 18 | 14 | 15 | £26
36-40 Rupert St., W1 (Piccadilly Circus), 020-7287 8989; fax 020-7287 8400

☒ Afishionados are hooked on the "simple menu of fresh seafood" (hooray for "fish 'n' chips as it should be") at this two-storey Soho spot, a "wonderful, relaxed" restaurant with a speedy, "handy-for theatre"-goers canteen one floor below; whilst fans applaud the "modern", "attractive setting", foes fume the "not very welcoming" "decor is straight from an NHS hospital"; P.S. there's a "good pre-theatre" menu for £11.50.

Café Grand Prix - | - | - | E
50A Berkeley St., W1 (Green Park), 020-7629 0808; fax 020-7409 4708

Named after its sister restaurant on Monaco's Grand Prix circuit, this enormous, three-floor Mayfair newcomer is comprised of three venues: chef Richard Turner (ex Hotel Tresanton in Cornwall, Quo Vadis and Pharmacy) turns

| **F** | **D** | **S** | **C** |

out light Mediterranean dishes in La Rascasse, a smart dining room with marble pillars, whilst Pit Brasserie serves casual French brasserie fare in a revved-up, F1-themed setting with a racing car display; snack food is available at the elegant Rosie's Bar downstairs.

Cafe Japan S | 24 | 10 | 17 | £25
626 Finchley Rd., NW11 (Golders Green), 020-8455 6854; fax 020-8455 6854

■ "Great value in Golders Green", this "no-nonsense" Japanese "cafeteria" offers some of the "best sushi in town"; the "decor is functional" (it "could be improved"), but the "cutesy service" "adds to the atmosphere", making this "favourite" "worth the journey."

Cafe Lazeez | 17 | 15 | 16 | £26
21 Dean St., W1 (Leicester Sq.), 020-7434 9393; fax 020-7434 0022 ☾ S
93-95 Old Brompton Rd., SW7 (Gloucester Rd./South Kensington), 020-7581 9993; fax 020-7581 8200 ☾ S
88 St. John St., EC1 (Farringdon), 020-7253 2224; fax 020-7253 2112

◪ "Think sophisticated rather than vindaloo" propose proponents of the "nouvelle Indian cuisine" at this "flock-free", "avant garde" trio in South Ken, Soho and Clerkenwell; the "Westernised" menu of "intelligent food" is flavoured with a "decent amount of spice" and "service is attentive", but traditionalists chide it's "glorifying its own eclecticism" and chafe at the "snotty" servers; P.S. the Clerkenwell glass conservatory is an "airy", "very pleasant place to eat."

Cafe, Level Seven S | 16 | 20 | 15 | £20
Tate Modern, Bankside, SE1 (Blackfriars/London Bridge), 020-7401 5020

■ "The beautiful view of London is a work of art in itself", and you may be "surprised by the quality" of the Modern British food, chorus visitors who appreciate this "buzzing" yet "casual escape" on the seventh-floor of the Tate Modern at Bankside; it's "great for dates and fun with friends", especially when you're craving "light, fresh food for mid-day sustenance"; P.S. "service can be a bit slow."

Cafe Med | 15 | 15 | 14 | £24
184A Kensington Park Rd., W11 (Ladbroke Grove/Notting Hill Gate), 020-7221 1150; fax 020-7229 5647 ☾ S
320 Goldhawk Rd., W6 (Stamford Brook), 020-8741 1994; fax 020-8741 9980 ☾ S
22 Dean St., W1 (Tottenham Court Rd.), 020-7287 9007; fax 020-7287 3529 ☾
21 Loudoun Rd., NW8 (St. John's Wood), 020-7625 1222; fax 020-7328 1593 ☾ S
370 St. John St., EC1 (Angel), 020-7278 1199; fax 020-7833 9046 S

■ "Comfy and cosy like your best mate's flat" concur surveyors who appreciate the "very chilled-out" "vibe"

www.zagat.com

F **D** **S** **C**

and "smart service" at this "better than average" Eclectic-Med chain of "reliable performers"; the "really good" menu makes you "want to try everything", and the "lovely" atmosphere is "perfect for a rainy Sunday."

Cafe Pacifico ●◐ S | 15 | 13 | 14 | £24 |

5 Langley St., WC2 (Covent Garden), 020-7379 7728;
fax 020-7836 5088

■ "Party time!" – this "loud", "crowded" Tex Mex haunt in Covent Garden is "hardly authentic", but it's "still fun" to do "shots of tequila or munch on fajitas" even "after all these years"; the "filling" fare is "unspectacular, but consistent" and "affordable", which may explain why most go for the "dangerous pitchers of margaritas"; purists, however, are still looking "to find a good Mexican restaurant in London."

Cafe Rouge S | 11 | 11 | 11 | £19 |

34 Wellington St., WC2 (Covent Garden), 020-7836 0998;
fax 020-7497 0738
31 Kensington Park Rd., W11 (Ladbroke Grove), 020-7221 4449;
fax 020-7792 3064
158 Fulham Palace Rd., W6 (Hammersmith), 020-8741 5037;
fax 020-8563 2761
98-100 Shepherd's Bush Rd., W6 (Shepherd's Bush),
020-7602 7732; fax 020-7603 7710
227 Chiswick High Rd., W4 (Chiswick Park), 020-8742 7447;
fax 020-8742 7557
15 Frith St., W1 (Tottenham Court Rd.), 020-7437 4307;
fax 020-7437 4442
39 Park Gate Rd., SW11 (Clapham Junction/Sloane Sq.),
020-7924 3565; fax 020-7924 3773
27-31 Basil St., SW3 (Knightsbridge), 020-7584 2345;
fax 020-7584 4253
120 St. John's High St., NW8 (St. John's Wood),
020-7722 8366; fax 020-7483 1015

▨ "Cheap and acceptable", this "no surprises" French bistro chain is "ideal for that quick food hit in between shopping" or when "you're tired or with children and need a refuge"; they're "cooking by numbers" cry critics who point to "ho-hum food in a ho-hum setting" that's become "so passé"; N.B. the Camden Town branch closed post-*Survey*.

Cafe Spice Namaste | 20 | 16 | 17 | £28 |

247 Lavender Hill, SW11 (Clapham Junction B.R.),
020-7738 1717; fax 020-7738 1666 ●◐ S
16 Prescot St., E1 (Aldgate/Aldgate East), 020-7488 9242;
fax 020-7488 9339

■ "Boldly goes where no curry house usually goes" enthuse lovers of this "fantastic" Indian duo in Clapham and near Tower Bridge, where chef/cookbook author Cyrus Todiwala tempts taste buds with "magic flavours and combinations"; whilst a handful bridle at the "D.I.Y.-ish" interior (it's "not a place for soaking up atmosphere"), few dispute that this "different experience" is "worth a second trip."

42 www.zagat.com

| F | D | S | C |

Calzone ⑤ 16 | 11 | 14 | £17
2A Kensington Park Rd., W11 (Notting Hill Gate), 020-7243 2003;
fax 020-7243 2006 ●
335 Fulham Rd., SW10 (South Kensington), 020-7352 9797;
fax 020-7352 9798 ●
66 Heath St., NW3 (Hampstead), 020-7794 6775;
fax 020-7794 1138
35 Upper St., N1 (Angel), 020-7359 9191; fax 020-7359 9192 ●
■ "Perfect for a simple and quick bite", this "kid-friendly" Italian quartet hits the spot with a "good value" menu of "excellent thin-crust pizzas, tasty salads", calzones and the like; the "cheerful", "happening service" secures its status as a "favourite."

Cambio de Tercio ●⑤ 21 | 17 | 18 | £34
163 Old Brompton Rd., SW5 (Gloucester Rd.), 020-7244 8970;
fax 020-7373 8817
■ "Small" and "superb", this "jolly" South Ken Iberian "never gets it wrong" with its "imaginative and sometimes witty take on Spanish food" that "comes blessed with a phenomenal wine list"; the "intimate" setting is "excellent for a date" and "good for business", plus the "tremendous service" translates to "presidential treatment for regulars."

Camden Brasserie ●⑤ 18 | 14 | 18 | £26
216 Camden High St., NW1 (Camden Town/Chalk Farm),
020-7482 2114; fax 020-7482 2114
■ An "oasis of calm and good food in Camden", this "friendly" "local find" is "comfortable after a tiring day"; the "consistent quality" Mediterranean fare is "dependable", "though not all that exciting", yet the "lovely people" behind this restaurant "set it apart."

Cantaloupe ●⑤ 16 | 14 | 13 | £23
35-42 Charlotte Rd., EC2 (Old St.), 020-7729 5566;
fax 020-7613 4111
■ A "laissez-faire ambience" reigns at this "grunge heaven" in Shoreditch, a "funky", "noisy" Mediterranean restaurant and bar that's "fun for a night out with a group"; the "earthy" "tapas-style food" is "great for peckish clubbers" or for "when you don't want a big meal", plus you can "spend hours here without breaking the bank"; but diners done in by the din sound off that it's "deafeningly loud."

Cantina del Ponte ⑤ 18 | 18 | 16 | £29
Butlers Wharf Bldg., 36C Shad Thames, SE1 (London Bridge/
Tower Hill), 020-7403 5403; fax 020-7403 4432
◪ "Location, location, location", including an "impressive view of Tower Bridge" from the Butler's Wharf terrace, is what makes this Conran Group Mediterranean an "absolute must on a summer's day"; thereafter opinions divide: some enjoy the "well-executed" dishes and the "social" setting, but others baulk at its "impersonal" "production-line" approach to cooking.

www.zagat.com

F	D	S	C

Cantina Vinopolis S 17 | 17 | 14 | £28
Vinopolis Museum, 1 Bank End, SE1 (London Bridge), 020-7940 8333; fax 020-7940 8334

◪ The "bible-size" *vino* list wins plaudits at this "wine lover's dream", a "charming", "cavernous" brick-walled Mediterranean restaurant housed in the Vinopolis Museum under the South Bank's railway arches; for a "complete experience, do the tasting first, then carry on" with a selection from the "imaginative menu"; critics counter that "the accolades end" after the bottle's been uncorked, lashing out at the "uninspiring food."

Cantinetta Venegazzu S ∇ 17 | 14 | 19 | £33
31-32 Battersea Sq., SW11 (Clapham Junction B.R.), 020-7978 5395; fax 020-7228 8946

■ "Creative" Venetian cooking, a "very good" wine list and "excellent service" coalesce to create a cosy "bit of Italy in Battersea"; terrace tables ease the crush on busy nights, though it can sometimes still feel a "little over-cramped."

Canyon S 17 | 20 | 15 | £32
Tow Path, Riverside, near Richmond Bridge (Richmond), Richmond, 020-8948 2944; fax 020-8948 2945

■ All is "resplendent in Richmond" declare diners who find this "amazing location by the river" the "perfect setting for Sunday brunch on an English summer's day" (if you're in "hangover land, recovery is guaranteed"); the American-Southwestern menu is "always delightful", as is the "stylish" decor; the "service is chaotic" and the "food mediocre" retort canyon-bashers who assert it's "past its prime."

CAPITAL RESTAURANT S 26 | 21 | 25 | £53
The Capital, 22-24 Basil St., SW3 (Knightsbridge), 020-7589 5171; fax 020-7225 0011

■ A "small hidden treasure of gastronomy" awaits at The Capital hotel's "consistently elegant" dining room in Knightsbridge, where chef Eric Chavot "excels" at creating "sumptuous" New French fare; "it's not just a meal, it's a pleasant dining experience", smoothed along by "keen" "service that's a paean to the food" and a wine cellar boasting 700 bins; the "prices can be hard to swallow" lament a few, who also suspect the "staid" "decor could use a rethink."

Caraffini ◐ 21 | 17 | 22 | £33
61-63 Lower Sloane St., SW1 (Sloane Sq.), 020-7259 0235; fax 020-7259 0236

■ The "charming" "waiters chatter and flatter" the "chic people" who frequent this "compact", "bright and airy" Italian "treat" near Sloane Square, making "you feel like it's always a special occasion, even if it's not"; the "delicious", "affordable" "food couldn't be better" – small wonder it's "great for a group" or a "lighthearted romantic dinner"; P.S. "noisy" environs can make it an "eavesdropper's paradise."

| F | D | S | C |

Caravaggio | 19 | 17 | 17 | £37 |
107-112 Leadenhall St., EC3 (Bank), 020-7626 6206; fax 020-7626 8108
■ "Popular with City executives", this "hustling, bustling" Modern Italian "power lunch" haunt, set in a "fantastic former bank", offers a "varied menu" of "reliably good" dishes with an emphasis on seafood; it's a "welcome oasis" thanks to "staff who know how to serve, not just look good"; cynics paint a different picture, declaring it's "a little too flashy" and a bit "on the pricey side."

Carluccio's Caffe | 19 | 14 | 15 | £20 |
5-6 The Green, W5 (Ealing Broadway), 020-8566 4458; fax 020-8840 8566 S
3-5 Barrett St., W1 (Bond St.), 020-7935 5927; fax 020-7487 5436 S
Fenwick, New Bond St., W1 (Bond St.), 020-7629 0699; fax 020-7493 0069
8 Market Pl., W1 (Oxford Circus), 020-7636 2228; fax 020-7636 9650 S
12 West Smithfield, EC1 (Farringdon), 020-7329 5904; fax 020-7248 5981 S
■ "Just what London needs" laud lovers of this "well-carried-out concept" from Antonio Carluccio: a burgeoning chain of "all-day" cafes, bars and food shops with "utterly delicious", "easy" Traditional Italian cooking at "reasonable prices"; naysayers find it "a little unimaginative given the chef's flair and charm" and object to "cramped" quarters, but most concede it's "perfect for a shopping lunch."

Carpaccio ● | – | – | – | M |
4 Sydney St., SW3 (South Kensington), 020-7352 3433
The team behind Como Lario and Ziani now have a third Chelsea restaurant, a promising, affordable Modern Italian newcomer in a Sydney Street location that's seen several ventures come and go; the moderate-size site has been cleverly renovated to include a retractable glass ceiling, and the menu, long on, what else, carpaccio, is just as innovative; wines are sensibly sourced and priced.

Casale Franco ● S | 19 | 16 | 15 | £27 |
134-137 Upper St., N1 (Angel/Highbury & Islington), 020-7226 8994; fax 020-7359 1114
■ "Love it! love it! love it!" swoon surveyors who fall for the "great homemade pizza" and Modern Italian "food as it should be" at this "nice, friendly" Islington Italian; whilst some like that staff "always remember you", a handful of groaners gripe that it's "overpoweringly friendly."

Catch ● S | 17 | 16 | 16 | £34 |
158 Old Brompton Rd., SW5 (Gloucester Rd./South Kensington), 020-7370 3300; fax 020-7370 3377
■ "Every neighbourhood should have one" insist insiders hooked on the "delightful" Modern British and seafood

| F | D | S | C |

dishes at this "small", "elegant" South Kensington spot where, after a "top-of-the-line" dinner, the "beautiful people" who want to be "seen" "head to the lounge downstairs"; the unimpressed wave away the food – it's "ok, but not memorable" – and consider the space "cramped."

Caviar Kaspia ◐ | 22 | 17 | 22 | £54 |
18-18A Bruton Pl., W1 (Bond St./Green Park), 020-7493 2612; fax 020-7408 1627

■ "For a decadent lunch on a gloomy day", this discreet, wood-panelled Mayfair caviar specialist, modelled after its Parisian predecessor, hits the bull's-eye, offering "delicate portions" of Beluga, Sevruga and Oscietra, plus "high-standard" Franco-Russian cooking; it's as "expensive" as it is "sophisticated", but you can still indulge in the "fun" with a £22 prix fixe lunch.

Cecconi's 🆂 | 21 | 20 | 19 | £46 |
5A Burlington Gardens, W1 (Green Park), 020-7434 1500; fax 020-7494 2440

◪ It's "like being in a Robert de Niro film" enthuse fans who "love" the "extremely sophisticated" atmosphere, "first-class service" and "food without fripperies" at Hani Farsi's lavishly revamped Bond Street "bastion of great Italian cuisine"; it's a "fat-cat dining" experience lament a handful who claim it "lost something in the remake"; P.S. there's a "great scene" most nights at the "funky bar."

Cellar Gascon ◐ | 22 | 19 | 18 | £27 |
59 West Smithfield, EC1 (Barbican), 020-7600 7561; fax 020-7796 0601

■ "Less snooty and less pricey" than Club Gascon, its "big brother" next door, this "small but perfectly formed" Smithfield wine bar offers a "super" *vino* selection plus the same "brilliant little dishes" of New French fare, served "tapas-style"; the "unusual setting, relaxed atmosphere and affordable prices" ensure a loyal "after-work" following.

Chamberlain's | – | – | – | VE |
23-25 Leadenhall Mkt., EC3 (Bank/Monument), 020-7648 8690

The handful who commented on fish wholesaler Les Steadman's new, "brilliant", business-oriented seafood restaurant and emporium, housed in a "striking" tri-level Victorian building, consider it a "wonderful addition" to Leadenhall Market; fans fawn over the "sophisticated", "expense-account"–worthy dishes and feel cared for by the "attentive service with a bit of difference"; N.B. the opening was delayed when Roman remains were discovered nearby.

Champor-Champor | ▽ 24 | 20 | 23 | £30 |
62 Weston St., SE1 (London Bridge), 020-7403 4600

■ "By rights" this "tiny, polished" Malaysian-Asian "jewel", "a well-kept secret near London Bridge", "should be packed with City suits in search of adventure"; the "exquisite",

| **F** | **D** | **S** | **C** |

"exotic" food and "special" setting, "lovingly decorated" to look like an Eastern "boudoir", explain why it's "quickly become a favourite" of those in-the-know, who confide they're "glad more people don't know about it."

Che ◐ | 16 | 18 | 16 | £40 |
23 St. James's St., SW1 (Green Park), 020-7747 9380; fax 020-7747 9382

◪ A "perennial favourite for expense-accounters", this "fun" St. James's eaterie offers "nicely prepared" but "pricey" Modern British cooking on the first floor and a "smart" cigar bar below, "packed with a glitzy crowd" of "young professionals"; but insurgents rise up against the "snail-paced service" and "rather pompous" atmosphere, charging the "cost isn't quite justified by results."

Chelsea Bun ⬛ | 16 | 9 | 14 | £14 |
70 Battersea Bridge Rd., SW11 (Clapham Junction B.R./ Sloane Sq.), 020-7738 9009
Limerstone St., SW10 (Earl's Court), 020-7352 3635 ◐

■ When you're craving a hangover brekkie" or a Traditional British "meal like mum would make", head to these "no-frills" sibs in Chelsea and Battersea; the "crowd-pleasing" fare comes close to "NY diner food", and the "quick service" goes down well too; a few baulk "it looks like an American breakfast place, but it doesn't taste like one."

CHEZ BRUCE ⬛ | 26 | 20 | 23 | £41 |
2 Bellevue Rd., SW17 (Balham/Wandsworth Common B.R.), 020-8672 0114; fax 020-8767 6648

■ "Close your eyes and you're in the countryside eating" "out-of-this-world" dishes enthuse loyalists who "never tire" of chef-owner Bruce Poole's "constantly changing", French-accented menu, ranked No. 1 in this *Survey* for Modern British fare, or the "really special", "romantic" Wandsworth setting that's "well worth the trip"; "nothing is too much trouble" for "friendly" staff, and most walk away with a "feeling of having received a value-for-money treat"; P.S. check out the "very reasonable lunchtime offers."

Chez Gérard | 16 | 15 | 14 | £28 |
119 Chancery Ln., WC2 (Chancery Ln.), 020-7405 0290; fax 020-7242 2649
Opera Terrace, The Market, 45 E. Terrace, 1st fl., WC2 (Covent Garden), 020-7379 0666; fax 020-7497 9060 ◐⬛
31 Dover St., W1 (Green Park), 020-7499 8171; fax 020-7491 3818 ◐⬛
8 Charlotte St., W1 (Tottenham Court Rd.), 020-7636 4975; fax 020-7637 4564 ◐⬛
9 Belvedere Rd., SE1 (Waterloo), 020-7202 8470; fax 020-7202 8474 ⬛
64 Bishopsgate, EC2 (Bank/Liverpool St.), 020-7588 1200; fax 020-7588 1122

(continued)

| F | D | S | C |

(continued)
Chez Gérard
84-86 Rosebery Ave., EC1 (Angel), 020-7833 1515;
fax 020-7833 9118
14 Trinity Sq., EC3 (Tower Hill), 020-7480 5500; fax 020-7480 5588

☑ "Chain dining at its best" fawn fans who find the "good bistro food" and "decently priced wine" *magnifique*, especially for those times when "you don't want to fuss", plus the "gracious service" is "just French enough"; it's "lacklustre" lament the underwhelmed, who suggest "go if you like steak frites, otherwise don't bother"; P.S. the Covent Garden location is "perfect on a nice day."

Chez Max 23 | 18 | 22 | £40
168 Ifield Rd., SW10 (Earl's Court), 020-7835 0874;
fax 020-7244 0618

■ It "still has that magic touch" enthuse the enchanted who burrow into the "tiny nooks and crannies" of this "quirky", "subterranean French" eatery on the Fulham-Chelsea border for a "romantic" BYO meal hosted by the "brilliantly eccentric owner/maitre'd" and "staff who love food"; a few protest the "hammy service" "tries too hard."

Chez Moi 22 | 19 | 22 | £39
1 Addison Ave., W11 (Holland Park), 020-7603 8267;
fax 020-7603 3898

■ "The formula is still working" at this "comfortably old-fashioned" "small spot" in Holland Park where locals count on the "interesting" New French cooking, "nice service" and a "sensible wine list" year after year; P.S. it's been in business since 1967 – perhaps that "says it all."

Chiang Mai ⑤ 20 | 13 | 15 | £26
48 Frith St., W1 (Leicester Sq./Tottenham Court Rd.),
020-7437 7444; fax 020-7287 2255

☑ "Consistently good for many years", this Thai venue in Soho still offers some of the "most authentic food around"; a recent revamp (including air conditioning) allays some concerns about "cramped seating" and "terrible decor."

China Dream ⑤ ▽ 26 | 21 | 20 | £26
68 Heath St., NW3 (Hampstead), 020-7794 6666

■ "A welcome addition to Hampstead" from "the owners of Hi Sushi" applaud admirers who make tracks to this "warm Oriental setting" in the former Horse and Groom pub that wins a pat on the back for "very authentic dim sum" and other "innovative" multiregional Chinese food; P.S. the "best seats are downstairs."

China House ☾ 16 | 18 | 15 | £25
160 Piccadilly, W1 (Green Park/Piccadilly Circus),
020-7499 6996; fax 020-7499 7779

■ It's like an "Oriental odyssey" fawn fans of the "plush, dark", "impressive interior" at this "imposing" 1920s

| F | D | S | C |

building, a former bank on Piccadilly endowed with a "great vibe" and an "amusing", "reasonably priced" menu of Chinese noodle and dumpling dishes; N.B. the Clipper Bar and Orient restaurant upstairs have closed.

Chinon ▽ | 24 | 17 | 16 | £34 |
23 Richmond Way, W14 (Olympia/Shepherd's Bush), 020-7602 5968; fax 020-7602 4082

◪ Well off-the-beaten-track behind Olympia, this slightly "bizarre" eaterie with a "well-lit garden" makes a "soothing backdrop" for "sensational" New French fare from self-taught Irish chef Jonathan Hayes; whilst a few report "off-putting service", most find it "charming and friendly" – "just another plus for this wonderful gem."

Chiswick, The S | 20 | 16 | 18 | £30 |
131 Chiswick High Rd., W4 (Turnham Green), 020-8994 6887; fax 020-8994 5504

◪ The "marvellous" Modern British "food is as good as ever" and, what's more, "surprisingly reasonable" at this "friendly", "relaxed", "down-to-earth" "local"; foes weigh in that it's "no longer the pride of Chiswick", as the food is "dull" and the decor "needs a face-lift."

Chives S | 21 | 16 | 17 | £35 |
204 Fulham Rd., SW10 (South Kensington), 020-7351 4747

◪ Now separated from the Red Pepper Group (who had been running it for the current owner), this bi-level Chelsea spot "carries on nicely", with a "friendly" approach and a "superb" Modern European menu that's "good for what you pay"; snipers snip that the dishes have "little substance."

Chor Bizarre ●S | 21 | 21 | 19 | £31 |
16 Albemarle St., W1 (Green Park), 020-7629 9802; fax 020-7493 7756

◪ "Kooky decor" makes dining at this Mayfair Indian "a very bizarre experience", and whilst some praise the "adventurous" cooking (with "some outstanding dishes") at a "reasonable" price, others cite "mediocre" fare and "poor service that spoils the experience"; still, at least it's not on the "lads' curry evening" circuit.

Christopher's American Grill S | 19 | 17 | 18 | £36 |
18 Wellington St., WC2 (Covent Garden), 020-7240 4222; fax 020-7836 3506 ●
Thistle Victoria Hotel, 101 Buckingham Palace Rd., SW1 (Victoria), 020-7976 5522; fax 020-7976 5521

◪ The "grand interiors" at both of these "buzzy" eateries in Theatreland and next to Victoria Station ensure a "great ambience", even if "low lighting" means some are "tempted to offer meter coins"; opinions on the American surf 'n' turf menu range from a "meat eaters' feast" to "disappointing", whilst "service varies" too; Covent Garden is "excellent" for a "quick pre-theatre" meal.

| F | D | S | C |

Chuen Cheng Ku ●S | 17 | 8 | 10 | £18 |
17 Wardour St., W1 (Leicester Sq.), 020-7437 1398; fax 020-7434 0533
■ "Wagon-style Hong Kong dim sum" and a "cheap" multiregional Chinese menu delight diners who crown this functional Chinatown standby "the best around, hands down"; it's especially "fun" for those "who want to try different dishes", plus staff are "friendly" (not so, pout a paltry few who claim they are "of little help").

Churchill Arms S | 21 | 14 | 14 | £15 |
119 Kensington Church St., W8 (High St. Kensington/ Notting Hill Gate), 020-7727 4242
■ "Thai for a tenner" – what "unbelievable value" fawn fans who "book ahead" to eat in this "great old traditional pub" in the "deepest Kensington"; the "yummy food" is "perfect for a casual meal" and so is the "wonderfully quirky atmosphere" – little wonder it's "invariably packed."

Chutney Mary ●S | – | – | – | E |
535 King's Rd., SW10 (Fulham Broadway), 020-7351 3113; fax 020-7351 7694
"Not your normal curry house", this 12-year-old, bi-level "Indian oasis" in Chelsea "deserves its reputation for fun and authenticity" more than ever thanks to an impressive post-*Survey* revamp, including teak panelling and dramatic lighting; there's also a sophisticated, new regional Indian menu from chef Nagarajan Rubinath, supported by a team of seven regional specialists from areas such as Goa, Kerala and Hyderabad; whilst it's now closed for weekday lunch, it's still open for the popular Sunday jazz brunch.

Chutney's ●S | 20 | 13 | 16 | £17 |
124 Drummond St., NW1 (Euston/Euston Sq.), 020-7388 0604
■ "The eat-all-you-want buffet is a bargain" at this modest Indian Vegetarian in Euston, and as "the à la carte menu does not disappoint" either, this "cheerful" spot has a loyal following – especially for the £5.45 prix fixe lunch.

Cibo S | 20 | 14 | 16 | £34 |
3 Russell Gardens, W14 (Olympia/Shepherd's Bush), 020-7371 2085; fax 020-7602 1371
◪ Not only is there "some celebrity spotting to be had" at this "relaxed", "lovely find down a back street" near Olympia, there's also "wholesome, rustic" Modern Italian cooking served in "substantial portions" by "attentive" staff; it's "nothing special" retort naysayers who deem the "service slow" and the "decor disappointing."

Cicada | 19 | 16 | 17 | £26 |
132-136 St. John St., EC1 (Farringdon), 020-7608 1550; fax 020-7608 1551
◪ "Hip and friendly, from the staff to the clientele", this "minimalist", "breath of fresh air" in Clerkenwell "tickles

| F | D | S | C |

your fancy" with "tasty cocktails" and "unusual" Chinese–Pan-Asian fare that's "worth returning for"; it's "best for groups because it's noisy, crowded" and "inexpensive"; critics chirp back that it's just "another trendy restaurant" where the "fusion-style food" is "often disappointing."

Cigala S | 20 | 13 | 17 | £33 |
54 Lambs Conduit St., WC1 (Holborn), 020-7405 1717; fax 020-7242 9949

■ An "excellent addition", this "lovely" "up-and-coming" Bloomsbury "local" "makes you rethink Spanish" cuisine thanks to its "superb seafood" and "well-executed" fare; it's "simple, and all the better for it", with a "reasonable wine list" and "friendly service" – in sum, it "just misses being excellent"; a disparaging few find it "somewhat cluttered", "cramped and not cheap."

Cinnamon Cay | ∇ 24 | 19 | 21 | £28 |
87 Lavender Hill, SW11 (Clapham Common), 020-7801 0932; fax 020-7924 5436

■ "Leagues ahead of its Clapham peers" chorus the adoring few who frequent this "stylish" Pacific Rim "revelation" that "deserves to do well"; the "refreshingly different tasty" dishes served by a "hardworking team" prove that this "gem" can readily go from "strength to strength."

Cinnamon Club | 23 | 23 | 21 | £41 |
The Old Westminster Library, Great Smith St., SW1 (Westminster), 020-7222 2555; fax 020-7222 1333

◪ "No teething problems here" enthuse admirers of Iqbal Wahhab's "very chic", "spacious", "civilized" yearling in two converted floors of the Old Westminster Library where executive chef Vivek Singh puts a "new slant on Indian food" with "truly inspirational" dishes that offer "depth and flavour"; cin-ics bark that it's "expensive, pretentious" and "over-hyped"; N.B. breakfast is served every weekday, and a second bar area (with DJ) opened post-*Survey*.

Circus ● | 19 | 19 | 17 | £37 |
1 Upper James St., W1 (Piccadilly Circus), 020-7534 4000; fax 020-7534 4010

■ It "looks daunting from the outside", but this "favourite" "all-rounder" is actually a "crisp, clean" and "cheerful" Soho spot that performs with "no airs and graces"; the "interesting" Modern British cooking doesn't clown around either – "media types" and other fans applaud that "it never disappoints"; the "very cool bar" downstairs strikes some as "more fun than the restaurant", as it "attracts the right crowd" with an entertaining "after-dinner atmosphere."

City Miyama | 23 | 15 | 20 | £40 |
17 Godliman St., EC4 (St. Paul's), 020-7489 1937; fax 020-7236 0325

■ The "decor is the only downer" at this laid-back City Japanese near St. Paul's Cathedral where the faithful flock

| F | D | S | C |

for the "fantastic experience" of "very good, traditional" cooking, as well as "excellent sushi, albeit at a price."

City Rhodes | 24 | 17 | 21 | £48
1 New Street Sq., EC4 (Blackfriars/Chancery Ln.), 020-7583 1313; fax 020-7353 1662

■ "A good bet for client lunches", Gary Rhodes' "smoothly run" first-floor Holborn eatery "has kept its edge over the years" by serving "perfectly cooked" Modern British fare in "stylish surroundings"; whilst it's "priced for pinstripes", acolytes are "willing to pay the price" and confide it's such a "winner", you should "try it not for business" too; still, a few sniff that the "dull setting" is "cold" and "uninviting."

CLARKE'S | 25 | 19 | 23 | £46
124 Kensington Church St., W8 (Notting Hill Gate), 020-7221 9225; fax 020-7229 4564

◪ "Just like at home", "kitchen whiz" Sally Clarke's "consistently excellent" Modern British "menu is set", which "absolves you from the effort" of making a decision at this "class act" in Kensington; the "satisfying" cooking, "charming service" and "cosy" setting are "fantastic" enough to spark a "romantic reverie"; still, sceptics dismiss the "no choice" scenario as "strangely unmemorable"; N.B. now open for Saturday brunch, lunch and dinner.

Clerkenwell Dining Room & Bar ● | 20 | 17 | 19 | £37
69-73 St. John St., EC1 (Farringdon), 020-7253 9000

■ "Trendy, but not precocious for its age", this "first-rate" Clerkenwell "newcomer" is a "thoroughly enjoyable experience" thanks to chef Andrew Thompson's "lovely" Modern British cooking served in a "relaxed" setting that's "stylish without being stuffy"; even if a circumspect few quibble about "overblown" service and an "awkward space", most agree it makes a "nice addition to EC1."

Cliveden Hotel, Waldo's | 23 | 24 | 23 | £61
Cliveden Hotel, Taplow, Berkshire, 01628 607166; fax 01628 607166

■ "Be landed gentry for a few hours" ("or stay the night and make an event of it") at this historic country-house hotel in Berkshire where "everything is done well" in the "small", "sumptuous" basement dining room/bar, from the "marvellous" New French cooking and "terrific wine list" to the "outstanding service"; it's a "unique experience" that's "worth the scenic drive from London"; P.S. the unrated Terrace dining room above looks out over "lovely gardens."

Clock Restaurant S | ▽ 18 | 17 | 16 | £31
130-132 Uxbridge Rd., W7 (Boston Manor), 020-8810 1011; fax 020-8405 5464

◪ It's about time that Hanwell had an "inventive" Modern British "gem" chime "food fans" who've found their way to this former bank near the Clock Tower; "admittedly, there's

| F | D | S | C |

not much competition" nearby, still, the few who know it say this "great local" is one of the "best in the area"; the wallet-pinched complain it's "a bit pricey."

CLUB GASCON   26 | 20 | 21 | £46
57 West Smithfield, EC1 (Barbican), 020-7796 0600; fax 020-7796 0601

■ "Don't bring a cardiologist" to this "foie gras sanctuary" tease touters of this "divine" New French "food nirvana" in Clerkenwell, an "ego-free zone" where the "service is unexpectedly friendly and very professional"; it's "worth mortgaging your flat" just to dine on the "rich but heavenly" tapas-style dishes "accompanied by wines that bring out" the "immense concentration of flavours" (it's a "veritable treat for the palate"); N.B. the same owners also run Comptoir Gascon, a delicatessen nearby, and Cellar Gascon.

Collection, The ⑤   14 | 19 | 13 | £38
264 Brompton Rd., SW3 (South Kensington), 020-7225 1212; fax 020-7225 1050

☑ The International "food is actually good, but who comes to taste it?" wonder surveyors who find "the pickup scene more important" to the hip and "trendy crowd that fills this spacious", "animated" bi-level Brompton Cross venue; the "music pumps till the bar closes", amplifying the "fun", "electrifying atmosphere", but deafened denizens sound off that it's "too loud to have a conversation", let alone "hear yourself think."

Como Lario ❶   18 | 14 | 17 | £34
22 Holbein Pl., SW1 (Sloane Sq.), 020-7730 2954; fax 020-7244 8387

■ "Mad but fun", this "crowded", "chaotic Italian affair" "hidden behind Sloane Square" may be "one of the noisiest experiences in town", but many "keep going back", as the fare is "solid" and the "friendly hospitality" "makes you feel welcome"; critics cry it's a "bit crammed" "for comfort."

Condotti ❶   17 | 14 | 17 | £20
4 Mill St., W1 (Oxford Circus/Piccadilly Circus), 020-7499 1308; fax 020-7491 2122

☑ "Upmarket pizzas" and other "reliable" Italian fare make this "decent" Mayfair haunt a "pleasant experience" for some; whilst loyalists applaud its "stylish" looks, detractors snipe it's "like stepping back to the early '80s", concluding there's "little to be excited about" here.

Connaught, The ⑤   – | – | – | VE
The Connaught Hotel, Carlos Pl., W1 (Bond St./Green Park), 020-7499 7070; fax 020-7495 3262

Change is afoot at this very famous Mayfair hotel, with a sumptuous revamp by designer Nina Campbell and Gordon Ramsay taking over the dining facilities, with his protégé, Angela Hartnett, at the stove; the recently reopened Grill

| F | D | S | C |

Room, an intimate setting, now serves Modern European fare and will offer interpretations of Connaught classics; scheduled to open this autumn are the main restaurant, Angela Hartnett's MENU at The Connaught, plus The Terrace which will have year-round alfresco dining; a chef's table with a plasma-TV view of the kitchen is also planned.

Coq d'Argent S | 18 | 20 | 16 | £42 |
No. 1 Poultry, EC2 (Bank), 020-7395 5000; fax 020-7395 5050

■ It "cuts away from the grey-suited norm" crow admirers who insist that "lunch doesn't get any better in the City" than the Conran Group's "beautiful" rooftop garden "dining mecca" offering "fantastic" views, "attentive servers" and "good-quality" New French fare; but cynics squawk about "snail-like service" and "expense-account" prices, dubbing it "Coq trop d'Argent."

Costa's Grill | ▽ 14 | 10 | 13 | £18 |
12-14 Hillgate St., W8 (Notting Hill Gate), 020-7229 3794

■ "One never fails to be amused" by this "unique", "crazy place" in Notting Hill where the "laid-back service" and "great-value" Greek-Cypriot menu continue to attract an "eccentric crowd"; "sitting under the stars and vines" in the garden seems to "make up" for any shortcomings.

Cotto | 20 | 14 | 17 | £34 |
44 Blythe Rd., W14 (Olympia), 020-7602 9333; fax 020-7602 5003

■ "A godsend for lunch after antiquing in Olympia", this "friendly", "offbeat", unassuming "local gem" is "bright in all respects", from chef-owner James Kirby's "innovative" Modern British cooking to the "intimate" surroundings; whilst a few are put off by "small, pricey portions", most agree this "nice neighbourhood place" is "promising."

County Hall Restaurant S | 19 | 20 | 19 | £35 |
London Marriott County Hall, Westminster Bridge Rd., Queens Walk, SE1 (Westminster), 020-7902 8000; fax 020-7928 5300

■ With "delicious" Modern European food, "good all-round service" and a "killer view of Big Ben", this "rather grand" hotel dining room "on the wrong side of the Thames by the Eye" strikes many as an "excellent" choice for "entertaining guests"; a handful caution that the "food is average" (the setting is the "best part"), so consider "going for a drink instead."

Cow, The S | 20 | 15 | 16 | £26 |
89 Westbourne Park Rd., W2 (Westbourne Park), 020-7221 0021; fax 020-7727 8687

■ The "last remaining gem in over-trendy Notting Hill", Tom Conran's "charming" first-floor eatery above the same-named bar downstairs is "an unexpected gastronomic experience in retro surroundings" agree mavens moo-ved by the Modern British menu that allows for "a seafood

| F | D | S | C |

indulgence"; whilst downstairs attracts a "grungy pub crowd", the dining room "always has the 'in' crowd."

Creelers 22 | 13 | 21 | £32
3 Bray Pl., SW3 (Sloane Sq.), 020-7838 0788; fax 020-7838 0788

■ Though "yet to be discovered" by the masses, this "small", "intimate" Modern British–seafooder set in a "simple setting" on a "wonderful street off King's Road" is "creating a loyal following" with "good-size portions" of "very high-quality fish" (straight from Scotland) and "superb service"; in sum, "well worth your time."

Crescent, The S 17 | 15 | 18 | £29
Montcalm Nikko Hotel, 34 Great Cumberland Pl., W1 (Marble Arch), 020-7402 4288

■ The few who frequent this Marble Arch hotel dining room are over the moon about its "effortless style", "benevolent service" and "fantastic value" Modern European menu (which includes half a bottle of wine per person); N.B. the decor was recently spruced up a bit.

CRITERION GRILL ● 19 | 25 | 16 | £39
224 Piccadilly, W1 (Piccadilly Circus), 020-7930 0488; fax 020-7930 8380

◪ "The most unexpected place under the neon of Piccadilly Circus", this "stunning" Marco Pierre White spot is the dining "equivalent of a Chanel suit: classy, grown-up and pricey", with "first-class" New French food to match; whilst some say staff "pamper" you "from arrival to departure", critics are irked by the "average food" and "condescending service", but even they admit that the "decor makes up for" lapses; N.B. a post-*Survey* shift to mostly grilled and rotisserie fare may impact the above Food score.

Crivelli's Garden S ▽ 16 | 16 | 13 | £22
National Gallery, mezzanine level, Sainsbury Wing, WC2 (Charing Cross/Leicester Sq.), 020-7747 2869; fax 020-7747 2438

◪ "A nice respite after immersion in the great art" on display in the National Gallery, this "spacious", "relaxing" dining area (run by the Red Pepper group) in the Sainsbury Wing offers "views of Trafalgar Square" and "surprisingly good" Mediterranean cooking; "it's much better than it has to be" concur most, but critics counter that things can be a "bit ad hoc"; N.B. closed for dinner except Wednesdays.

Cucina S 16 | 13 | 15 | £33
45A South End Rd., NW3 (Belsize Park), 020-7435 7814; fax 020-7435 7147

◪ An "imaginative" Modern British menu of "good-value", "honest food in the desert of Hampstead" and "warm, willing service" make this restaurant a "local to enjoy time and again"; dissenters "would not go out of their way to visit", as it's "losing consistency."

www.zagat.com

| | | | F | D | S | C |

Dakota ⑤   17 | 17 | 14 | £32
127 Ledbury Rd., W11 (Notting Hill Gate/Westbourne Park), 020-7792 9191; fax 020-7792 9090
■ "Interesting, friendly and not incredibly expensive", with American-Southwestern eats and a "nice vibe", this comfortable Notting Hill sibling to Canyon, Montana et al., is a "great family brunch place" and "pleasant for a tête-à-tête"; bashers blast that it's a "mixed bag", bemoaning the "variable quality" and "casually arrogant service."

Dan's ⑤   17 | 17 | 18 | £31
119 Sydney St., SW3 (Sloane Sq./South Kensington), 020-7352 2718; fax 020-7352 3265
■ It's "still like home" exclaim enthusiasts drawn to this "long-lived" Chelsea "local" as much for the "fantastic welcome" from "friendly" servers as for the "frequently changing" Modern British–European menu; the "pretty patio" is just right for "alfresco evenings", plus there are two private rooms available for larger parties.

Daphne ◐   19 | 19 | 19 | £34
83 Bayham St., NW1 (Camden Town), 020-7267 7322; fax 020-7482 3964
■ "The place has a certain charm" say smitten surveyors who give this "welcoming, cosy Greek restaurant" a "strong showing all-round"; the "excellent menu" includes "very good fish", and the servers are "friendly", which may explain why some are happy to "drive 30 minutes to get there."

Daphne's ◐⑤   19 | 19 | 17 | £43
112 Draycott Ave., SW3 (South Kensington), 020-7589 4257; fax 020-7225 2766
■ Though "no longer the No. 1 glamour hangout", fans say this Modern Italian "high-class nosheria" in Brompton Cross is not only "getting back on its feet again" but is "better than before", as witnessed by the "delicious food" and "polite service", all "improved since the guys from Le Caprice" took over last year; it's "living on its former glory" declare doubters "underwhelmed" by the "snooty" servers and "high prices."

Daquise ⑤   15 | 10 | 16 | £18
20 Thurloe St., SW7 (South Kensington), 020-7589 6117
■ Admirers love this "time warp" Polish standby in South Kensington for its "old-world charm" and "unassuming" fare, dubbing it a "great experience"; detractors "can forgive the dowdy decor but not the indifferent food", though even they allow that it's "worth trying once."

Deca   – | – | – | E
23 Conduit St., W1 (Green Park), 020-7493 7070; fax 020-7493 7090
Named after the Greek word for 'ten', this new, bi-level Incognico sibling (Nico Ladenis' tenth eatery to date), set in a classily designed Mayfair townhouse, has hit the ground

F | D | S | C

running, offering a polished New French menu including several of the restaurateur's classics; dinner is served from 5:30 PM to attract pre-theatre diners, who may also be lured by the £12.50 prix fixe; a small, elegant room is available for private parties.

De Cecco 17 | 12 | 15 | £29
189 New King's Rd., SW6 (Parsons Green), 020-7736 1145; fax 020-7371 0278
◪ "Reliable and tasty", this "faithful neighbourhood Italian" lures locals with one of the "best spaghetti and lobster" dishes, a "super atmosphere" and "affordable" prices; dissenters can't "understand what all the fuss is about", as it's "good, yes, outstanding, no."

Defune S 23 | 15 | 17 | £47
34 George St., W1 (Bond St.), 020-7935 8311; fax 020-7487 3762
◪ It "took time to bed down" in its "new location" near Marble Arch, but this "modern" Japanese spot is now "back to its previous brilliance"; the "food is exceptional" rave reviewers who say it affects your "senses like fine wine" yet warn about the "astronomical expense" – "heavenly sushi, hellish prices"; the address change has been "to its detriment" say those put off by the "bland, boring" decor.

Del Buongustaio S 19 | 13 | 16 | £31
283-285 Putney Bridge Rd., SW15 (East Putney/Putney Bridge), 020-8780 9361; fax 020-8780 9361
◪ Though it's "a little out of the way" across Putney Bridge, this "unpretentious" "longtime favourite" rewards trekkers with "simple, authentic" Italian dishes and a "very pleasant" ambience; the "food disappoints and the decor does not work" retort buon-bashers, convinced it's "going downhill"; P.S. the adjoining pasticceria is "perfect for lunch."

Dibbens 19 | 19 | 20 | £30
2-3 Cowcross St., EC1 (Farringdon), 020-7250 0035; fax 020-7250 3080
■ "Brilliant" for a "low-key business lunch" that offers "adventurous variations on UK standards", this "friendly" Modern British "find" in Smithfield is "worth making a detour for"; a couple of critics carp that the "disappointingly indifferent food" is "not very impressive"; N.B. there's live entertainment on Friday nights.

Diverso ●S 20 | 17 | 18 | £38
85 Piccadilly, W1 (Green Park), 020-7491 2222; fax 020-7495 1977
◪ "Nothing is lacking" at this "well-kept secret" on the edge of Green Park, where customers gather for "great" Italian food; the "quiet" setting and "wide-set tables" come in handy for "nice business lunches" and just plain "talking", though quibblers cite "slow service" and "overpriced food" as bug-bears.

www.zagat.com

| | | | | F | D | S | C |

Don, The 23 | 20 | 20 | £37
The Courtyard, 20 St. Swithins Ln., EC4 (Bank), 020-7626 2606; fax 020-7626 2616
■ An "unexpected pleasure in the City" bolstered by "efficient" service, Bleeding Heart's "baby" sib proffers "superb" Modern European–French food in its "posh" ground-floor restaurant and "lovely" bare-brick basement brasserie; "full of historical interest", the circa 1798 building was once the House of Sandeman headquarters, and fittingly enough, a "good" "choice of port" and wine are available; N.B. The Don is actually a tip of the sombrero to the Sandeman's trademark image.

Dorchester, Grill Room S 24 | 23 | 25 | £51
The Dorchester, 53 Park Ln., W1 (Hyde Park Corner/ Marble Arch), 020-7629 8888; fax 020-7317 6464
■ Decorated in an "opulent" style that evokes the spirit of "Victorian England at its finest", this "elegant" Mayfair hotel dining room is still the kind of "place to entertain VIPs"; the "gracious" service is "welcoming", and chef Henry Brosi's "excellent" Traditional British fare, accompanied by a "wonderful wine list", meets "very high standards"; but you may need to be a member of the "Rolex owner's club" warn the wallet-sensitive, who think it "could be better for the price"; N.B. jacket is preferred.

Dorchester, Oriental 23 | 22 | 22 | £52
The Dorchester, 53 Park Ln., W1 (Hyde Park Corner/ Marble Arch), 020-7317 6328; fax 020-7317 6464
◪ It's the "champion of Chinese food in London" declare devotees who claim the "impeccably done" fare is "as good as the best in Hong Kong" at this "oasis of calm", a "civilised" dining room within Mayfair's Dorchester; a handful, however, dismiss it as an "amazingly expensive" spot that's "stuck in a time warp"; P.S. the three "slick" private rooms have different Asian themes.

Drones S 20 | 20 | 20 | £44
1-3 Pont St., SW1 (Sloane Sq.), 020-7235 9555; fax 020-7235 9566
◪ Marco Pierre White's "fabulous reincarnation" of this Belgravia "classic" is "excellent in every way", with "elegant, chic" decor, "well-drilled staff", an "imaginative wine list" and a "superb" Classic French menu that's "up with the best"; a snooty few think the "formula's boring" and "somewhat overpriced", but they are outvoted: "another great MPW dining experience."

Duke of Cambridge S 20 | 16 | 15 | £22
30 St. Peter's St., N1 (Angel), 020-7359 3066
■ "If you want organic, this is the place" declare devotees of this "laid-back" Islington "gastro-pub" with "innovative yet comforting" Modern British food and "excellent" pesticide-free potables; it's "bustling", so "service is

| F | D | S | C |

hard-pressed (but cheerful)", and the "wonderful" ambience gives it a "very 'in' feel."

Dumela — — — E
42 Devonshire Rd., W4 (Turnham Green), 020-8742 3149
"Eat exotic animals" (like "warthog and zebra!") at this "excellent, family-run" sibling of Fish Hoek, a Chiswick haunt where "amazing South African food" is "lovingly prepared by owner" and chef Pete Gottgens; the "friendly, efficient service" and an interesting wine list also make this "meat lover's" spot worth pursuing.

Eagle, The 🆂⊘ 22 14 13 £20
159 Farringdon Rd., EC1 (Farringdon), 020-7837 1353; fax 020-7689 5882
■ "Be prepared to fight for a table" (no reservations) at "one of London's most famous gastro-pubs"; this Clerkenwell stalwart is "strong on character" and offers "unfussy" Mediterranean food at "reasonable prices", and if some object to "cramped" quarters, others are reassured by their fellow diners: "all those Guardian hacks can't be wrong."

E&O 🆂 21 20 19 £32
14 Blenheim Crescent, W11 (Ladbroke Grove), 020-7229 5454
■ This "cool place shouts 'now'" cry "chic" champions of this "fun" Notting Hill newcomer that offers a "perfect blend" of "London style" and "tasty" Pan-Asian cooking, along with "awesome cocktails" and some of "the best celeb-spotting"; snipers sniff it's "all sass, no substance", but most say this "innovative" venue has staying power.

East One 15 14 13 £21
175-179 St. John St., EC1 (Farringdon), 020-7566 0088; fax 020-7566 0099
■ "If you can avoid the wok queues", this "create-your-own-stir-fry" eaterie (select "raw ingredients and watch chefs cook" them) near Smithfield Market is "great fun for a group" and also boasts a "pleasant environment"; N.B. an à la carte Chinese menu is also available.

Ebury Wine Bar & Restaurant 🆂 16 15 16 £26
139 Ebury St., SW1 (Victoria), 020-7730 5447; fax 020-7823 6053
■ A "lovely little secret" where you "may find yourself next to the odd MP", this wine bar on the Pimlico-Belgravia border "can get crowded" thanks to "surprisingly good" International food that's "perfect [for] informal evenings"; a few say it's "middle of the road", but this "cheerful" spot fits the bill as a "reliable standby" for most.

ECapital ●🆂 — — — E
(fka Capital)
8 Gerrard St., W1 (Leicester Sq./Piccadilly Circus), 020-7434 3838; fax 020-7434 9991
Claiming to be Chinatown's only restaurant offering genuine insight into "authentic Shanghai" cooking, this upbeat

| F | D | S | C |

newcomer, overseen by experienced chef David Tam, serves up more than the standard noodle dishes, tempting diners with regional favorites, including cold appetizers and adventurous specials; there's also a strong wine list with an emphasis on Burgundies.

Eco
| 19 | 12 | 12 | £15 |

4 Market Row, SW9 (Brixton), 020-7738 3021; fax 020-7720 0738
162 Clapham High St., SW4 (Clapham Common), 020-7978 1108; fax 020-7720 0738 S

■ There's "never a dull moment" at this "frenetic" duo in Clapham ("favourite" of many) and Brixton where a "great-value" Italian menu includes "excellent pizzas" and "huge salads", and whilst most "can't complain" about anything, a minority do: it's "noisy" and "difficult to get a table."

Ed's Easy Diner S
| 14 | 14 | 14 | £14 |

London Trocadero Ctr., 19 Rupert St., W1 (Piccadilly Circus), 020-7287 1951; fax 020-7287 6998 ◐
12 Moor St., W1 (Leicester Sq./Tottenham Court Rd.), 020-7439 1955; fax 020-7494 0173
362 King's Rd., SW3 (Sloane Sq.), 020-7352 1956; fax 020-7352 4660
Brent Cross Shopping Ctr., NW4 (Brent Cross), 020-8202 0999; fax 020-8202 7526 ◐
O₂ Ctr., 255 Finchley Rd., NW3 (Finchley Rd.), 020-7431 1958; fax 020-7431 9837

■ "The 1950s hit you in the face" at this "fun" American diner-themed chain providing "a nostalgia trip" that's perfect for "those occasions when your hot dog and onion ring cravings get the better of you" (they dole out "decent burgers" and "heavenly shakes" as well); it "could be better", as it's "all image" retort dissenters, still everyone agrees they've got one thing right: "the jukeboxes work!"

Efes Kebab House ◐
| 18 | 12 | 16 | £21 |

175 Great Portland St., W1 (Great Portland St.), 020-7436 0600; fax 020-7636 6293 S
80-82 Great Titchfield St., W1 (Oxford Circus), 020-7636 1953; fax 020-7323 5082

■ "Catch the belly dancer" for a "complete Turkish night out" at this "lively" West End pair where "good, tasty kebabs" and other "traditional" dishes are deemed "honourable" and the overall experience "always a pleasure"; although a few detractors skewer this twosome as "disappointing", defenders "don't regret going" to these "entertaining places."

El Blason
| 18 | 13 | 14 | £35 |

8-9 Blacklands Terrace, SW3 (Sloane Sq.), 020-7823 7383; fax 020-7589 6313

■ "The magnificent owner, Carlos, creates an atmosphere that makes customers feel special" at this neighbourhood Iberian eatery in Chelsea off King's Road; the proprietor

| F | D | S | C |

Electric Brasserie, The ⑤ — | — | — | M
191 Portobello Rd., W11 (Ladbroke Grove/Notting Hill Gate), 020-7908 9696; fax 020-7908 9595
Attached to the impressively revamped Electric Cinema in Portobello Road, this all-day brasserie from the team behind Soho House serves Modern European fare, sparking interest with a domed trolley of roast dishes and a stylish setting that clicks with leisurely meals; look for a casual bar with communal tables for snacks and drinks at the front; N.B. there is also a private member's club on site.

Elena's l'Etoile   20 | 19 | 21 | £36
30 Charlotte St., W1 (Goodge St.), 020-7636 1496; fax 020-7637 0122
■ "The tradition's maintained under Elena's eagle eye" at this Fitzrovian bistro where longtime hostess Elena Salvoni is "the star" who provides her guests with a "personal welcome" and a "sense of occasion"; the combination of "simple, well-executed" French cooking, "courteous, efficient service" and "old-fashioned" atmosphere makes it "excellent for a business lunch."

El Gaucho ⑤∌   19 | 15 | 15 | £29
88 Ifield Rd., SW10 (Earl's Court/Fulham Broadway), 020-7823 3333; fax 020-8769 6586
Chelsea Farmers Mkt., 125 Sydney St., SW3 (Sloane Sq./South Kensington), 020-7376 8514; fax 020-8769 6586
■ "For red-meat fans only", these "unpretentious, informal" (hence "child-friendly") Argentinean twins in Chelsea Farmers Market and near Earl's Court (dinner only) serve "juicy steaks" "cooked to perfection"; though a few el grouchos insist the "service is weak", supporters shrug and say "you go there for the beef."

Elistano ⑤   18 | 14 | 16 | £28
25-27 Elystan St., SW3 (South Kensington), 020-7584 5248; fax 020-7584 8965
■ Although it gets "incredibly loud", *amici* of this "friendly" Chelsea trattoria "challenge anyone to walk away unhappy" thanks to "big portions" of "honest" Traditional Italian cooking at "reasonable prices"; though serenity seekers chafe at the "chaotic" environs, sociable sorts consider it a "good neighbourhood hangout" for "everyday dining out."

Embassy ⓓ   21 | 19 | 18 | £40
29 Old Burlington St., W1 (Piccadilly Circus), 020-7437 9933
■ On the former premises of Legends nightclub near Bond Street comes this new venture from entrepreneur Mark Fuller and chef Garry Hollihead, and whilst it's still early days, the place draws a mixed reaction: diplomats

			F	D	S	C

Emporio Armani Caffe | 17 | 16 | 15 | £24
Emporio Armani, 191 Brompton Rd., SW3 (Knightsbridge), 020-7581 0854; fax 020-7823 8854
■ "Stylish and pricey – just like the clothes" at Emporio Armani sums up reactions to this "great" in-store "pit stop" away from the "hustle and bustle" of Knightsbridge; "light", "fashionable" Modern Italian–Euro fare comes in "diet-friendly portions", ensuring its popularity as a "ladies-who-lunch cafe" (it closes at 6 PM).

Engineer, The S | 19 | 15 | 15 | £26
65 Gloucester Ave., NW1 (Camden Town/Chalk Farm), 020-7722 0950; fax 020-7483 0592
■ This "true gastro-pub" in Primrose Hill is a "homely", "comfortable" spot for "consistently good" Modern British fare from an "imaginative" menu that includes organic produce; whilst wallet-watchers whisper it's "overpriced", all agree the "great garden" is "magical on a summer's evening" – if you can engineer a table.

English Garden S | 19 | 21 | 20 | £40
10 Lincoln St., SW3 (Sloane Sq.), 020-7584 7272; fax 020-7584 1961
◪ Richard Corrigan's Modern British eaterie ensconced in a bloomin' "beautiful" townhouse off King's Road in Chelsea attracts admirers with "excellent" Modern British cooking, a "romantic" atmosphere and "very good service"; naysayers declare the fare "disappointing" and the ambience "a bit formal"; N.B. the eponymous garden is in fact a conservatory.

Enoteca Turi | 21 | 18 | 20 | £32
28 Putney High St., SW15 (Putney Bridge), 020-8785 4449; fax 020-8785 4449
■ "Truly worth [crossing] the bridge for" say lovers of Giuseppe Turi's "thoroughly enjoyable" "Putney jewel" offering "exceptional", "good-value" Modern Italian food and an "awesome wine list", all served by "friendly" staff that "remember returning guests"; "the refit two years ago" still provokes a divided response: "much more airy" vs. "not as cosy."

Enterprise, The S | 18 | 17 | 15 | £29
35 Walton St., SW3 (South Kensington), 020-7584 3148; fax 020-7784 2516
◪ With "the spontaneous atmosphere of a pub", this "crowded" "neighbourhood-sy" Chelsea spot makes a "nice meeting" point, and even if some sceptics feel the "food's not the reason to come here", defenders report "delicious", "unpretentious" Eclectic tucker, along with "good service"; the biggest gripe: "very smoky at dinner."

Esarn Kheaw S |20| |8| |12| |£22|
314 Uxbridge Rd., W12 (Shepherd's Bush), 020-8743 8930; fax 020-7243 1250

◪ It may not be "posh", but this "family-run" Shepherd's Bush spot keeps many happy with "good, authentic" Thai cooking and "ready smiles" from the staff; yet dissenters report "bland" food, adding it's "overrated."

Eyre Brothers |24| |21| |19| |£40|
70 Leonard St., EC2 (Old St.), 020-7613 5346; fax 020-7739 8199

◪ The founders of the Eagle pub, David and Rob Eyre, are the force behind this "excellent newcomer" in Shoreditch that sets off "culinary fireworks" with "creative" Spanish-Portuguese cooking proffered in an "urban" atmosphere; even if knockers proclaim it's a "pretentious" venue with occasionally "stony" service, most feel it'll give local rivals "a run for their money."

Fairuz S |21| |17| |18| |£26|
27 Westbourne Grove, W2 (Bayswater/Queensway), 020-7243 8444; fax 020-7243 8777 ●
3 Blandford St., W1 (Bond St.), 020-7486 8108; fax 020-7935 8581

◪ "Book ahead" urge loyalists of this "gem" in Marylebone that's "great as an introduction to Lebanese" cooking, with "fabulous food" ("the mezze platter's tops") served by "hospitable" staff; although a handful deem the dishes "Anglofied" and "pricey for what you get", it's valued by many as a "classic neighbourhood" spot for a "pleasant" meal; N.B. the new Bayswater sibling opened post-*Survey*.

Fakhreldine ●S |18| |13| |16| |£34|
85 Piccadilly, W1 (Green Park), 020-7493 3424; fax 020-7495 1977

Fakhreldine Express ●S
92 Queensway, W2 (Bayswater/Queensway), 020-7243 3177

◪ This longtime Lebanese overlooking Green Park is "worth a visit" for "surprisingly excellent" cooking (and "lovely house wine"), and it's popular with the "club crowd after partying" (thanks to a midnight license); impatient sorts warn you "wait ages" for dinner in a space that "feels like an airport waiting room"; N.B. Fakhreldine Express is a "fast-food fave", mainly for takeaway.

Fat Duck, The S |24| |18| |22| |£57|
High St., Bray, Berkshire, 01628 580333; fax 01628 776188

◪ "Audacious" chef-owner Heston Blumenthal "tries to astound" adventurous palates with a "wacky, wonderful", even "psychedelic" New French menu at this "unique" pub/restaurant in a "cute [Berkshire] village"; critics range from the "indifferent" ("drab decor") to those who find the experience "ludicrously pretentious" and "expensive"; still, most feel it's "worth the drive" from London – just "be ready for surprises."

| F | D | S | C |

Feng Shang Floating Restaurant ⑤ | 17 | 18 | 18 | £31 |
Cumberland Basin, Prince Albert Rd., NW1 (Camden Town), 020-7485 8137; fax 020-7267 2990

◪ It's "like going back in time" aboard this "old faithful" Chinese located in houseboat docked beside Regent's Park, where sailors cross a drawbridge for "very good" multiregional Chinese food and "highly attentive service"; whilst "disappointing" to some – "tacky", "not worth the price" – others insist it makes "for a fun night out."

ffiona's ●⑤ | 20 | 18 | 21 | £28 |
51 Kensington Church St., W8 (High St. Kensington/Notting Hill Gate), 020-7937 4152; fax 020-7937 4152

◪ "Ffantastic Ffiona" Reid-Owen is "the star" at this "dark, intimate" Kensington "bôite" where she not only "welcomes you herself" but also produces "reliable", "homestyle" Traditional British cooking and "adds much character" to the "charming" place; if the place is a little "small and smoky" for some, the "inexpensive" fare gets everyone's "vote."

Fifth Floor ⑤ | 19 | 17 | 16 | £38 |
Harvey Nichols, 109-125 Knightsbridge, SW1 (Knightsbridge), 020-7235 5250; fax 020-7823 2207

◪ Temporarily closed for refurbishment at press time and slated to reopen early autumn, this "perfect, posh shopper's lunch spot" on the top floor of Knightsbridge's "fashionable" Harvey Nichols will re-emerge with a glass-domed ceiling and a bright new look (good news for those who thought it was "looking old"), plus chef Simon Shaw plans to spruce up his "excellent" Modern British menu; expect to walk past an "unashamedly materialistic crowd" ("very *Ab Fab*!") in the "fun bar."

Fifth Floor Cafe ⑤ | 16 | 14 | 13 | £25 |
Harvey Nichols, 109-125 Knightsbridge, SW1 (Knightsbridge), 020-7823 1839; fax 020-7823 2207

◪ "If you can be bothered to queue", boosters say this "buzzing, happening" Knightsbridge in-store cafe is "handy" for a "quick shopper's lunch" of "well-cooked, light" Mediterranean food; foes, however, find it "steeply priced" and "too hectic", complaining about "deafening mobiles"; "do they have customers who are not blond and slim?" wonders one wag.

Fina Estampa | 22 | 13 | 20 | £28 |
150-152 Tooley St., SE1 (London Bridge), 020-7403 1342; fax 020-7403 1342

■ "Distinctive", "excellent" Peruvian cooking is the magnet at this "popular" spot in an "offbeat location" near Tower Bridge; it's best "to go when hungry, as they serve large courses" (there's also a "tapas-style bar downstairs"), and although "it can be noisy", "friendly" staff and "comfortable surroundings" ensure an "excellent" experience.

| F | D | S | C |

First Floor S   18 | 19 | 16 | £30
186 Portobello Rd., W11 (Ladbroke Grove/Notting Hill Gate), 020-7243 0072; fax 020-7221 9440
■ "Feels like you're miles away from Portobello Road" below when you dine at this first-floor Notting Hill "neighbourhood eaterie" where the "cozy" atmosphere evokes "a friend's impromptu dinner party"; the Modern British menu offers "quality", "irresistible" choices.

Fish! S   17 | 13 | 14 | £25
1 Lawn Terrace, Blackheath Village, SE3 (Blackheath B.R.), 084-5100 4555; fax 020-7234 3343
Cathedral St., Borough Mkt., SE1 (London Bridge), 084-5100 4555; fax 020-7234 3343
County Hall, 3B Belvedere Rd., SE1 (Waterloo), 084-5100 4555; fax 020-7234 3343
33 Westferry Circus, Hanover House, E14 (Canary Wharf), 084-5100 4555; fax 020-7234 3343
■ There's a "modern, fresh feel" to this seafood chain, but opinions on the fin fare are fiercely divided: afishionados adore the "superbly simple" Traditional British menu with "choices of sauce" to "tailor your requirements", whilst detractors decry "disappointingly bland" dishes, adding it's "too pricey to do regularly"; N.B. several branches closed post-*Survey*.

Fish Hoek S   – | – | – | E
6-8 Elliot Rd., W4 (Turnham Green), 020-8742 0766
Pete Gottgens, a media commentator on South African food, runs this Dumela sibling in Chiswick, an easygoing seafood spot that offers an "interesting", "daily changing" Eclectic menu dominated by "fantastic varieties of exotic fish" plus "very knowledgeable" servers who "fall all over themselves to help" with selections; "tables are a little too close" for some, but that doesn't stop hooked fans from pledging to "go back ASAP."

Fishmarket   18 | 17 | 17 | £34
Great Eastern Hotel, Liverpool St., EC2 (Liverpool St.), 020-7618 7200; fax 020-7618 7201
■ The "great decor" at this "typical Conran" Group eaterie inside the Great Eastern Hotel in Bishopsgate makes this a "nice room to eat in"; whilst some are taken by the "excellent" seafood, "well-cooked" Modern British fare and "slick lunchtime service", others suggest the food is "distinctly average" and "overpriced."

Floriana   20 | 20 | 18 | £49
15 Beauchamp Pl., SW3 (Knightsbridge), 020-7838 1500; fax 020-7584 1464
■ Riccardo Mazzuchelli's "elegant", "pretty" Knightsbridge "gem" hits the spot for many with a "perfect menu" of "memorable" Modern Italian dishes ("great in truffle season") "made [even] better by congenial staff"; on the

| F | D | S | C |

downside, a few think it's "perhaps too adult" and warn that "the bill will not be a pleasant surprise", but most who know this well-"kept secret hope it stays that way."

Florians S
∇ | 18 | 15 | 19 | £26

4 Topsfield Parade, Middle Ln., N8 (Highgate), 020-8348 8348; fax 020-8292 2092

■ "Worth travelling to" Crouch End suggest supporters of this "good local" with a "fun atmosphere", "surprisingly nice" Modern Italian food and a wine list that's strong on Tuscans; "not worth the trip" retort a "disappointed" few.

FOLIAGE S
25 | 22 | 23 | £52

Mandarin Oriental Hyde Park, 66 Knightsbridge, SW1 (Knightsbridge), 020-7235 2000; fax 020-7201 3811

■ "You'll forget you're in a hotel" at this "flagship Mandarin" in Knightsbridge where the "sophisticated" dining room (which attracts "lots of aristocrats") "combines" "fantastic" Modern European–French food with "faultless" service, making it a "great addition to top restaurants" in London; a few protest it's "pretentious" and "chilly", but those who warn of "expensive" prices should warm up to the "good deal" prix fixe lunch; N.B. the arrival of chef Chris Staines (ex Oak Room) post-*Survey* may impact the above Food score.

Food for Thought S ⊄
21 | 9 | 12 | £12

31 Neal St., WC2 (Covent Garden), 020-7836 9072; fax 020-7379 1249

■ Voted the *Survey's* No. 1 Bang for the Buck, this Covent Garden "veggie heaven" serves some of the "best food in London for the money", with an "excellent", daily-changing selection of "comforting", "wholesome" Vegetarian fare; those who think the basement premises are "cramped" and "dreary" looking say it's "better as a takeaway"; N.B. last orders are at 8 PM, and it's BYO too.

Formula Veneta ●
15 | 13 | 16 | £32

14 Hollywood Rd., SW10 (Earl's Court), 020-7352 7612; fax 020-7352 8305

■ Although this Chelsea Italian "changed hands" during *Survey* period, no major adjustments are planned to the "tried-and-tested formula" of "good", "robust" Modern Italian fare served in a "jolly", "noisy" environment that attracts its share of "City geezers and barrow boys"; detractors grumble about "overpriced", "unremarkable food" and "tables too close together" for comfort.

Fortnum's Fountain
16 | 16 | 16 | £24

Fortnum & Mason, 181 Piccadilly, W1 (Green Park/Piccadilly Circus), 020-7973 4140; fax 020-7437 3278

■ Many find it "hard not to like" this "unique" Piccadilly "institution", Fortnum & Mason's "old-fashioned" all-day eaterie that "can always be relied upon" for "simple" Traditional British "comfort food" (the "best Welsh rarebit");

| F | D | S | C |

though a few sniff at "spotty service", nostalgic noshers proclaim it a "prime stop" after you've "shopped till you dropped", especially with "grandma or grandkids" in tow.

Four Regions ●🆂 ▽ | 19 | 16 | 18 | £27 |
County Hall, Riverside Bldg., SE1 (Waterloo/Westminster), 020-7928 0988; fax 020-7928 9060
■ "Stunning views" of the Houses of Parliament are "reason enough" to visit this spacious riversider within Westminster's County Hall, but it also provides a "nice eating experience" with "consistently" "very good" multiregional Chinese cooking; factor in the decent "value" and cognoscenti "can't understand why it's not busier."

Four Seasons Chinese ●🆂 | 23 | 10 | 12 | £23 |
84 Queensway, W2 (Bayswater), 020-7229 4320
☑ What it "lacks [in] decor" and "smiley service", this "crowded, boisterous" Bayswater Chinese makes up for with its "worldwide renowned" roast duck (it's their "heavenly" specialty) and other "magnificently prepared" multiregional dishes "at reasonable prices"; N.B. "even with a booking", diners should expect "long waits" for a table.

Four Seasons Hotel, | 23 | 24 | 24 | £47 |
Lanes Restaurant 🆂
Four Seasons Hotel, Hamilton Pl., W1 (Green Park/Hyde Park Corner), 020-7499 0888; fax 020-7493 6629
■ "Absolutely delightful" is the consensus on this spacious, "comfortable" hotel dining room overlooking Park Lane, serving a Modern European–International menu; added benefits include "pampering" service from "real pros" and views of Hyde Park; N.B. a post-*Survey* chef shuffle, with Bernhard Mayer from the Four Seasons Hong Kong replacing longtime chef Eric DeBlonde, may impact the above Food score.

FOUR SEASONS HOTEL, | 24 | 21 | 23 | £43 |
QUADRATO 🆂
Four Seasons Canary Wharf, 46 Westferry Circus, E14 (Canary Wharf), 020-7510 1999; fax 020-7510 1998
■ The "ultramodern interior" "heightens the experience" in the dining room of this Four Seasons Canary Wharf outpost, which is "by far the best restaurant in Docklands", attracting a local "business" crowd at lunch (although evenings can be "under-patronised"); "attentive" service and "excellent", "original [Modern] Italian specialities" get the thumbs-up, as does the "outstanding-value Sunday brunch."

Frederick's ● | 20 | 20 | 18 | £38 |
106 Camden Passage, N1 (Angel), 020-7359 2888; fax 020-7359 5173
☑ "As good as it has always been" assess acolytes of this "elegant but casual" Islingtonian, a longtime "favourite" for "gorgeous" Modern British cooking and "obliging" service

that also boasts three private rooms, making it "reliable for corporate outings"; though protesters posit it's "passed its sell-by date", all agree the garden is "great in summer".

FRENCH HORN S 24 | 23 | 22 | £48
French Horn Hotel, Sonning-on-Thames, Berkshire, 01189 692204; fax 01189 442210
■ Rated No. 1 in the *Survey* for Traditional British cuisine, this "reassuringly old-fashioned" family-run hotel alongside the Thames near Henley is "perfect [for] serious dining" on "superb" dishes such as "exquisite duck" "cooked on an open fire", accompanied by a selection from the 1,000-bottle strong wine list; although views on the service range from "professional" to "snobby", most concede the place "well deserves its fine reputation" and is "delightful [in] summer"; P.S. it makes a "good anniversary destination."

French House Restaurant 21 | 17 | 17 | £32
49 Dean St., W1 (Piccadilly Circus), 020-7437 2477; fax 020-7287 9109
■ Following a refurb last year, this "quaint" "piece of Paris above a Soho pub" is still an "intimate", "understated affair", serving "perfectly prepared" French "comfort food" ("fabulously tasty vegetables") in a "great setting"; though old-timers tut it "will never live up to" its past reputation, its new *amis* answer it's "busy and buzzy" nonetheless.

Friends ◐ S 19 | 14 | 16 | £25
6 Hollywood Rd., SW10 (South Kensington), 020-7376 3890; fax 020-7352 6368
◪ "When you're not in the mood to cook", this "bustling" Chelsea "hangout" comes up trumps, with "fab pizzas" from a wood-burning oven plus "good" Traditional Italian fare; even if foes find it "average" and too "cramped" for comfort, most say it's a "lively" spot that's "great for kids."

Fung Shing ◐ S 21 | 12 | 15 | £29
15 Lisle St., WC2 (Leicester Sq.), 020-7437 1539; fax 020-7743 0284
◪ "Better if you order adventurously" say champions of this Chinatown Chinese that's "worth going to for the genuine article": "tasty, consistently good" Cantonese fare with "some real gems on the menu"; critics claim it's "nothing special", citing "so-so service", a "bland interior" and "average" food, but even after 30 years it remains "a great dinner spot before or after the theatre."

Galicia ◐ S ▽ 21 | 13 | 17 | £22
323 Portobello Rd., W10 (Ladbroke Grove), 020-8969 3539
■ "The finest tapas this side of the Pyrenees" gush groupies of the "excellent" Spanish provisions at this "cheerful", down-to-earth Notting Hill Gate eaterie; "friendly", "bend-over-backward" service and "cheap" tariffs complete the rosy picture; P.S. "book early and sit near the bar – the ambience is better."

68   www.zagat.com

| F | D | S | C |

Gallipoli ⑤   _ | _ | _ | M |
102 Upper St., N1 (Angel), 020-7359 0630
120 Upper St., N1 (Angel), 020-7359 1578
A "party atmosphere" prevails (you may "need earplugs") at these Turkish twins just doors apart in Islington that are "great places to go with friends"; admirers "adore" the "flavourful", "very reasonably" priced "food without frills", including "mezze that enables grazing"; they may be a "bit cramped", but this "favourite twosome" never disappoints.

Garbo's ⑤   15 | 14 | 16 | £25 |
42 Crawford St., W1 (Baker St./Marylebone), 020-7262 6582; fax 020-7262 6582
◪ "Photos of Greta Garbo adorn" this Marylebone "jewel" that's "full of Swedes" seeking "interesting" Scandinavian sustenance; although a minority find the atmosphere "depressing", "cheerful, welcoming staff" and the "very good-value buffet lunch" (under £10) may compensate.

Gate, The   21 | 17 | 18 | £26 |
72 Belsize Ln., NW3 (Belsize Park), 020-7435 7733; fax 020-7435 7711 ⑤
51 Queen Caroline St., W6 (Hammersmith), 020-8748 6932; fax 020-8563 1719
■ "You soon forget there's no meat on the menu" at this Hammersmith Vegetarian and its newer Belsize Park sibling, as the "creative" cooking suits "all tastes"; brownie points also go to "friendly service" and "funky" environs; P.S. you "need to book, as they are rightly very popular."

GAUCHO GRILL   20 | 17 | 16 | £31 |
125-126 Chancery Ln., WC2 (Chancery Ln.), 020-7242 7727; fax 020-7242 7723 ◐
19 Swallow St., W1 (Piccadilly Circus), 020-7734 4040; fax 020-7734 1076 ⑤
89 Sloane Ave., SW3 (South Kensington), 020-7584 9901; fax 020-7584 0045 ◐⑤
64 Heath St., NW3 (Hampstead), 020-7431 8222; fax 020-7431 3714 ◐⑤
1 Bell Inn Yard, EC3 (Bank/Monument), 020-7626 5180; fax 020-7626 5181
29 Westferry Circus, E14 (Canary Wharf), 020-7987 9494; fax 020-7987 9292 ◐⑤
◪ For "steaks as big as a paving stone", this mushrooming chophouse chain has many devotees, although some sceptics lament the "limited" scope of the Argentinean menu; the "eclectic" decor ("cowhide everywhere") and "friendly" staff contribute to the "fun" atmosphere.

Gaudí   20 | 21 | 16 | £37 |
63 Clerkenwell Rd., EC1 (Farringdon), 020-7608 3220; fax 020-7250 1057
■ "You feel like you are in Barcelona" at this "wonderfully bizarre" and "beautiful" Clerkenwell dining room "inspired

| F | D | S | C |

by the [Catalan] architect" Antonio Gaudí; "everything is done so well", from the "refreshingly different" Spanish food and "excellent wine list" to service that "treats you like royalty", and though it's "certainly not cheap", it's "worth it."

Gay Hussar | 17 | 17 | 18 | £34 |
2 Greek St., W1 (Tottenham Court Rd.), 020-7437 0973; fax 020-7437 4631
■ There's a "cosy feel" to this "old-fashioned" Soho "time warp" that's "still a treat" after 50 years; "winter warmer" Hungarian fare comes in "hearty portions", the "delightful" staff make you feel "special" and if a few knock the food as "uninspired", longtime loyalists will "always" go back.

Geale's Fish Restaurant S | 18 | 10 | 14 | £20 |
2 Farmer St., W8 (Notting Hill Gate), 020-7727 7528; fax 020-7229 8632
■ This "genuine", "no-frills" Notting Hill Gate seafooder "is to the point" with its "egalitarian atmosphere" and offerings of "genuine fish 'n' chips" made with "crunchy, fresh batter"; a few demurrers deride "dire" fare ("more like con-geales"), nevertheless the place gets "crowded" with "lots of regulars."

George | 21 | 22 | 22 | £45 |
Private club; inquiries: 020-7491 4433
■ Mark Birley's "newest, hippest creation" is a private restaurant/bar in Mayfair where a "well-heeled, loyal membership" appreciate "attentive service", "terrific atmosphere" and "always good" Modern European cooking; spoilsports say the "stuffy crowd make it a bore", but in the main, most vote this "another success story" in the owner's celebrated stable of clubs.

George Bar & Restaurant S | ▽ 15 | 16 | 13 | £22 |
Great Eastern Hotel, 40 Liverpool St., EC2 (Liverpool St.), 020-7618 7300; fax 020-7618 7301
■ "Good pies" and "great fish 'n' chips" are part of the appeal of Sir Terence Conran's pub-style restaurant in an "unusual public school dining-hall setting" within the City's Great Eastern Hotel; dissenters are unimpressed by "dull food" from a "rather limited" Traditional British menu and warn "service is not quick at all."

Getti | 16 | 15 | 16 | £27 |
42 Marylebone High St., W1 (Baker St./Bond St.), 020-7486 3753
74 Wardour St., W1 (Leicester Sq./Piccadilly Circus), 020-7437 3519 ●
16-17 Jermyn St., SW1 (Piccadilly Circus), 020-7734 7334; fax 020-7734 7924
■ According to supporters of this "stylish" but casual Italian trio in Marylebone, St. James's and Soho, the "decent, well-priced" fare and "very passable wines" (27 "available by the glass") are a "good idea", especially "at lunchtime",

| F | D | S | C |

but not everyone is so sanguine: "promises a lot, delivers nothing" some lament; still, "cheerful service" is appreciated.

Ginger S | 18 | 16 | 17 | £25 |
115 Westbourne Grove, W2 (Notting Hill Gate), 020-7908 1990; fax 020-7908 1991

"For an exotic meal" of "carefully spiced" Bangladeshi cooking, this bright, "turquoise" Notting Hill yearling is "surprisingly great" as an "interesting" "alternative to Indian curries", though there are those who bemoan "variable" dishes and "polite but erratic service."

Giraffe S | 17 | 13 | 16 | £19 |
27 Battersea Rise, SW11 (Clapham Junction), 020-7223 0933; fax 020-7722 1037
6-8 Blandford St., W1 (Baker St./Bond St.), 020-7935 2333; fax 020-7935 2334
46 Rosslyn Hill, NW3 (Hampstead), 020-7435 0343; fax 020-7431 4090
29-31 Essex Rd., N1 (Angel), 020-7359 5999; fax 020-7359 6158

"Friendliness pervades" this "colourful", handy herd that's become a "family favourite" thanks to a "fast-paced" atmosphere, "wholesome" Eclectic cooking and service that can handle "hordes of children"; if "you can avoid" the throngs, "one of the best brunches in London awaits."

Gladwins ▽ | 20 | 16 | 18 | £36 |
Minster Ct., Mark Ln., EC3 (Bank/Monument), 020-7444 0004; fax 020-7444 0001

"Still a favourite" of many, chef-patron Peter Gladwin's lunch-only City "staple" serves "reliably good" Modern British food in a basement setting with well-spaced tables; storytellers taunt "it's lost the plot completely" and is "too expensive for what you get"; closed weekends.

Glaister's Garden Bistro S | 14 | 14 | 14 | £28 |
36-38 White Hart Ln., SW13 (Barnes Bridge B.R.), 020-8878 2020; fax 020-8876 8478
8-10 Northcote Rd., SW11 (Clapham South), 020-7924 6699; fax 020-7924 5733
4 Hollywood Rd., SW10 (Earl's Court/South Kensington), 020-7352 0352; fax 020-7376 7341

These "relaxed" "yuppie hangouts" in Chelsea, Clapham and Barnes are "fine for weekday dining" with a "varied" Anglo–French bistro menu (including "excellent hangover" fare); nonsayers knock them as "underwhelming and overpriced" but admit the "garden seating" at Hollywood Road is one "reason to go."

Glasshouse, The S | 22 | 19 | 20 | £39 |
14 Station Parade (Kew Gardens), Kew, 020-8940 6777; fax 020-8940 3833

"Never lets us down" insist enthusiasts of this Kew outpost of the Chez Bruce/The Square group, which

| F | D | S | C |

"continues" to offer "beautifully presented", "superior" Modern British dishes; though some throw stones at service that's "snooty unless you're a regular", most say this "polished" venture is "excellent" to "celebrate or take someone special"; N.B. a post-*Survey* refurbishment may impact the above Decor score.

Globe S   18 | 15 | 18 | £28
100 Avenue Rd., NW3 (Swiss Cottage), 020-7722 7200; fax 020-7722 2772

■ "Trying hard and often succeeding" sums up the outlook on Neil Armishaw's "excellent neighbourhood" Swiss Cottage eaterie that has been "recently nicely refurbished"; "consistently good" Modern British cooking, a "lively" ambience and "willing-to-please" service have global appeal; P.S. it's "convenient for the Hampstead Theatre."

Golden Dragon ◐ S   19 | 11 | 12 | £21
28-29 Gerrard St., W1 (Leicester Sq.), 020-7734 2763; fax 020-7734 1073

◪ This "always busy" Chinatown eaterie is a "favourite" of many thanks to a "wide, delicious range" of "excellent" multiregional dishes and "fine dim sum", all at "reasonable prices"; a few grousers gripe about "inattentive staff" and a too-bright, "not romantic" atmosphere, but for "a light meal before the theatre, this fits the bill admirably."

Good Earth ◐ S   20 | 14 | 17 | £29
233 Brompton Rd., SW3 (Knightsbridge/South Kensington), 020-7584 3658; fax 020-7823 8769
143-145 The Broadway, NW7 (Mill Hill), 020-8959 7011; fax 020-8959 1464

◪ "Can't go wrong" say supporters of the "high-end", "consistently good" multiregional cooking at this well-established duo in Knightsbridge and Mill Hill; whilst the "decor needs freshening up" and "indifferent service" leaves some unimpressed, most concede both venues provide a "useful standby" when in the area.

Gopal's of Soho ◐ S   ∇ 18 | 11 | 16 | £24
12 Bateman St., W1 (Tottenham Court Rd.), 020-7434 0840; fax 020-7434 0840

◪ "Fresh", "tasty", "better than ordinary [South] Indian" food on a "good-value" menu is the main attraction at this "old-fashioned" Soho eaterie; however, foes rail against "rather slow service."

GORDON RAMSAY AT CLARIDGE'S S   27 | 24 | 24 | £63
Claridge's Hotel, Brook St., W1 (Bond St.), 020-7499 0099; fax 020-7376 7170

◪ Although it "would be impossible to live up to all the hype" of Gordon Ramsay's arrival at this "elegant", revamped Mayfair hotel dining room, most agree the eponymous

| F | D | S | C |

chef has succeeded in creating a "culinary temple" where "flawless" New French cooking and "well-trained" service create "a wonderful experience" that's "like a beautifully orchestrated symphony"; the less-enamoured deem the staff "slow" and the ambience "too quiet", but in truth, it's "best-behaviour stuff" here and "a must for that special occasion."

GORDON RAMSAY AT 68 ROYAL HOSPITAL RD.   28 | 23 | 27 | £70

68 Royal Hospital Rd., SW3 (Sloane Sq.), 020-7352 4441; fax 020-7352 3334

■ "The best London has to offer", Gordon Ramsay's Chelsea flagship, rated No.1 (once again) in this *Survey* for Food, New French cuisine and Service is something "everyone must enjoy once in their lives", with "incredibly innovative", "mouthwateringly delicious" modern Gallic cooking, "pampering" servers and a "top-notch wine list"; "the only criticism" comes from those who find "the formula" "a trifle studied" and the atmosphere "cold", but most tout this "treasured" spot as "an unforgettable experience at every level"; P.S. it's also "a prix fixe haven" at lunch (£35).

Goring Dining Room S   20 | 22 | 24 | £43

The Goring Hotel, Beeston Pl., SW1 (Victoria), 020-7396 9000; fax 020-7834 4393

◪ It's "unknown to many", but this "elegant" hotel dining room in Victoria has a loyal following for "steady, reliable", "traditional" cooking that's "as British as it gets", served "by an army of top-class waiters"; sure, it's a tad "staid", but no one quibbles over its "quintessential English" qualities: "the best breakfast" and "loveliest high tea."

Granita S   19 | 14 | 16 | £32

127 Upper St., N1 (Angel/Highbury & Islington), 020-7226 3222; fax 020-7226 4833

◪ Now under the ownership of Huseyin Ozer (of Sofra fame), this Islingtonian "favourite" proffers a "superb, simple" Modern European menu that "consistently delivers", as well as a few "impressive" design touches; the jury is still out "since the change of management" say some surveyors, whilst others dismiss it as "nice, but nothing special"; N.B. a post-*Survey* change of chef may impact the above Food score.

GRAVETYE MANOR S   24 | 25 | 24 | £51

Gravetye Manor Hotel, East Grinstead, West Sussex, 01342 810567; fax 01342 810080

■ It's "like dining in a Merchant Ivory film" at this "formal", "lovely country house" hotel in Sussex that's "one of the UK's grandest settings" ("I scarcely dared speak") offering "fabulous" Modern British cooking that's "a real, rare treat" and "smoothly" "served by grown-ups"; it's certainly "pricey" and a "long way for lunch", so "save it for a romantic occasion and stay the night."

| F | D | S | C |

Great Eastern Dining Room   19 | 18 | 16 | £32
54 Great Eastern St., EC2 (Liverpool St./Old St.), 020-7613 4545; fax 020-7613 4137
◪ "Go for the buzz – you'll be pleasantly surprised by the food" say supporters of the "imaginative", "well-prepared" Modern Italian cuisine at this "very happening place" full of "beautiful people" swanning about a "great, airy" Hoxton warehouse; opponents opine it's "ordinary" and suggest it's "no longer a novelty."

Great Nepalese ●S   ▽ 16 | 9 | 16 | £19
48 Eversholt St., NW1 (Euston), 020-7388 6737; fax 020-7388 6737
◪ "For an exotic bite before catching a Euston train", this "bright" eaterie serves "good, solid" Nepalese-Indian food (like "curry with a difference"); critics counter that it's "gone off", citing "boring" dishes and "uncomfortable" digs; still, the £6.50 set lunch is "a great value."

Greek Valley   ▽ 15 | 10 | 16 | £21
130 Boundary Rd., NW8 (Swiss Cottage), 020-7624 3217; fax 020-7372 2042
■ It "could use a makeover", but mavens maintain this "very cheerful", family-run St. John's Wood taverna is an "excellent local" option, offering "tasty dishes" of "genuine, good Greek" eats from a "moderately priced" menu; N.B. the vegetarian selection has been expanded post-*Survey*.

Green Cottage ●S   17 | 10 | 14 | £20
9 New College Parade, Finchley Rd., NW3 (Finchley Rd./Swiss Cottage), 020-7722 5305
◪ "Perfect for a quick bite, but don't go out of your way" sums up views on this Finchley Road Chinese institution ("been here for years") serving "good", "solid" multiregional cooking; whilst a few vociferous voices object to "seedy decor" and "second-rate food", everyone agrees on one thing: it's "cheap."

Greenhouse, The S   22 | 20 | 20 | £42
27A Hay's Mews, W1 (Green Park), 020-7499 3331; fax 020-7499 5368
◪ After a "fresh makeover" by designer David Collins, this 25-year-old Mayfair stalwart has reopened to reveal a modern, "upscale" look with green leather mini-banquettes, bamboo screens and hand-painted wallpaper; chef Paul Merrett's "marvelous" Modern British menu remains largely unchanged, much to the delight of those who appreciate the "very high standards", but wallet-watchers warn it's for "expense accounts only."

Green Olive S   20 | 17 | 19 | £34
5 Warwick Pl., W9 (Warwick Ave.), 020-7289 2469; fax 020-7289 2463
◪ In a "cute" location "near the canal" in Maida Vale, this "tightly packed" member of the Red Pepper family serves

| F | D | S | C |

"excellent" Modern Italian dishes from an "interesting menu"; detractors have more of a "lasting memory of the bill" and think the place "just misses", but at least the "friendly service" gets a round of applause; one pressing tip: "don't get stuck in the basement."

Greens S | 20 | 19 | 22 | £41 |
36 Duke St., SW1 (Green Park), 020-7930 4566; fax 020-7930 2958

■ "Simon Parker-Bowles gets it so right" at this "charming" St. James's seafooder with "spot-on" service and "solid" Traditional British "comfort food" and "delicious fish"; even if a few jest about the "stuffy" clientele, all appreciate the "clubby" atmosphere, replete with "great booths for private conversations"; N.B. closed Sundays from October–April.

Grenadier S | 14 | 21 | 14 | £25 |
18 Wilton Row, SW1 (Hyde Park Corner), 020-7235 3074; fax 020-7235 3400

■ "Tourists" "love the quaintness" and "interesting history" of Belgravia's "tiniest pub" (once the mess hall of the Duke of Wellington's guards), and whilst the "reliable" Traditional British cooking is "good for what it is", many prefer their "great Bloody Marys"; on "crowded" nights, expect "smoke so thick you'd think you'd gone back a hundred years to foggy olde London!"

Grissini S | 19 | 18 | 17 | £41 |
Carlton Tower, 2 Cadogan Pl., 1st fl., SW1 (Knightsbridge/ Sloane Sq.), 020-7858 7171; fax 020-7823 1708

◪ This "stylish" first-floor dining room of Knightsbridge's Carlton Tower boasts a "lovely view" over gardens and gets the thumbs-up for "organised service"; "after shopping", the "sound" Modern Italian cooking hits the spot, as does the "good-value Sunday brunch" where children can eat for free, though the less-ardent lament the "lax atmosphere."

Groucho Club, The ◐ | 16 | 15 | 17 | £34 |
Private club; inquiries: 020-7439 4685

◪ Now owned by Matthew Freud and Joel Cadbury (as is 192), this "louche" (in a "good" way) Soho private club – "for the unconservative" – has "a less adventurous but more consistent" Modern British menu and "cheerful service"; however, it remains "strictly a place to see and be seen" ("high celeb quota") with "food an afterthought", but in any case, the "drinks are generous."

Grumbles S | 18 | 15 | 20 | £25 |
35 Churton St., SW1 (Pimlico/Victoria), 020-7834 0149; fax 020-7834 0298

■ No one grumbles about this "unpretentious" Pimlico "haunt" with a "great ambience" and "cosy" setting; its "reliable" Anglo–French bistro menu offers "great" "simple" fare and "good" wine, all at "excellent prices", and "friendly service" rounds out the experience.

www.zagat.com

| F | D | S | C |

Gung-Ho ●⑤   20 | 15 | 16 | £26
330 West End Ln., NW6 (West Hampstead), 020-7794 1444; fax 020-7794 5522

■ Acolytes aver this Hampstead "local" is "without doubt the best Chinese in North London" thanks to a "diverse selection" of "tasty", "classic Szechuan" dishes and other "gourmet" multiregional fare that "always satisfies"; the less gung-ho point to "poor service", but the fact that it's "best to book" suggests the ayes have it.

HAKKASAN ⑤   22 | 26 | 17 | £40
8 Hanway Pl., W1 (Tottenham Court Rd.), 020-7927 7000; fax 020-7907 1889

☑ "What a vibe" there is at Alan Yau's (of Wagamama fame) "sexily designed" newcomer off Tottenham Court Road in an "awesome" underground space that's "like a movie set"; enthusiasts extol the "excellent", "tasty" Chinese cooking, "great dim sum" (lunch only) and "amazingly hip cocktail bar", and though party-poopers pan it as "pricey" and "noisy" with "arrogant" service, there's no disputing the "decadence" – it's one of London's most "exciting" additions.

Halepi ⑤   20 | 13 | 18 | £28
18 Leinster Terrace, W2 (Lancaster Gate/Queensway), 020-7262 1070; fax 020-7262 2083 ●
48-50 Belsize Ln., NW3 (Belsize Park/Swiss Cottage), 020-7431 5855; fax 020-7431 5844

■ These "authentic" Greek-Cypriots in Belsize Park and near Hyde Park are "good fun" for "the whole family", with an "excellent" choice of dishes from "Hellenic pastures and sea"; even if a few find them "impossibly crowded", both venues remain "local favourites"; P.S. the "great" guitarist in NW3 "makes you feel like you're in Greece."

Harbour City ●⑤   18 | 9 | 12 | £20
46 Gerrard St., W1 (Leicester Sq./Piccadilly Circus), 020-7439 7859; fax 020-7734 7745

☑ Opinions on this functional, tri-level Chinatown eatery are polarised: to admirers it's a "genuine" spot with "fresh-tasting" Chinese fare, "excellent dim sum" and "friendly" staff, but dissenters are "disappointed" with the "quality" and slam "slapstick service" and "crowded" conditions.

Hard Rock Cafe ●⑤   13 | 17 | 14 | £22
150 Old Park Ln., W1 (Green Park/Hyde Park Corner), 020-7629 0382; fax 020-7629 8702

☑ "The best [rock 'n' roll] memorabilia" can be found at this "big, brash", "loud" Hyde Park Corner outpost of the famed pop chain, but even if some think the "formula's getting tired", it's "still attractive" to "homesick Yanks" looking for "enormous servings" of "dependable" American diner fare; critics object to "waiting outside" for a table and then "being rushed" over a meal.

| F | D | S | C |

HARRY'S BAR   23 | 22 | 22 | £51
Private club; inquiries: 020-7408 0844
■ "Look forward to it all day long" say lovers of Mark Birley's "elegant" private dining club in Mayfair with an "unbeatable atmosphere" that combines a "high-energy" power scene with "superb", "consistent" Modern Italian cooking and "polished", un-harryed service; though it may dish out the "most expensive pasta in town", it's "worth it" for this "unique experience."

Harry's Social Club S   – | – | – | E
30 Alexander St., W2 (Royal Oak) 020-7229 4043; fax 020-7229 7051
Well-concealed down a dead-end street in Notting Hill Gate, this "buzzing" bohemian private club has a "retro kitsch" upstairs restaurant (that's open to the public) featuring Nick Nosh's "short menu" of simple Modern British fare and a low-lit downstairs bar offering entertainment; an added perk: members are given their own club door key to use after hours.

Hartwell House S   22 | 24 | 22 | £47
Hartwell House, Oxford Rd., Aylesbury, Buckinghamshire, 01296 747444; fax 01296 747450
☑ "If you go for grand", this "beautiful, historic" country house hotel nestled in 90 acres of Buckinghamshire parkland "cannot be bettered", with the added bonus of Daniel Richardson's "very enjoyable" British cooking and a "great wine list"; sceptics say the admittedly "impressive" dining room "lacks atmosphere", but few deny it's "a lovely place to recharge the batteries."

Havelock Tavern S⊄   21 | 16 | 14 | £21
57 Masbro Rd., W14 (Olympia/Shepherd's Bush), 020-7603 5374; fax 020-7602 1163
☑ This "wonderful" "gastro-pub in charming Brook Green" has fans raving about "outstanding", "inspired" Modern British cooking at "a good price" served in a "great atmosphere", but others are unimpressed by "sloppy service" from "pressured staff"; still, its perennial popularity means "it's a headache to get a table", not helped by the no-reservations policy.

Hi Sushi S   18 | 12 | 14 | £21
40 Frith St., W1 (Leicester Sq.), 020-7734 9688; fax 020-7734 9882
16 Hampstead High St., NW3 (Hampstead), 020-7794 2828; fax 020-7794 7328
☑ The "strange, deli-like setting" of this duo in Soho and Hampstead may not appeal to everyone ("a bit sterile", "best for takeaway"), but proponents are "pleasantly surprised" by the "fresh", "tasty" sushi, suggesting they make "a nice change" from similar spots ("more authentic"); "fast service" means they're also "great for pre-cinema snacks."

| F | D | S | C |

Home House ◐ 🆂
Private club; inquiries: 020-7670 2100   17 | 23 | 18 | £37

◪ Home-lovers hail this "quite nice [private] club in Portman Square", with its cosy Bison Bar and "beautiful", high-ceilinged first-floor dining room; however, the Traditional British fare with Thai accents divides opinion ("surprisingly good" vs. "tries too hard"), and "friendly service" can get "muddled" on occasions; still, it's perfect for "people-watching", particularly if you prefer "media types."

Honest Cabbage 🆂
99 Bermondsey St., SE1 (London Bridge), 020-7234 0080; fax 020-7403 1119   19 | 15 | 18 | £21

■ Alex Thompson's "casual" Bermondsey patch is a little "off-the-beaten-track", but its "charming bohemian spirit" makes for a "nice rendezvous" over "large portions" of "good, honest" British cooking from an "ever-changing menu"; though a few hiss it's "not as cheap as its image" would suggest, more maintain it's a "wonderful value."

House on Rosslyn Hill 🆂
34 Rosslyn Hill, NW3 (Hampstead), 020-7435 8037; fax 020-7431 3610   13 | 14 | 12 | £26

◪ "New management" have given this "lively" Hampstead "hangout" a lick of paint and expanded next door, and whilst complaints rain in on "chaotic service", it remains a "reliable place to eat" "nice" Modern European fare.

Hunan
51 Pimlico Rd., SW1 (Sloane Sq.), 020-7730 5712; fax 020-7730 8265   23 | 11 | 17 | £33

■ Let "gourmand" chef-owner Mr. Peng "do the ordering" – "you can trust him" to "tailor a wonderful selection" of "regional Chinese dishes" "to your likes and dislikes" at this low-key Pimlico eaterie where the "unusually bold" fare "often comes close to perfection"; the "real issue is the cost, which is quite high", but loyalists feel it's "worth it."

Hush
8 Lancashire Ct., W1 (Bond St.), 020-7659 1500; fax 020-7659 1501   18 | 20 | 16 | £38

■ "Secluded off Bond Street" in a pretty mews, this "good all-rounder" is a "fun" spot for "the 'in' crowd", with a "noisy" ground-floor brasserie serving "delightfully simple" Modern British fare and a "quieter upstairs" eaterie offering an upscale New French menu; there's a "chic" bar for those who'd rather "be seen than eat", plus "great outside tables"; N.B. chef Henry Harris' post-*Survey* departure (to Racine) may impact the above Food rating.

Ibla
89 Marylebone High St., W1 (Baker St./Bond St.), 020-7224 3799; fax 020-7486 1370   21 | 14 | 17 | £39

◪ Insiders insist that the "rather drabby surroundings" of this "spartan" Marylebone venue are overshadowed by

| F | D | S | C |

the "gorgeous", "singular" Modern Italian cooking ("when in form" it's among the "best"), a "great wine list" and "helpful service"; sceptics warn that "the bill quickly mounts" ("Sicilian food at Milanese prices") and bristle at the "not so friendly service."

Ifield, The S | 17 | 17 | 14 | £24 |
59 Ifield Rd., SW10 (Earl's Court), 020-7351 4900; fax 020-7351 1100

◪ It feels like your "second living room" rave admirers of Ed Baines' and Jamie Poulton's "boisterous" Modern British gastro-pub on the Chelsea-Fulham border, a "neighbourhood favourite" where you can "take your friends"; the dining room is as much a draw for the "hip crowd" that hangs here as the "see-and-be-seen" bar; N.B. at press time a Belsize branch was due to open late summer.

Ikeda | ▽ 24 | 15 | 21 | £40 |
30 Brook St., W1 (Bond St.), 020-7629 2730; fax 020-7628 6982

■ "Hefty on the pocket, light on the palate" is the consensus on Mr. Ikeda's tiny, "formal" Mayfair venue, which may not look like much ("decor, what decor?") but nevertheless steps up to the plate with "wonderfully fresh" sushi and "excellent, authentic" Japanese fare; "attentive service" completes the picture.

Ikkyu S | 17 | 10 | 14 | £22 |
7 Newport Pl., WC1 (Leicester Sq.), 020-7439 3554; fax 020-7773 4150
67A Tottenham Court Rd., W1 (Goodge St.), 020-7636 9280; fax 020-7323 5378

◪ "Excellent for a quick meal" say devotees of this "slightly shabby" Tottenham Court Road basement site that satisfies many with "wonderful" fare at "great prices" and even "feels like Tokyo"; the separately owned Chinatown venue is less popular, and some say it "helps if you speak Japanese" at both sites to ensure "attentive service."

Il Convivio | 21 | 19 | 17 | £41 |
143 Ebury St., SW1 (Sloane Sq./Victoria), 020-7730 4099; fax 020-7730 4103

■ "Mangia bene", the "quality rustic-style" Modern Italian cooking is "excellent" exclaim enthusiasts who also admire the "creative wine list" and "most attentive" staff at this "elegant", "stylish" bi-level venue on the Pimlico-Belgravia border; even though a few foes claim it's "easy to forget", most argue it "will not disappoint"; N.B. an electric room opens at the rear on warm days.

Il Falconiere ◐ | 15 | 12 | 17 | £27 |
84 Old Brompton Rd., SW7 (Gloucester Rd./South Kensington), 020-7589 2401; fax 020-7589 9158

◪ Supporters of this "old faithful" in South Kensington appreciate the "quiet" ambience and "basic" Italian dishes

| F | D | S | C |

that are "usually pleasant enough", especially for a "lovely lunch"; critics counter that it's "not exciting at all", indeed, it's "a letdown."

Il Forno
63-64 Frith St., W1 (Tottenham Court Rd.), 020-7734 4545; fax 020-7287 8624

| 18 | 16 | 16 | £26 |

■ "Tasty" Modern Italian food, including "excellent pizzas" from a wood-burning oven, and "friendly staff" lure loyalists to Claudio Pulze's "cheerful", "relaxed" Soho eaterie; a smattering snap it's "too noisy" and "erratic" and are happy to "give it a miss"; N.B. artwork is sometimes on display.

Il Posto S
6 Clarendon Rd., W11 (Holland Park), 020-7727 3330

| – | – | – | E |

Small and welcoming, with art on the walls and a lively feel, this split-level Holland Park newcomer serves authentic Modern Italian fare with a creative seafood slant, all prepared by chef Andrea Gazzabin, formerly of Cibo.

Imperial City
Royal Exchange, Cornhill, EC3 (Bank), 020-7626 3437; fax 020-7338 0125

| 17 | 17 | 15 | £32 |

◪ "Roomy", with "vaulted ceilings", this "large basement" venue under the City's Royal Exchange is "popular among brokers" and expense-accounters who head here for "high-standard", "expensive" Chinese cooking; knockers retort it's "resting on its laurels" and could, in fact, "do far better."

INCOGNICO ●
117 Shaftesbury Ave., WC2 (Leicester Sq.), 020-7836 8866; fax 020-7240 9525

| 22 | 18 | 18 | £37 |

■ The "fantastic" New French dishes, including a "bargain-treat" pre-theatre menu, are "smashing value considering its location" say fans who "keep returning" to this "stylish" Theatreland "find" run by Nico Ladenis' daughter Natasha Robinson; the "ultra-chic" yet "relaxed ambience" ("at last, a nice place to eat and talk") and "hospitable" staff add to the "feel-good experience"; it's "disappointing given its heritage" fret a few who find the "atmosphere stark" and caution that "service can range from fluent to haphazard."

Independence, The S
235 Upper St., N1 (Highbury & Islington), 020-7704 6977

| – | – | – | M |

Transformed from a run-down pub in Highbury, this bi-level restaurant/bar spin-off of The Perseverance makes its own mark with animal hides on the walls and a reasonably priced Modern European menu; most of the action can be found downstairs on the ground level in the large saloon.

Indigo ●S
One Aldwych Hotel, 1 Aldwych, WC2 (Charing Cross/Covent Garden), 020-7300 0400; fax 020-7300 0401

| 21 | 21 | 20 | £38 |

■ "Comfy seats", a "soothing atmosphere" and a "very original menu" of "impeccable" Modern British–European

| F | D | S | C |

cooking make this mezzanine dining area within the One Aldwych Hotel "spot on" for a "business lunch", pre-show suppers or "watching celebs pass through the lobby"; although a few report feeling "let down by the service" and think the "food could use a bit more zest", they're outvoted by those who find it a "pleasant", "peaceful" experience.

Innecto S ▽ | 13 | 17 | 11 | £36 |
66 Baker St., W1 (Baker St.), 020-7935 4545; fax 020-7486 6888

◪ Only a few found their way to this "tasty, if a tad pricey", Modern Italian newcomer "in the wilds of Baker Street", a strikingly designed addition to Marylebone from the owners of Eco; whilst fans adore the "great vibe" in the downstairs bar, sensitive sorts are "deafened by the music."

ISHBILIA ◐ S | 25 | 15 | 21 | £31 |
9 William St., SW1 (Knightsbridge), 020-7235 7788; fax 020-7235 7771

■ "Great value", "flavoursome" food – that's the "formula" that makes this "excellent" Lebanese local a "home away from home" for "Middle Eastern diners"; P.S. it's "good for takeaway", and there's a belly dancer on weekends.

Isola | 17 | 18 | 15 | £40 |
145 Knightsbridge, SW1 (Knightsbridge), 020-7838 1055; fax 020-7838 1099

◪ Views on Oliver Peyton's "modern", bi-level Knightsbridge venue are polarised: "what an experience" fawn fans who flock to this "chic", "sexy, sleek" destination for "excellent", "creative" Modern Italian fare from new chef Graziano Bonacina (who took over from Bruno Loubet); bashers baulk that it "does not distinguish itself" thanks to a "cold interior" and "scant portions" of "uneven cooking"; P.S. the "fun" Isobar upstairs is "great" "for a drink" and antipasti.

I-Thai S | 20 | 23 | 19 | £53 |
Hempel Hotel, 31-35 Craven Hill Gardens, W2 (Lancaster Gate), 020-7298 9000; fax 020-7402 4666

■ "A completely unique and pleasing experience until you get the bill" chorus acolytes of this "fabulous minimalist" dining room in the Hempel Hotel in Bayswater, one of "London's most unusual settings" for "innovative" Pacific Rim–Thai dishes; the "interesting flavours are brought together" in an "outstanding presentation" that's even "perfect" for a "modern candlelit dinner"; N.B. the hotel's famous founder Anoushka Hempel is no longer involved.

itsu S | 18 | 17 | 15 | £25 |
103 Wardour St., W1 (Leicester Sq./Piccadilly Circus), 020-7479 4794; fax 020-7479 4791
118 Draycott Ave., SW3 (South Kensington), 020-7590 2401; fax 020-7590 2403

■ "Sushi addicts – go, go, go" urge admirers of these "novel, fun and fast" "modern-style conveyor belt" Chelsea

| F | D | S | C |

and Soho siblings; the "urban, dynamic" atmosphere makes a "nice refuge" for "when you're dining alone", and the self-serve concept is also "a great" way to discover Japanese food; whilst the "original fun factor" has waned "a bit" for a few, most claim it's "still reliable."

IVY, THE ●S 23 | 21 | 22 | £45
1 West St., WC2 (Leicester Sq.), 020-7836 4751; fax 020-7240 9333
◪ Though ousted from this *Survey*'s Most Popular position for the first time since 1998, this "very chichi" Theatreland "institution" remains "one of the most difficult reservations" in town ("unless you're Tom Cruise"), with "stunningly simple" Modern British–European fare proffered by "service that rocks"; the "buzzy surroundings" and "wall-to-wall celebrities" make it "quite an experience" for most, but critics snipe that "the good food is foiled by the starstruck staff" and the "more-sizzle-than-substance" "hype."

Iznik ●S 19 | 21 | 17 | £24
19 Highbury Park, N5 (Highbury & Islington), 020-7704 8099; fax 020-7354 5697
■ "Tucked away" in Highbury, this "interesting" standby blessed with "outstanding decor" is "perhaps London's best Turkish" venue insist surveyors who've sampled the "tasty" Ottoman-inspired cooking; those who prefer to keep this "lovely local" close to the vest "don't want to recommend it, otherwise" they "won't be able to get a table!"

Jade Garden S 18 | 14 | 15 | £23
15 Wardour St., W1 (Leicester Sq./Piccadilly Circus), 020-7437 5065; fax 020-7429 7851
◪ "Excellent for dim sum at lunchtime", this "peaceful" multiregional Chinatown eaterie also serves a "very good-value" prix fixe theatre menu; whilst supporters say "staff make an effort to make you feel comfortable", hard-core critics suggest "service is slow" and conclude it "does not stand out from the crowd."

Jason's S 18 | 17 | 16 | £32
Jason's Wharf, opp. 60 Blomfield Rd., W9 (Warwick Ave.), 020-7286 6752; fax 020-7266 4332
◪ "Fun" and "unique", this Little Venice seafooder boasts a "picture-perfect" "unusual canalside setting" that's "good on a warm night" and also "great" for a "winter's meal"; the "excellent fish courses" and "seaside atmosphere" make it "worth a visit", but wave-makers who now deem it "disappointing" wonder "what happened?"; N.B. two cruising boats are also available for private charter.

Jen Hong Kong Cuisine ●S ▽ 19 | 10 | 14 | £21
7 Gerrard St., W1 (Leicester Sq.), 020-7287 8193; fax 020-7734 9845
■ "Distinctly better than other Chinatown restaurants", this "unpretentious" Chinese "favourite" specialises in "really

authentic Hong Kong dishes" like "brilliant crispy duck"; a snippet of snipers bemoan that it's "run of the mill" with "typically rude service", but no one knocks the set lunch for under a fiver.

Jim Thompson's   17 | 21 | 14 | £24 |
Flaming Wok S

141 The Broadway, SW19 (Wimbledon), 020-8540 5540; fax 020-8540 8728
408 Upper Richmond Rd., SW15 (East Putney), 020-8788 3737; fax 020-8788 3738
617 King's Rd., SW6 (Fulham Broadway), 020-7731 0999; fax 020-7731 2835
889 Green Lanes, N21 (Southgate/Wood Green), 020-8360 0005; fax 020-8364 3006

There are "lots of things hanging from the roof" and they're all for sale in the "cosy and exotic" "bazaar atmosphere" at this "friendly" and "casual" Southeast Asian chain; whilst some find the "yummy", "consistent" Thai-Asian fusion fare up to scratch, others suggest it "can be very iffy", "varying enormously" from restaurant to restaurant, adding "service leaves a lot to be desired" ("still lousy after all these years"); N.B. the Goldhawk Road branch closed post-*Survey*.

JIN KICHI S   24 | 10 | 18 | £27 |
73 Heath St., NW3 (Hampstead), 020-7794 6158

What an "authentic experience" exclaim enthusiasts smitten by the "yummy" yakitori and "awesome sushi" at this "small, intimate" Japanese "time warp" in Hampstead; sure, the "decor needs updating", but that only adds to the "just like in Tokyo" "feel."

Joe Allen ● S   16 | 16 | 16 | £29 |
13 Exeter St., WC2 (Covent Garden), 020-7836 0651; fax 020-7497 2148

Dine on Eclectic-"American comfort food" "with actors straight off the West End stages" at this "'80s throwback", a "vibrant", "informal" Theatreland basement where there's "still a buzz whenever you go"; it's "an old reliable friend for after theatre", but even admirers admit the "basic" fare is "secondary" to the "showbiz-style atmosphere"; foes fume the "old boy has not moved on", to which the faithful retort "don't write him off yet."

Joe's S   16 | 16 | 13 | £28 |
126 Draycott Ave., SW3 (South Kensington), 020-7225 2217; fax 020-7584 1133

■ "Delightfully quiet", this "very cool" Brompton Cross lunch spot is where daytime diners come to eat "good" Modern British soups and salads whilst taking a "rest from shopping expeditions"; a thimbleful of nitpickers gripe about the "look-at-me service" that's "waiting to be discovered by *Vogue*"; N.B. closed from 5 PM.

			F	D	S	C

Joe's Restaurant Bar ▽ | 18 | 16 | 17 | £26 |
16 Sloane St., SW1 (Knightsbridge), 020-7235 9869; fax 020-7235 3218
■ Supporters are "always assured of a welcome smile" and "good Modern" British fare "with substance" at this "stylish", often "crowded" basement cafe in the Marni store in Knightsbridge; though some say it's a "be-seen-in place", others call it an "ideal neighbourhood meeting" spot that affords a bit of "peace away from the bustle."

John Burton-Race | 24 | 17 | 23 | £65 |
Landmark London Hotel, 222 Marylebone Rd., NW1 (Marylebone), 020-7723 7800; fax 020-7723 4700
◪ The "ethereal textures and flavour combinations" of chef-owner John Burton-Race's "stunning" New French fare are "superb" rave admirers who also feel cosseted by the "impeccable service" at Marylbone's "well-kept secret" tucked inside the Landmark London Hotel; whilst some are smitten by the "gorgeous", "wonderful setting", sceptics carp that the "dining room is overupholstered and overwhelming"; P.S. *mais oui,* it's "very expensive."

Joy King Lau ●S | 20 | 11 | 14 | £20 |
3 Leicester St., WC2 (Leicester Sq./Piccadilly Circus), 020-7437 1133; fax 020-7437 2629
■ "It's reassuring to see the place constantly packed with Chinese" assert loyalists of this "popular pit stop" in Chinatown; it's "great all-around, from the dim sum to the à la carte menu", plus it "tastes authentic", "prices are still reasonable" and the food comes in "generous portions."

J. SHEEKEY ●S | 25 | 21 | 23 | £43 |
28-32 St. Martin's Ct., WC2 (Leicester Sq.), 020-7240 2565; fax 020-7240 8114
■ "Catch a glimpse of your favourite politician" or "celebrity crawling about" this "fish lover's mecca" in Theatreland, a "marvellous" seafooder that was voted No. 1 in this *Survey* for Modern European cuisine; it edges out its siblings, The Ivy and Le Caprice, and it's somewhat "easier to get into" enthuse the enthralled, who adore the "imaginative starters and carefully prepared mains" as well as the "old English club atmosphere"; the "courteous", "fantastic service" makes this "winner" "run like clockwork."

Julie's ●S | 17 | 21 | 16 | £35 |
133-137 Portland Rd., W11 (Holland Park), 020-7229 8331; fax 020-7229 4050
◪ "The romantic atmosphere is infectious" and the Modern British cooking "honest and unpretentious" at this "hidden pearl" near Holland Park, a "favourite" that's had "a good long run" of over three decades; adoring surveyors say the "great booths" and "cosy couches" make it a "wonderfully charming", "convivial" spot to "relax"; critics, however, contend that "complacency" blights this "tired" venture.

Julono ●🅂   ▽ 16 | 21 | 19 | £24
73 Haverstock Hill, NW3 (Chalk Farm), 020-7722 0909; fax 020-7428 9481

■ "Superlatives should be heaped" on this "wonderful" Med-Moroccan establishment in Haverstock Hill laud the few who know it; the "funky", lavish Moorish-inspired decor makes you feel "coddled", and the "interesting" fare, including "excellent couscous", is "never a letdown"; N.B. there's a live belly dancer upon request, plus a Bedouin-style bar downstairs with low-level seating.

Just St. James 🅂   16 | 20 | 17 | £38
12 St. James's St., SW1 (Green Park), 020-7976 2222; fax 020-7976 2020

◪ "The decor is eye-catching" and the Modern British fare "lovely" at this "informal", "spacious" bank lobby-cum-restaurant in St. James's; "personable staff" "know how to look after you in great surroundings" that include a second "fantastic bar downstairs"; detractors opine that the "food hasn't caught up with the spellbinding" setting.

Just the Bridge Restaurant & Bar 🅂   – | – | – | M
1 Paul's Walk, Millennium Bridge North Side, EC4 (Blackfriars), 020-7236 0000; fax 020-7329 9299

The long-awaited opening of the Millennium Bridge (aka "the wobbly bridge") that straddles the Thames between St. Paul's and South Bank is a boost for Peter Gladwin's (of Just St. James and Gladwin's fame) fish-themed, glass-fronted, all-day Eclectic brasserie that also features a pretty riverside terrace for alfresco dining; the reasonably priced menu has "a slight Oriental edge" and is deemed "good for business"; N.B. the view is stunning.

Kai 🅂   24 | 20 | 21 | £42
65 S. Audley St., W1 (Bond St./Marble Arch), 020-7493 8988; fax 020-7493 1456

■ A "top-flight" Mayfair destination, this Chinese stalwart satisfies surveyors with a "good selection" of "exquisite" dishes offset by an "excellent wine list"; admirers applaud the "knowledgeable service" as well as the "serene", "sophisticated atmosphere"; it's "becoming overpriced" pout a handful who cringe at the "expense-account prices"; N. B. a live harpist performs several nights a week.

Kaifeng 🅂   19 | 12 | 15 | £39
51 Church Rd., NW4 (Hendon Central), 020-8203 7888; fax 020-8203 8263

■ "You don't have to be Jewish" to enjoy the perks of this "friendly", "welcoming" Hendon venue that offers the "rarity" of "kosher food with a real Oriental twist"; the "fantastic" fare "combines the best of each" ethnicity claim loyalists who say it's "still as incredible" – and as "expensive" – "as ever."

	F	D	S	C

Kalamaras Taverna S
▽ 19 | 10 | 18 | £23

66 Inverness Mews, W2 (Bayswater/Queensway), 020-7727 9122; fax 020-7221 9411

☑ This "very understated", "family-run" Greek BYO "nosherie" in a Queensway mews may "revel in its original decor", but fans insist there's "nothing faded" about the "wonderful food"; "lovely service" adds to the "feels like Greece in England" encounter, but foes retort "there are better places."

Kandoo ◐S
▽ 24 | 13 | 18 | £18

458 Edgware Rd., W2 (Edgware Rd.), 020-7724 2428

■ "Don't go for the atmosphere, go for" the "perfect Persian cuisine" at this "great value" Edgware Road BYO venue that "proves simple is best"; "charming" service heightens the "cheerful" experience.

Kastoori S
▽ 23 | 11 | 19 | £20

188 Upper Tooting Rd., SW17 (Tooting Bec/Tooting Broadway), 020-8767 7027

■ It's "Tooting's triumph" trumpet the few who've made the "worth the visit" trek to this "unusual and unusually good" family-run Indian Vegetarian with a Ugandan slant; "you forget that you ever eat meat" cry carnivores who also go gaga for this "little-known gem" that "never disappoints."

Kennington Lane S
▽ 18 | 18 | 17 | £29

205-209 Kennington Ln., SE11 (Kennington/Oval), 020-7793 8313; fax 020-7793 8323

☑ A "smart", "West End local" with a "wonderfully creative" Modern European menu and "warm staff" is how supporters sum up this "terrific" Kennington spot kitted out with a "fantastic summer courtyard"; the less convinced, however, cite food that's "reasonably executed" but "no longer outstanding", topped with "lax service."

Kensington Place ◐S
19 | 16 | 17 | £36

201-209 Kensington Church St., W8 (Notting Hill Gate), 020-7727 3184; fax 020-7229 2025

☑ "See and be seen, but not heard" at this "crowded", "bright", glass-fronted Kensington "goldfish bowl" that remains a "long-standing favourite" of many as a "good all-rounder" with "consistent", "interesting" Modern British cooking, "swift service" and a sprinkling of "celebs"; "looking dated" dismiss detractors who also lament "amateur service" and "stressful" "noise levels."

Kettners ◐S
13 | 16 | 14 | £25

29 Romilly St., W1 (Leicester Sq.), 020-7734 6112; fax 020-7434 1214

☑ "Long may it continue" cry cultists of this "comfy" Soho "institution" that's a "bit worn around the edges" (aka "faded boarding-house chic") but remains "essential to London" life; it serves a "great" pizza (same owners as

| F | D | S | C |

Pizza Express) and other "simple but effective" (some say "average") Italian dishes, and though the "*Fawlty Towers*" service is a "shame", the "to-die-for" bubbly selection in the Champagne bar makes it "worth it on the right occasion."

Khan's ●S | 18 | 10 | 12 | £17 |
13-15 Westbourne Grove, W2 (Bayswater/Queensway), 020-7727 5420; fax 020-7229 1835

■ "Sit, order, eat and pay the bill in the blink of an eye" quip the khan-tented of the "very fast" service at this Bayswater "bargain" that offers up "excellent, authentic" Indian cooking; merrymakers maintain it "lost its charm" when it became "unlicensed" ("when the Cobras return, so will we"), but most agree it's "enormous fun with a group."

Khan's of Kensington ●S | 17 | 13 | 13 | £23 |
3 Harrington Rd., SW7 (South Kensington), 020-7584 4114; fax 020-7581 2900

■ There's a "big choice" of "reliable" Indian dishes at this "shabby"-looking South Kensington eatery that serves especially "lovely curries"; even if some knock it as "only marginally better than average" and suggest it "needs a kick in the pants service-wise", "low prices" get the thumbs-up.

Koi S | 23 | 16 | 16 | £38 |
1E Palace Gate, W8 (Gloucester Rd./High St. Kensington), 020-7581 8778; fax 020-7589 2788

■ "An alternative to Nobu" suggest rosy-viewed vaunters of this little-known Japanese near Kensington Gardens serving "delicious sushi and teppanyaki" that a few regard as some of the "best in town" but antagonists aver is "average" and "overpriced"; though the setting is "small", a koi-stocked aquarium provides a nice touch.

Kulu Kulu Sushi | 20 | 9 | 13 | £17 |
76 Brewer St., W1 (Piccadilly Circus), 020-7734 7316; fax 020-7734 6507
39 Thurloe Pl., SW7 (South Kensington), 020-7589 2225

■ "Fast", "uncomplicated" and "cheap", this "popular" pair in Piccadilly and now South Kensington are a "great example of authentic sushi bars"; even if some are left cold by the "conveyor belt" "gimmick", others are reassured by the sight of "many Japanese customers which signifies the real thing, not a trendy fad."

La Bouchée S | 19 | 16 | 16 | £29 |
56 Old Brompton Rd., SW7 (South Kensington), 020-7589 1929; fax 020-7584 8625

■ Tables are "a bit squeezed together" at this "dark" South Kensington French bistro, but that's part of its "romantic" charm; the fare is "delicious" according to its *amis*, who also adore "friendly" staff, but adversaries mouth off about waiters "who need to realise they're north of the Channel now."

| | | | | F | D | S | C |

La Brasserie ●S 16 | 14 | 13 | £29
272 Brompton Rd., SW3 (South Kensington), 020-7581 3089; fax 020-7581 1435

◪ "A slice of Paris in the heart of London", this "convenient, unpretentious" Brompton Cross "all-rounder" is "open all the time" (from breakfast to dinner), offering "authentic French" fare; it's a "classic Sunday brunch" spot, and even if bashers are brassed off by "rude servers", others say things have "greatly improved [since] its surly old days!"

La Cage Imaginaire S ▽ 17 | 17 | 18 | £29
16 Flask Walk, NW3 (Hampstead), 020-7794 6674

■ Even though this "sweet little place" in a Hampstead mews has been around for 20 years, it's something of "an unexpected gem" to many, with its "charming atmosphere" and "pretty" decor; the cuisine's "simple", "good" and "reasonably priced", and the service is "caring."

L'Accento Italiano ● 21 | 17 | 18 | £28
16 Garway Rd., W2 (Bayswater/Queensway), 020-7243 2201; fax 020-7243 2201

■ "Don't judge a book by its cover", as this "unpretentious" Bayswater trattoria is a "terrific local" with "consistent" "great" Modern Italian cooking (it pays to "stick to the set menu for best value"); although *si*-sayers insist the "service is well above the mark", a few carp it can be "let down by lackadaisical" lapses.

La Famiglia ●S 20 | 15 | 18 | £36
7 Langton St., SW10 (Sloane Sq.), 020-7351 0761; fax 020-7351 2409

◪ "They make you feel like family" at this "hectic", "noisy" Chelsea eaterie that's "full of character" and blessed with a "great" covered patio for year-round dining; the "wonderful", "consistent" Traditional Italian fare ("the essence of mama's cooking") is *buono* to boosters and "expensive" and "overrated" to outsiders, but all in all, this "happy" "old favourite" is like "a little holiday."

La Fontana ●S 19 | 13 | 18 | £37
101 Pimlico Rd., SW1 (Sloane Sq.), 020-7730 6630; fax 020-7730 5577

■ For nearly 40 years, this "unpretentious" Pimlico "old faithful" has been known for its "meticulously prepared" Traditional Italian specialties (including "scrumptious zabaglione" for dessert); the service is "chirpy", "graceful" and "warm" and the environs are "comfortable" and "intimate", making it a "great place for a romantic evening."

Lahore Kebab House ●S⌀ 23 | 5 | 11 | £14
2 Umberston St., E1 (Aldgate East/Whitechapel), 020-7481 9737; fax 020-7488 1300

■ The "worst decor of any restaurant just adds to the great experience" at this "cult curry classic" that's "always worth an excursion" to Commercial Road for "top Pakistani cooking" that's "cheap and tasty"; a few think it's "living off past glories", nevertheless this "no-frills" BYO is "still packing them in" and is "excellent for a group."

Lanesborough Conservatory ● S | 21 | 24 | 21 | £46 |
The Lanesborough, 1 Lanesborough Pl., SW1 (Hyde Park Corner), 020-7333 7254; fax 020-7259 5606
◪ "Bring your life savings" for a "brilliant experience" at this glass-domed hotel dining room on Hyde Park Corner where you can soak up the "romantic atmosphere" all day, from "super power breakfast" to "the best high tea" to "dinner dancing" with live jazz; although most are "delighted" with the "memorable" Eclectic dishes and "ultra-attentive staff", a few sigh it's "sooo not worth it."

Langan's Bistro | 19 | 18 | 17 | £37 |
26 Devonshire St., W1 (Baker St.), 020-7935 4531; fax 020-7493 8309
◪ This "very tiny, narrow" Marylebone dining room with walls jam-packed with art continues to do the "business after all these years" thanks to "reliable" French bistro cooking and "attentive service"; if some "have never warmed to it" and feel it's "looking its age", haven-seekers suggest it's "an absolutely safe place to take anyone."

Langan's Brasserie ● | 19 | 19 | 18 | £40 |
Stratton St., W1 (Green Park), 020-7491 8822; fax 020-7493 8309
◪ "Still got something about it" is the consensus on Richard Shepherd's "old-school" "winner" in Mayfair where loyalists "love" the "unbeatable atmosphere" ("rub elbows with celebs"), "great", "solid" Anglo-French cooking and "friendly staff"; bashers believe it's "gone off the boil", with "so-so food" and "slow service", yet it manages to remain "eternally popular."

Langan's Coq d'Or S | 18 | 18 | 18 | £38 |
254-260 Old Brompton Rd., SW5 (Earl's Court), 020-7259 2599; fax 020-7370 7735
◪ It's "in a difficult location" in Earl's Court, but "Langan's newest outpost" is a "good place to relax" and "enjoy the art on the walls", along with "lovely" Anglo-French fare; whilst a few avow that the victuals are "variable" and "pricey" to boot, they concede the front terrace "in summer is a redeeming feature."

Lan Na Thai | – | – | – | E |
2 Lombard Rd., SW11 (Vauxhall), 020-7924 6090
Owned by the Hazarindo catering group, which also operates offshoots in Shanghai and Jakarta, this Thai newcomer summons culinary influences from China and India in a converted riverside pub near Battersea Village with a timber terrace overlooking the Thames; exotic

| F | D | S | C |

---

artifacts from all over Asia lend a faraway feeling to the space; P.S. the bar offers a wide range of innovative drinks.

Lansdowne, The ⑤ | 18 | 16 | 14 | £26

90 Gloucester Ave., NW1 (Camden Town/Chalk Farm), 020-7483 0409; fax 020-7586 1725

◪ "So happy it's my local" boast boosters of this "busy, buzzy" Primrose Hill gastro-pub with a dining room upstairs (which takes bookings) and bar area downstairs serving "interesting", "good-value" Modern British pub fare; "all show, no go" is the counterview, but the majority maintain it's "worth the wait for a table."

La Perla Bar & Grill | 17 | 14 | 15 | £25

28 Maiden Ln., WC2 (Covent Garden), 020-7240 7400; fax 020-7836 5088 ⑤
11 Charlotte St., W1 (Tottenham Court Rd.), 020-7436 1744
803 Fulham Rd., SW6 (Parsons Green), 020-7471 4895; fax 020-7736 9309 ⑤

■ "Go for after-work beers" and "tasty cocktails" first, then go for the "good-quality" eats "when you get hungry" advise acolytes who fill these "always busy" Mexican spots; the "relaxed", "cheap and cheerful" vibe and "enjoyable food" add up to a "good mix"; N.B. a third branch opened post-*Survey* on Charlotte Street.

La Piragua ●⑤∅ | ▽ 15 | 7 | 13 | £17

176 Upper St., N1 (Angel/Highbury & Islington), 020-7354 2843; fax 020-7226 5480

◪ Overlook the "grotty decor" and study the "great choices" on the "interesting menu" of "authentic" South American food instead advise admirers of this "very individual" Islingtonian; the "value"-priced dishes are "quite good" and even have a "home-cooked feel", plus "smiling staff" make you feel "catered" to.

La Porchetta Pizzeria ●⑤ | 18 | 11 | 15 | £15

147 Stroud Green Rd., N4 (Finsbury Park), 020-7281 2892; fax 020-7281 2892
141-142 Upper St., N1 (Highbury & Islington), 020-7288 2488

■ "Fabulous, authentic pizzas the size of wagon wheels at rock-bottom prices" lure loyalists to this pair of "hectic" pizzerias in Finsbury Park and Islington; sure, these sibs get "incredibly noisy" (it "feels like you're eating in a Concorde test tunnel") what with the "mad" "singing waiters" and "queues" that can stretch to the "street outside", but most think the nosh is "worth it."

La Porte des Indes ●⑤ | 21 | 24 | 19 | £37

32 Bryanston St., W1 (Marble Arch), 020-7224 0055; fax 020-7224 1144

■ "You'll feel like you've stepped into another country" at this "colourful" Marylebone cousin of The Blue Elephant, where the "wonderful waterfalls", "exotic" decor and

F | D | S | C

"amazing Indian food" add up to a "real experience" "like no other"; the "fantastic flavours" are a "change from run of the mill", giving you a "chance to experiment", but critics claim the "novelty value" wears off quickly.

LA POULE AU POT ●S 21 | 22 | 19 | £38

*231 Ebury St., SW1 (Sloane Sq.), 020-7730 7763;
fax 020-7259 9651*

■ "Dates adore" this "romantic dinner-for-two venue" (some say it's "still best for mistresses") near the Pimlico Green antique shops, where "perfectly executed" French bistro cooking helps set the scene for "seduction"; "take a step back in time – but quite a pleasant step" – into the "cosy" setting that feels like "Paris in London without the pretension", made all the more "divine in the summer with the outside tables."

La Rueda ●S 15 | 11 | 14 | £24

*102 Wigmore St., W1 (Bond St.), 020-7486 1718;
fax 020-7486 1718
642 King's Rd., SW6 (Fulham Broadway), 020-7384 2684;
fax 020-7384 2684
66-68 Clapham High St., SW4 (Clapham North), 020-7627 2173;
fax 020-7627 2173*

◪ Expect "great party nights" and "dancing on the tables" at this "lively", "noisy" Spanish trio that's "hard to beat for fun on a Friday night", especially "if you are a bunch"; whilst some surveyors deem the "fabulous tapas" and "good-value" fare a "tasty treat", dissenters say there's "room for improvement", declaring it's more about "drinking and pulling" than dining.

LA TANTE CLAIRE 26 | 21 | 24 | £63

Berkeley Hotel, Wilton Pl., SW1 (Knightsbridge), 020-7823 2003; fax 020-7823 2001

◪ "Surely a textbook example of how to get everything right" rave acolytes of this "sophisticated" Berkeley Hotel dining room where "master craftsman" Pierre Koffmann turns out "exceptional", "to-die-for" French fare ("pure heaven" on a plate) and the "delightful" "invisible-when-they-should-be" servers treat diners "like royalty"; but a smattering of snipers say it's "not all it's cracked up to be", whilst wallet-watchers exclaim "ouch, ouch, ouch", wish "it were not so expensive."

LA TROMPETTE S 27 | 22 | 23 | £40

*5 Devonshire Rd., W4 (Turnham Green), 020-8747 1836;
fax 020-8995 8097*

■ "Civilisation – yippee!" chorus customers who claim this "stellar" New French yearling, a sibling of Chez Bruce and The Glasshouse, is "worth the detour" to Chiswick; chef Ollie Couillaud's "mouthwatering" fare is "absolutely delicious and exquisitely served", plus it's offered at "non–West End prices"; in sum, a "brilliant all-rounder."

www.zagat.com

| | | | | F | D | S | C |

La Trouvaille
▽ | 23 | 20 | 21 | £33

12A Newburgh St., W1 (Oxford Circus), 020-7287 8488; fax 020-7434 4170

■ "What a find" exclaim the lucky few who've stumbled upon this "piece of Paris in Soho" near Carnaby Street, a "fun, fun, fun" French bistro where the "waiters, like extras from *'Allo 'Allo*", greet guests with a "warm welcome"; the "simply outstanding" fare offers "quality at good-value prices", which seals its standing as a "great newcomer."

Launceston Place ◐ S
22 | 20 | 20 | £42

1A Launceston Pl., W8 (Gloucester Rd.), 020-7937 6912; fax 020-7938 2412

■ "It all fits like a glove" at this "wonderful quiet haven" set in a "discreet" Kensington townhouse, thanks to the "homely surroundings" and "reliably excellent" Modern British cooking; the "warm feel-good factor" is at work here say insiders who appreciate the "elegant comfort" of the "classy setting" as well as the "charming service"; if a few pose that "perhaps it's a little predictable", most maintain it's "still a favourite"; N.B. now open for Sunday dinner.

Laurent ◐ S
▽ | 17 | 13 | 20 | £21

428 Finchley Rd., NW2 (Golders Green), 020-7794 3603

◪ Things have yet to settle down since new owners (from the Domino's pizza team) took over this Golders Green Tunisian spot; opinions swing wildly, with fans praising it for "the best couscous in town" and "friendly service", whilst foes retort it "used to be good, but now it's a no-no."

L'Aventure
21 | 17 | 19 | £40

3 Blenheim Terrace, NW8 (St. John's Wood), 020-7624 6232; fax 020-7625 5548

■ "Cosy in winter" with a "great terrace in summer" – yes, the "old formula still works" at this "lovely, romantic" French bistro in St. John's Wood; the "food continues to be excellent", and the service, led by owner "Catherine [Parisot] the Greatest", is "hospitable", which may explain why this "pleasant neighbourhood" spot is "always full"; if a few gripe that it can get a "bit cramped inside", most concede it's still a "treat."

Le Boudin Blanc S
20 | 16 | 16 | £32

5 Trebeck St., Shepherd's Mkt., W1 (Green Park), 020-7499 3292; fax 020-7495 6973

■ "Exactly what a good [French] bistro should be" declare lovers of this "old favourite" "nicely tucked away in Shepherd's Market"; the "consistently tasty", "no-fuss" offerings, "rustic surroundings" and "friendly service" make you feel "like you've been whisked away to Paris or Lyon for the afternoon"; whilst some say it can be a "claustrophobe's nightmare with tables so close and crowded", others say all is forgiven on "warm nights" when you can sit outside.

| F | D | S | C |

Le Cabanon | 22 | 17 | 18 | £37 |
(fka Nico Central)
35 Great Portland St., W1 (Oxford Circus), 020-7436 8846; fax 020-7436 3455

◪ Formerly Nico Central, but now renamed (by the same owners) with no link to Nico Ladenis, and refurbished, this "pleasant", "compactly organised" New French spot near Oxford Street remains "ideal for business lunches"; views on the service range from "excellent" to "uninterested."

Le Cafe du Jardin ●S | 19 | 18 | 18 | £32 |
28 Wellington St., WC2 (Covent Garden), 020-7836 8769; fax 020-7836 4123

■ Bag a window seat and "watch the world go by" while dining on "imaginative" Modern British–Eclectic fare at this "bright" bi-level Covent Garden eatery; the "dependably delicious prix fixe menu" is an "excellent value" that's "just right for a pre- or post-theatre" supper.

Le Café du Marché | 22 | 20 | 20 | £35 |
22 Charterhouse Sq., EC1 (Barbican), 020-7608 1609; fax 020-7336 7459

■ "Just off Smithfield Market", this "adorable" French bistro in a converted warehouse "lends itself to long, happy lunches" and "dinner à deux"; it feels like the "real thing", with "tasty" fare that "never changes – but doesn't need to" and Gallic "service that adds to the experience"; "upstairs is better" for "business", whilst "downstairs is for romance."

LE CAPRICE ●S | 24 | 21 | 22 | £44 |
Arlington House, Arlington St., SW1 (Green Park), 020-7629 2239; fax 020-7493 9040

■ "It's still a thrill to walk through the door" gush fans of The Ivy's "classic" sibling, a "cool, minimal" Modern British–European "classic" in Piccadilly that's "unrivalled" for a "bit of glitz" and "stargazing"; "consistency is the watchword", with "energy and ambience" that "can't be duplicated", food so "delicious" you "never tire of it" and "pampering service" that makes you feel "very special."

Le Colombier S | 19 | 18 | 19 | £36 |
145 Dovehouse St., SW3 (South Kensington), 020-7351 1155; fax 020-7351 0077

■ "All that a local should be", this Chelsea "favourite" is "a revelation", with "solid" French fare, an "A+" setting (including a "lovely terrace") and *sympathetique* staff; although a few grumblers gripe about "variable food and service", most claim it's an "enjoyable experience."

Le Deuxieme ●S | ▽ 21 | 22 | 23 | £34 |
65A Long Acre, WC2 (Covent Garden), 020-7379 0033; fax 020-7379 0066

◪ From the team behind Le Cafe du Jardin comes this Covent Garden newcomer, a "worthy successor" to the

| F | D | S | C |

now-defunct Magno's that's made a promising start with an "excellent" Modern European menu of "value"-priced prix fixe options and a "pleasant, minimalist" setting; the less-enthused find the cooking "heavy-handed" and the decor "a bit clinical", but most seem to "trust" their progress thus far.

Lee Fook ●S ▽ 20 | 8 | 13 | £26
98 Westbourne Grove, W2 (Bayswater/Notting Hill Gate), 020-7727 0099; fax 020-7727 8773

"A real stroke of luck for locals" say fans who head to this Queensway standby for "generous portions" of "great" Chinese food; still, critics suggest there's "nothing unusual on the menu to elevate it beyond the ordinary" and are just as unimpressed by the "callous service" and "poor decor."

Lee Ho Fook ●S 16 | 10 | 12 | £21
15-16 Gerrard St., W1 (Leicester Sq./Piccadilly Circus), 020-7494 1200; fax 020-7494 1700

"Great dim sum" and "authentic" Cantonese fare are the main attractions at this "bustling", functional 35-year-old Chinatown stalwart; "if only the service could be improved" lament surveyors deterred by "surly" staff.

LE GAVROCHE 27 | 22 | 26 | £65
43 Upper Brook St., W1 (Marble Arch), 020-7408 0881; fax 020-7491 4387

■ Rated No. 1 for Classic French fare, Mayfair's "old dame" of "pricey perfection" – "the Ungaro, Harry Winston and Bentley" of restaurants – "remains a gourmet paradise" where Michel Roux (son of Albert) prepares dishes that "can only be deemed heavenly", especially when accompanied by the "superb wine list"; the servers "never miss a beat" and the "grand" setting feels "exactly right", and if a few find it "stuffy", most laud it as "fantastic" and "only wish they were open on Saturdays."

LE MANOIR AUX QUAT'SAISONS S 27 | 25 | 26 | £69
Le Manoir aux Quat'Saisons, Church Rd., Great Milton, Oxfordshire, 01844 278881; fax 01844 278847

■ "All serious foodies should try it once" say surveyors smitten by Raymond Blanc's "exquisite" New French fare served by "unbeatable" staff in this "magical" 15th-century Cotswold manor house, now owned by Orient-Express Hotels; it's "clearly worth the drive" ("go when the gardens are green") and "every pence" because this is "food on a higher plane"; a handful baulk at "over-the-top prices", but most claim it's "utterly perfect in every way."

Le Mercury ●S 16 | 15 | 16 | £19
140A Upper St., N1 (Angel/Highbury & Islington), 020-7354 4088; fax 020-7359 7186

"If you like candlelight", this "charming", "cheery" Islington bistro hits the mark with "wholesome", "simple

F | D | S | C

French cuisine" that's "fantastic for the money", "backed up by a great wine list"; "on the downside", naysayers declare it's "cramped" and "dark", with "mediocre food."

Le Metro 🆂 ▽ 15 | 13 | 16 | £25
L'Hotel, 28 Basil St., SW3 (Knightsbridge), 020-7591 1213; fax 020-7823 7826

■ "A great lunchtime pit stop" for Modern British fare fawn fans who find this "stylish" "hidden cafe" inside L'Hotel "affordable for Knightsbridge" and convenient "when shopping"; in sum, it's "more fun than eating in Harrods."

Lemonia ◐🆂 18 | 15 | 18 | £25
89 Regent's Park Rd., NW1 (Chalk Farm), 020-7586 7454; fax 020-7483 2636

■ It's "a bit of a trek", but this "festive, casual" Greek taverna in Primrose Hill is still the "place of choice for a fun evening" of "wonderful", "inspired cuisine" and drink; the "lively setting" is "ideal for a family outing" and "perfect for a small party", plus staff "treat you like old friends" – no wonder most say "it never fails to satisfy"; "wish our local wasn't sooo popular" lament loyalists who claim it's "always packed."

Le Palais du Jardin ◐🆂 20 | 18 | 16 | £35
136 Long Acre, WC2 (Covent Garden), 020-7379 5353; fax 020-7379 1846

◪ "Consistently high-quality seafood" is "generously served" from the Classic French menu at this "bustling", "buzzy" "reliable bet", a Covent Garden brasserie and "ace bar" that's "especially great for a drink when they open the front panels up" in the summertime; it's "surprisingly huge", yet the "varied character of the seating areas" ensures that "one doesn't feel lost"; some surveyors say "service can be slow" and "uneven."

LE PONT DE LA TOUR ◐🆂 21 | 21 | 19 | £47
Butlers Wharf Bldg., 36D Shad Thames, SE1 (London Bridge/ Tower Hill), 020-7403 8403; fax 020-7403 0267

◪ The "magnificent" "view alone is worth the effort of getting to" Sir Terence Conran's "dramatic" riverside setting next to Tower Bridge, boasting a "romantic terrace" that's "unbeatable on a hot day"; the "interesting" Modern European cooking is "perfect for the discerning diner", a "real treat" matched by an "excellent wine list" and "great service" that's "discreet, but always on hand"; critics, however, carp the "food could be better at those prices" and deride "indifferent" staff.

L'ESCARGOT ◐ 24 | 22 | 21 | £43
48 Greek St., W1 (Leicester Sq./Tottenham Court Rd.), 020-7437 6828; fax 020-7439 7474

◪ With a recent David Collins makeover under its belt, this "seriously special" French "gastronomic delight", spread

| F | D | S | C |

over several floors of a "stylish" Soho townhouse, is "thoroughly up to [Marco Pierre] White's usual standards"; the "superb" fare and "scrumptious wine" are "simply yum, yum, yum", plus it's all "beautifully" served by "just the right kind" of staff; P.S. it's a "great place to linger with a partner or a friend."

LE SOUFFLÉ S   24 | 18 | 24 | £55
Hotel Inter-Continental, 1 Hamilton Pl., W1 (Hyde Park Corner), 020-7318 8577; fax 020-7491 0926

◪ "Lovely for a bit of posh", this "comfortable" dining room within Hyde Park Corner's Hotel Inter-Continental serves "excellent" New French fare that's "still good", even after the departure of chef Peter Kromberg; the "hard-to-beat" signature dish is one of the "best soufflés ever tasted" and the "magnificent service" "makes you feel at home", however deflated dissenters deem it "pricey"; N.B. chef Michael Coaker, who joined the staff post-*Survey*, does not intend to dramatically revamp the menu.

L'Estaminet   22 | 19 | 21 | £37
14 Garrick St., WC2 (Covent Garden/Leicester Sq.), 020-7379 1432; fax 020-7379 1530

■ "As French as you can get", this "lovely little" Covent Garden bistro is "excellent for a quick, tasty" pre- and post-theatre meal or just a "nice evening out"; the menu offers a "real taste of Paris", with "well-presented cheeses" and "great classic cooking", all served by "professional" staff; "why aren't there more places like this?" wonder fans.

LES TROIS GARCONS   19 | 26 | 20 | £47
1 Club Row, E1 (Liverpool St.), 020-7613 1924; fax 020-7613 5960

◪ "Love it or hate it", the "outrageous" decor, featuring bejewelled stuffed animals and the like, "has to be seen to be believed" at this East End eaterie; whilst most say the "heavenly" French fare lives up to the "decorative feast-for-the-eyes" setting, a miffed few think the "food is nothing to write home about", proclaiming it's all about "style over substance"; still, even foes admit it's "great for a giggle."

Le Suquet ●S   21 | 16 | 18 | £40
104 Draycott Ave., SW3 (South Kensington), 020-7581 1785; fax 020-7225 0838

■ "A French seaside restaurant plopped right in the middle of London", this "lively" Gallic seafooder in Brompton Cross features a "broad selection" of fin fare that's "wonderful", particularly the "irresistible plat du mer"; P.S. the "discreet service is best for business meals" and "romance."

Levant ●S   19 | 22 | 17 | £37
Jason Ct., 76 Wigmore St., W1 (Bond St.), 020-7224 1111; fax 020-7486 1216

◪ "Interesting" Levantine fare (Eastern Mediterranean–North African), plus a "beautiful" "atmospheric" basement

F | D | S | C

and "cool bar", lures a "smart crowd" to this Marylebone haunt; whilst some say it's worth the "splurge", others say the "food is not worth the price, but the 'in'-ness is."

Light House S
▽ | 19 | 17 | 16 | £33

75-77 Ridgway Pl., SW19 (Wimbledon), 020-8944 6338; fax 020-8946 4440

☒ Expect a "perfect evening" at this "lovely", "consistently excellent" Wimbledown Village spot where the "offbeat" and "very unusual" Modern Italian "dishes always delight"; critics counter it's "rather a letdown", citing "erratic service" and a "pretentious" menu.

L'Incontro ◐ S
22 | 19 | 20 | £47

87 Pimlico Rd., SW1 (Sloane Sq.), 020-7730 3663; fax 020-7730 5062

☒ "A veritable joy" exclaim enthusiasts of this "elegant" eaterie in Pimlico, an "above-average" option for "excellent" Modern Italian cooking; surveyors chorus "love the food, hate the bill", still the "expensive spaghetti" is "justified by the attentive service."

Little Bay S
16 | 11 | 17 | £14

171 Farringdon Rd., EC1 (Farringdon Rd.), 020-7278 1234
228 Belsize Rd., NW6 (Kilburn Park), 020-7372 4699; fax 020-7372 8282 ◐ ⇄

■ "It's not much to look at", but this modest "little favourite" "off-the-beaten-track" in Kilburn "never fails to deliver a fantastic time" thanks to an "unbelievable bargain" of a Mediterranean menu and a "relaxed" atmosphere; it's "always packed, and it's no surprise why": "always leaves you satisfied"; N.B. a new City branch opened post-*Survey*.

Little Italy ◐ S
17 | 14 | 16 | £25

21 Frith St., W1 (Leicester Sq./Tottenham Court Rd.), 020-7734 4737; fax 020-7734 1777

■ The "rustic" Italian food tells just one side of the story at this "fun, buzzy" Soho stalwart; insiders reveal that it really "ignites after 11 PM", when it turns into a "loud", "excellent" bar and club with dancing, "great cocktails" and a "fantastic atmosphere" that just keeps "swinging" till 4 AM.

Livebait
18 | 15 | 15 | £30

21 Wellington St., WC2 (Covent Garden), 020-7836 7161; fax 020-7836 7141 ◐
175 Westbourne Grove, W11 (Notting Hill Gate), 020-7727 4321; fax 020-7792 3655 S
2 Northside, Wandsworth Common, SW18 (Clapham Junction B.R.), 020-7326 8580; fax 020-7326 8581 S
43 The Cut, SE1 (Waterloo), 020-7928 7211; fax 020-7928 2279 ◐
1 Watling St., EC4 (Bank/Mansion House), 020-7213 0540; fax 020-7213 0541

☒ As "close as you'll get to the seaside" without leaving town, this expanding seafood chain is particularly "fantastic

| F | D | S | C |

if you're a fish lover", with "nice, helpful" staff and a "tasty selection" of "beautiful", "quality fare" that also includes some "exciting, refreshing dishes"; sceptics moan that the "cold" tile-wall decor "lacks atmosphere" but concede that perhaps the "minimal effect" is "an acquired taste."

LMNT S   ▽ 19 | 24 | 18 | £27
316 Queensbridge Rd., E8 (Highbury & Islington), 020-7249 6727; fax 020-7249 6538

■ The few who commented on this "weird" Hackney pub conversion were more intrigued by the "certainly different" "surreal ambience" that pays homage to Roman, Greek and Egyptian history than by the "ok" New French cooking; N.B. the risqué antique pictures on display in the loos are also worth a peek.

Lobster Pot, The   ▽ 21 | 16 | 18 | £32
3 Kennington Ln., SE11 (Kennington), 020-7582 5556

■ With its "fab" but "strange decor" and "soundtrack of seagulls" shrieking, this Gallic seafooder "hidden" in a corner of Kennington guarantees "eccentric evenings"; the "sublime", "fresh fish" and dishes made with "excellent produce" come in "healthy servings", and it's all served by "very knowledgeable", "efficient, not intrusive" staff.

Locanda Locatelli ⌿   – | – | – | E
Churchill Inter-Continental Hotel, 8 Seymour St., W1 (Marble Arch), 020-7935 9088

Having made his name at Zafferano before dabbling at Cecconi's, popular chef Giorgio Locatelli now has his own "stylish" Modern Italian restaurant in the Churchill Inter-Continental Hotel on Portman Square to show off his "*bellissimo*" cooking; fans laud the "imaginative dishes cooked to perfection", "extensive, reasonably priced wine list" and, what else, "celebrity clientele", concluding it's a "great new addition to the London scene."

Lola's S   18 | 17 | 17 | £34
The Mall Bldg., 359 Upper St., N1 (Angel), 020-7359 1932; fax 020-7359 2209

■ A "gem in the heart of the Angel" proclaim lovers of the "fun ambience found in this old tram shed", an "interesting location" for dining on Modern European fare; the "excellent food, good wine list", "attentive service" and "wonderful decor" all lend "a sense of occasion" to this "pleasant surprise", but cynics cite "mediocre" food that "lacks flair"; N.B. the post-*Survey* arrival of chef Hywel Jones, formerly of Foliage, may impact the above Food rating.

Lomo ●S   16 | 14 | 14 | £23
222 Fulham Rd., SW10 (Earl's Court/Fulham Broadway), 020-7349 8848; fax 020-7349 8848

■ More of a "drink and snack" spot than a restaurant, this "casual", "buzzy" Fulham Road Spaniard is "great for a quick bite" of "good tapas" washed down with "killer sangria"; a few faultfinders complain that it can get "very noisy and overcrowded."

L'ORANGER   25 | 22 | 22 | £51
5 St. James's St., SW1 (Green Park), 020-7839 3774; fax 020-7839 4330

◪ His "heavenly" New French "food is up there with the best of them" declare enthusiasts of chef Kamel Benamar's "superb" cooking at this "elegant, but not stuffy" "splurge restaurant" in St. James's; the "incredible food" (including an "amazing selection of cheeses"), "impressive setting" and "impeccable service" just "get better and better every time"; whilst some say it's "perfect for a romantic evening", others save it for "expense-account" outings, as it's a "great power-lunch venue."

Lou Pescadou ●S   18 | 13 | 16 | £34
241 Old Brompton Rd., SW5 (Earl's Court), 020-7370 1057; fax 020-7244 7545

■ This "neighbourhood fish house" in Earl's Court may not quite qualify as a "French masterpiece", nevertheless it has a loyal following who appreciate its "reasonably priced" "delicious food" and "friendly" service that offers "the right amount of attention"; a handful rate it as "nothing special."

Lucky Seven S⇗   ▽ 16 | 18 | 13 | £15
127 Westbourne Park Rd., W2 (Royal Oak/Westbourne Park), 020-7727 6771

◪ "Great burgers" are in the cards at Tom (son of Terence) Conran's "cool" American-style diner near Westbourne Park "where the genuine U.S. theme extends to friendly service" and a "terrific" atmosphere; critics would rather cast their die elsewhere, as there's "not much space" and "they run out of stuff", concluding you "can't replicate an American diner in London."

Luigi's of Covent Garden ●   19 | 16 | 18 | £33
15 Tavistock St., WC2 (Covent Garden), 020-7240 1789; fax 020-7497 0075

◪ "Once hooked, it can become a favourite" applaud admirers drawn by the "theatrical ambience" and "large menu" of "absolutely delightful", "moderately priced" Italian dishes at this "welcoming" Covent Garden destination; even those who think it's getting "tired", with "unmemorable" cooking, concede it's "reliable pre-theatre" and a "good fallback if everywhere else is full."

Lundum's S   21 | 20 | 21 | £35
119 Old Brompton Rd., SW7 (Gloucester Rd./South Kensington), 020-7373 7774; fax 020-7373 4472

■ Perhaps "one can do better in Copenhagen, but one can't in London" fawn fanciers of this "charming", family-run Danish "gem" in South Kensington; "all the ingredients of

| F | D | S | C |

an incredibly superb dinner" are here, from the "sensational smorgasbord" to the "heavenly herring" to the "smooth service"; whilst only a "little room", it's "perfect for low-key entertaining" or "a quiet dinner."

Made in Italy ◐ S | 19 | 14 | 13 | £23 |
249 King's Rd., SW3 (Sloane Sq.), 020-7352 1880; fax 020-7351 5098

◪ "It's easy to understand why Italians" as well as "locals" "love" this "lively" King's Road haunt that turns out "yummy" fare, including "heavenly pizzas" (some of the "best in the 'hood"); the servers "really seem to enjoy themselves", and "in the summer you can eat on the roof" – two more reasons why it's a "fun group dinner place"; bashers retort it can be "slow and noisy" and say "staff are very rude."

Maggie Jones's S | 18 | 18 | 17 | £30 |
6 Old Court Pl., W8 (High St. Kensington), 020-7937 6462; fax 020-7376 0510

■ "Great for nostalgia" (as "untrendy as it gets") this "wonderfully rustic" 50-year-old Kensington spot feels like a "Devon cottage in W8", with Traditional British "comfort food" that "never disappoints" "chunky appetites"; it's a "bit hokey, but just right if ambience is what you're after", especially on "winter evenings."

Ma Goa S | 21 | 15 | 17 | £23 |
242-244 Upper Richmond Rd., SW15 (East Putney), 020-8780 1767; fax 020-8246 6878

■ "Indian with a difference" – it "never disappoints" say admirers of this "recently refurbished" "local favourite" in Putney; the "delicious" Goan dishes "taste home-cooked", and the prices are "kind on the wallet too"; P.S. there's now a takeaway in Sheen – "home-delivered Ma Goa Express, the ultimate indulgence."

Maison Novelli ◐ | 22 | 16 | 18 | £42 |
29 Clerkenwell Green, EC1 (Farringdon), 020-7251 6606; fax 020-7490 1083

◪ Respected chef Jean-Christophe Novelli is "back in form" at this "elegant" Clerkenwell "delight", producing "truly gorgeous" New French dishes that reveal "fascinating contrasts and garnishes" and "exquisite" "artistry in presentation"; what a "wonderful atmosphere – it's relaxed, even though it's posh" swoon the smitten, also taken by the "attentive service"; critics, however, consider the "very ordinary" setting "a bit stark" and the "menu uninspired", griping it "doesn't live up to its reputation."

Malabar ◐ S | 20 | 14 | 16 | £25 |
27 Uxbridge St., W8 (Notting Hill Gate), 020-7727 8800; fax 020-7743 8350

■ A "trendy", "snazzy Indian" ("no flock wallpaper here") "tucked away" in a "charming Notting Hill setting", this

| F | D | S | C |

"great little find" is worth seeking out for its "unique menu" of "original" dishes and "prompt, cordial" service; whilst a few "don't like eating on metal plates", they're in the minority, as "lots of regulars" rate this "neighbourhood favourite" "a winner all-around."

Malabar Junction ◐🅂 22 | 16 | 18 | £25
107 Great Russell St., WC1 (Tottenham Court Rd.), 020-7580 5230; fax 020-7436 9942

■ "A treasure waiting to be discovered", in a "spacious" "conservatory setting", this "rare treat" in Bloomsbury produces "delicious" Kerala dishes with "fascinating combinations of flavours" at "such a reasonable price", with separate vegetarian and non-vegetarian chefs to boot; a handful pass it off as "disappointing", but they're outnumbered by the cognoscenti who confide "if you like South Indian food, this is the place."

Mandalay 21 | 9 | 20 | £19
444 Edgware Rd., W2 (Edgware Rd.), 020-7258 3696

■ "An absolute must for a cheap night out with sensational" Burmese cuisine, this "genuinely warm", family-run Edgware Road spot is "wonderful" enough to "make a fan" out of you; whilst it's "not a place to linger" (you "don't go for the decor, you go for the food"), it's still necessary to "reserve if you're going at a busy time"; P.S. the prix fixe lunch is under £6.

Mandarin Kitchen ◐🅂 23 | 10 | 14 | £29
14-16 Queensway, W2 (Bayswater/Queensway), 020-7727 9012; fax 020-7727 9468

■ "Seafood like nowhere else", particularly "lobster noodles to die for", lures regulars to this "busy" Queensway Chinese "reliable" with a "bustling Hong Kong feel"; sure, the "strange decor" may be in "need of refurbishing" and it sometimes seems "impossible to get a table" ("even if you've booked, be prepared to wait"), but all shortcomings are excused in honour of "the excellent yummy dishes."

Mandola 🅂 21 | 16 | 14 | £19
139-143 Westbourne Grove, W11 (Notting Hill Gate), 020-7229 4734

■ The "simply sumptuous Sudanese" cooking, "wonderful service and atmosphere" are all "out-of-this-world" say fans who come to this "cosy", "unpretentious" Bayswater "spot for something different"; the "high-quality food" is not only "delicious" but "reasonably priced", thanks in part to the fact that you "bring your own wine"; a scant few find staff so "slow it's painful."

Mango Tree 🅂 22 | 21 | 21 | £32
46 Grosvenor Pl., SW1 (Victoria), 020-7823 1888; fax 020-7838 9275

◪ "Spice up your life" with "very impressive" Thai dishes at this "attractive newcomer" near Buckingham Palace where the "extremely gracious service" exhibits a real "willingness to please"; a handful feel "let down" by the "disappointing" fare and find staff too "fussy."

Manor ●S ▽ 22 | 20 | 17 | £29
6-8 All Saints Rd., W11 (Westbourne Park), 020-7243 6363; fax 020-7243 6360
■ Matthew du Cann's sophisticated restaurant and bar near Portobello Road only garners a few comments, but those who know it consider it a "real find"; a fashionable "Notting Hill crowd" hangs out at this evenings-only (plus Sunday brunch) spot as much for the "good" International–Southern European cooking as for the cosy downstairs cocktail bar that's "fun on Saturday nights."

Manzi's ●S 19 | 13 | 17 | £35
1-2 Leicester St., WC2 (Leicester Sq./Piccadilly Circus), 020-7734 0224; fax 020-7437 4864
■ "Nothing changes" – this Leicester Square "institution" (since 1928) keeps "soldiering on", with "very fresh, old-fashioned" seafood dishes (including the "tastiest Dover sole") and "wonderful waiters" who make everyone "feel at home"; if a few wonder whether it's "time for a re-think" (it's "a museum really"), the majority aren't unashamed in their appreciation, visiting "as often as possible."

Mao Tai ●S 20 | 18 | 17 | £33
58 New King's Rd., SW6 (Parsons Green), 020-7731 2520; fax 020-7471 8992
96 Draycott Ave., SW3 (South Kensington), 020-7225 2500; fax 020-7225 1965
◪ "So good not to have to travel to Chinatown for authentic" Szechuan food say supporters of this "attractive" pair in Parson's Green and Brompton Cross, where "excellent" staff greet you with "a very nice welcome"; but detractors beg to differ, citing "expensive" food and "snooty" servers and conclude the "new site [SW3] is considerably inferior" to its long-established sibling; your call.

Maquis S ▽ 20 | 17 | 19 | £35
111 Hammersmith Grove, W6 (Hammersmith), 020-8846 3851
■ "Hurrah for fondue" fete fans who also champion the "good" French fare at this "off to a good start Hammersmith fledgling", partly owned by Sam Clark of Moro fame; the pace is "relaxed and leisurely" in the "beautifully lit", "spacious" dining room, making it an "excellent place for day or night"; N.B. there's also a takeaway deli next door.

MARK'S CLUB 24 | 25 | 26 | £62
Private club; inquiries: 020-7499 2936
■ The "height of luxury", Mark Birley's "tip-top" Mayfair private dining club is "always on the ball", with "perfect" staff serving "great, no-nonsense" Traditional British fare in a "truly special" setting; a few quibble that it's "very

pricey for simple cooking", but most are appreciative: it's the "most wonderful membership I have."

Maroush ●S 21 | 13 | 15 | £23

21 Edgware Rd., W2 (Marble Arch), 020-7723 0773; fax 020-7723 3161
68 Edgware Rd., W2 (Marble Arch), 020-7224 9339; fax 020-7723 3161
62 Seymour St., W2 (Marble Arch), 020-7724 5024; fax 020-7723 3161
4 Vere St., W1 (Bond St.), Mayfair, 020-7493 5050; fax 020-7723 3161
38 Beauchamp Pl., SW3 (Knightsbridge), 020-7581 5434; fax 020-7723 3161

■ "London wouldn't be the same without this late-night" Middle Eastern quintet that delivers "really tasty", "hearty" Lebanese "comfort food" in spades; meat lovers say they'd "kiss their feet for the kebabs", whilst nibblers suggest "go for the mezze" – whatever you order, it's "always a good bet" and a "brilliant value"; sure the wee hours attract "everyone, including half the world's paparazzi", but it's also "perfect for lunching" or "any time of day."

Masala Zone S 20 | 16 | 16 | £19

9 Marshall St., W1 (Oxford Circus), 020-7287 9966; fax 020-7287 8555

◪ "A super find for a quick satisfying nosh" of "deliciously" "creative Indian" cooking, this "cheerful", "convenient" Soho "canteen" is also "outstanding value for the money", prompting fans to gush "what more could you ask for?"; it's "not your ordinary curry house", as witnessed by the "cool setting" that "combines tribal art and modern industrial design", but even the few unimpressed by the "plain decor" admit "what it lacks in style, it makes up for in gastronomic delights"; P.S. "takeaway is dirt cheap."

Mash 14 | 15 | 12 | £28

19-21 Great Portland St., W1 (Oxford Circus), 020-7637 5555; fax 020-7637 7333

◪ A "great funky setting" – think "'70s kitsch meets '90s London" – Oliver Peyton's place off Oxford Street attracts a "loud, trendy, young" crowd who are happy enough with the "average", "standard" Modern European cooking but even more enthralled by the "fab cocktails" and housemade microbrew beers dispensed at the "cool bar"; get a "great start to a long night out" here, but "go somewhere else for food" advise "deafened" surveyors who find it's not the setting to "dine in if you want any conversation"; N.B. the Mayfair sibling has closed.

Matsuri 23 | 17 | 20 | £43

15 Bury St., SW1 (Green Park), 020-7839 1101; fax 020-7930 7010

■ "The art of Japanese cuisine comes alive" at this "formal" Mayfair basement venue where a "real festival"

| F | D | S | C |

of "fantastic food", including "fresh" "great sushi" and the "famous teppanyaki", takes center stage; it's a "great place to impress business clients" and a "sure success for a night out" – yes, it "lives up to your expectations" – though wallet-watchers warn, it "can be a bit expensive."

Maxwell's ●S | 14 | 11 | 13 | £21 |

8-9 James St., WC2 (Covent Garden), 020-7836 0303; fax 020-7240 3562
76 Heath St., NW3 (Hampstead), 020-7794 5450; fax 020-7435 5158

"Fun for kids" and "full of teenagers" and "day-trippers", these "noisy", "cavernous" and "friendly" American diners in Covent Garden and Hampstead are "good for a relaxed meal" of "juicy burgers" and the like; the "big portions of passable", "bland" food "need a little work", and so does the slightly "scruffy", "dated decor" observe detractors.

Mediterraneo ●S | 20 | 15 | 16 | £30 |

37 Kensington Park Rd., W11 (Ladbroke Grove), 020-7792 3131; fax 020-7229 7980

For "a nice night out for two" head to Osteria Basilico's sibling, a "charming" place in Notting Hill where "friendly" "staff make you feel welcome"; the "simple but delicious" Modern Italian fare is "satisfying", and it's "not too pricey" either; cynics contend it "doesn't stand out from the crowd", plus "slack service" could do with some "schooling."

Mela ●S | 19 | 14 | 17 | £25 |

152-156 Shaftesbury Ave., WC2 (Leicester Sq.), 020-7836 8635; fax 020-7379 0527

Expect "deft touches from the chef at this new wave Indian" that's set in a "handy location" near Cambridge Circus but is "far removed from your average curry house"; the "regional variations" of "out of the ordinary" dishes are a "revelation" and "reasonably priced" to boot, but critics counter it's "nothing special"; N.B. there's now a dining/bar area in the basement as well.

Melati ●S | 18 | 9 | 13 | £20 |

21 Great Windmill St., W1 (Piccadilly Circus), 020-7437 2745; fax 020-7734 6964

■ "Cheap and cheerful", this Soho stalwart "impresses visitors" with its "generous portions" of "the most delicious" Indonesian-Malaysian "fancy grub"; mavens "love the unpretentious" setting, but aesthetes are less impressed, finding it a bit "plain."

Memories of China S | 22 | 18 | 18 | £37 |

353 Kensington High St., W8 (High St. Kensington), 020-7603 6951; fax 020-7603 0848 ●
65-69 Ebury St., SW1 (Victoria), 020-7730 7734

"About as good as Chinese food gets" declare admirers of this "comfortable, quiet" Belgravia and Kensington duo

F | **D** | **S** | **C**

(part of the A to Z Group) where the "excellent" dishes are "generously presented" by "courteous" staff; the older Ebury Street venue has a "great new look" after "a good revamp", still many find this pair "unmemorable" apart from "the big price tag."

Memories of India ●🇸   ▽ 19 | 14 | 18 | £29
18 Gloucester Rd., SW7 (Gloucester Rd.), 020-7581 3734; fax 020-7589 6450
160-162 Thornbury Rd. (Osterley), Osterley, 020-8847 1548
■ "The aroma of the Indian food – thought I was in India" sums up how fans feel about this "traditional" "old favourite" in Kensington and its younger Osterley sibling; whilst some say it's a "good everyday" kind of haunt, the less-impressed dismiss it as little more than a "standard curry house."

Mesclun 🇸   ▽ 20 | 18 | 19 | £35
24 Stoke Newington Church St., N16 (Manor House), 020-7249 5029; fax 020-7275 8448
■ "The best 'nice' restaurant in N16" with "excellent" Modern British cooking and "outstanding service" is one take on this little-known Stoke Newington spot, but foes suggest it's "quite pricey" with "not much ambience", plus it's "nowhere near as good as it used to be"; deuce.

Meson Don Felipe ●   17 | 14 | 13 | £23
53 The Cut, SE1 (Southwark/Waterloo), 020-7928 3237; fax 020-7736 9857
■ "The war for a table is anything but civil at this Spanish hot spot" in Southwark thanks to the "great-value" tapas ("keep the dishes coming!") and "good, solid" Iberian fare, all served in a "laid-back" "atmosphere reminiscent of Spain", complete with a live guitarist; it's "always enjoyable before or after the theatre" and a "favourite spot for an after-work drink and a light bite", though insiders advise you "best be prepared for the crush"; P.S. there's now "top-notch access with the Jubilee line open."

Metrogusto   20 | 16 | 18 | £33
153 Battersea Park Rd., SW8 (Battersea Park B.R.), 020-7720 0204; fax 020-7720 0888
11-13 Theberton St., N1 (Angel), 020-7226 9400; fax 020-7226 9400 🇸
■ "Interesting, inventive", "high-quality" Modern Italian fare and "welcoming service" are "much appreciated" by "locals" at these "relaxed eateries" in Battersea and Islington; a handful consider the "atmosphere cold" and the "food fussy", but most say they're "worth the trip."

Mezzo ●   16 | 17 | 14 | £34
100 Wardour St., W1 (Leicester Sq./Piccadilly Circus), 020-7314 4000; fax 020-7314 4040
■ "Best for entertaining a group and for people-watching", Sir Terence Conran's "lively", "giant"-size "creation"

| F | D | S | C |

"makes you feel like you have had a crazy night just by eating there"; the Modern European food is "secondary to the scene" – "enjoy a meal, then dance to the live music" (for a £5 surcharge); bashers blast it's "too noisy" ("tap if you can hear" your friends), with "uneven cooking" to boot.

Mezzonine ◐S   16 | 14 | 13 | £25
100 Wardour St., W1 (Leicester Sq./Piccadilly Circus), 020-7314 4000; fax 020-7314 4040

◪ "Fast-paced by design", Conran's "cheerful Soho cafe" on the ground floor above Mezzo is "good" for "cheap" Thai fare, "before a play" or "with friends for a midweek" meal; most agree there's "much room for improvement" when it comes to the "poor service" and note that on busy nights, a "loud" "yuppie crowd" tends to overflow into the dining room from the adjacent "cool bar area."

Mildreds   19 | 10 | 14 | £16
45 Lexington St., W1 (Oxford Circus), 020-7439 2392; fax 020-7494 1634

◪ An "excellent antidote to the excess and pretentiousness of Soho", this Vegetarian "institution" is still "jam-packed" despite moving a few streets across town from its previous location; the "fantastic", "homemade" fare is "value"-priced, prompting fans to enthuse it's "always a winner"; a few gripe that service can be "terrible."

Mimmo d'Ischia ◐   20 | 16 | 18 | £41
61 Elizabeth St., SW1 (Sloane Sq./Victoria), 020-7730 5406

■ "Bathtub-size portions" of Traditional Italian cooking, "cheery waiters" and the presence of owner Mimmo, a "real character", are the hallmarks of this "old-fashioned" Belgravia stalwart where a "great time is guaranteed"; whilst a few faultfinders knock it as "absurdly overpriced" and merely "ordinary", most insist this 30-year-old's reputation as "a 'feel good' restaurant" is unassailable.

MIRABELLE ◐S   23 | 22 | 21 | £49
56 Curzon St., W1 (Green Park), 020-7499 4636; fax 020-7499 5449

◪ "Magical and marvelous", this "chic, discreet" Mayfair "jewel in Marco Pierre White's crown" exudes "effortless glamour" that seems to "get better with age" (there's even a "throwback-to-the-'70s disco ball" to admire); it's a "place to pamper yourself" with "delectable" Classic French fare that steps "out of the box", "service that's magnificent in all respects" and "great celeb spotting"; dissenters, however, declare it's "patchy for the price" and feel "let down by the snooty" servers.

Mitsukoshi S   21 | 14 | 19 | £38
Dorland House, 14-20 Lower Regent St., SW1 (Piccadilly Circus), 020-7930 0317; fax 020-7839 1167

■ "Japanese food could not taste better" fawn fans of the "excellent sashimi" and "fresh, yummy" cooked fare at

F | D | S | C

this "best-kept secret", a low-key basement dining room in an Asian department store near Piccadilly Circus; the "full-on menu delivers" with "wonderful" food that's "properly prepared, properly served" by "serene" staff; N.B. the prix fixe lunch is under £10.

Miyama ⑤   23 | 14 | 21 | £40
38 Clarges St., W1 (Green Park), 020-7499 2443; fax 020-7493 1573

■ "Delightful, kimono-clad service" greets diners at this "dependable" Japanese in a discreet Mayfair townhouse that remains "a sushi favourite"; it's a "pity the teppanyaki area closed" on the lower ground floor groan grill fans.

MJU   24 | 16 | 23 | £59
Millennium Knightsbridge Hotel, 17 Sloane St., SW1 (Knightsbridge), 020-7201 6330; fax 020-7201 6302

■ An "excellent new spot to try" suggest supporters of this modern Knightsbridge hotel dining room where the main talking point is "innovative" Japanese-Asian "fusion fare" – an "orgasmic" "treat" – albeit at a "hefty price"; the less-enamoured say the "soulless" premises "lack fun" and urge "staff to relax a little more"; P.S. though Sydney's "sought-after" chef Tetsuya Wakuda no longer makes monthly forays, his apprentice chef cooks on-site full-time.

MOMO ●⑤   18 | 25 | 17 | £38
25 Heddon St., W1 (Piccadilly Circus), 020-7434 4040; fax 020-7287 0404

■ "The next best thing to being in Morocco", this "exotic" "fairy-tale setting" "transports you to Marrakech" by way of Piccadilly, helped along by "delicious North African" fare and "excellent" Arabic music; it's a "fab experience", one of the "best escapes within London", plus if you want to "prolong the evening", "you can always move" to the Mô tearoom next door or Cameo, the "cool" members-only bar downstairs; sceptics say it's "more about great atmosphere than great food", still, most "never want to leave."

Monkeys   21 | 18 | 19 | VE
1 Cale St., SW3 (Sloane Sq./South Kensington), 020-7352 4711

■ There's "lots of game" in season, including "grouse to die for", on the Anglo-French menu at this "unusual", "intimate" "gem" "hidden away" off Chelsea Green; the "friendly" husband-and-wife proprietors maintain a "high standard of cuisine", creating a "homely atmosphere" that feels "like a dinner party at a friend's house"; a few grumblers gripe that the "hosts are too familiar"; P.S. there's "a minimum £50 per person charge" at dinner.

Mon Plaisir ●   20 | 18 | 18 | £33
21 Monmouth St., WC2 (Covent Garden/Leicester Sq.), 020-7836 7243; fax 020-7240 4774

■ "Ever popular", this "rustic", "friendly" Soho bistro "goes on and on" – it's "still reliable" after 60 years for "typically

| F | D | S | C |

French" fare, plus the "best cheeseboard this side of the Channel"; the "comfortable yet stylish" setting and "simple but high-quality" dishes are "ideal for a theatre supper", "intimate meals or family gatherings"; "perhaps your pleasure, but not mine" mutter the nonplussed, who find it too "chaotic" and "cramped" for their liking.

MONSIEUR MAX S   26 | 19 | 25 | £43
133 High St. (Fulwell B.R.), Hampton Hill, 020-8979 5546; fax 020-8979 3747
■ Following Max Renzland's departure, the elevation of Alex Bentley to head chef "has not diminished this extraordinary place" in Hampton Hill, a "cosy", "understated" "treat" with "rich", "hearty" French bistro cooking that's "so intense" you may want to "lie down between courses"; staff are "friendly and attentive", as indicated by a three-point rise in the Service rating; P.S. "you can still bring your own wine."

Montana S   18 | 16 | 17 | £33
125-131 Dawes Rd., SW6 (Fulham Broadway), 020-7385 9500; fax 020-7386 0337
◪ "Sunday brunch is a must" and so is the "good" live jazz (Thursday–Saturday) say fans of this "comfy", "lively" haunt that, after a big makeover, expanded into adjacent premises; diners are divided when it comes to the varied American Regional cooking – some insist it's "excellent", whilst others claim it can vary from "fantastic to dire" to "pretty average"; too "noisy and crowded" complain critics.

Monte's   20 | 20 | 18 | £46
Private club; inquiries: 020-7245 0896
◪ The "very pleasant", bright first-floor dining room at this smart Knightsbridge private club (open to non-members for lunch) plays host to high-profile Jamie Oliver, who as consultant oversees a Modern Italian menu of "good, gusty" dishes that "never disappoint"; "too much 'naked', not enough chef" quip quibblers who find the cooking "ordinary" and conclude "the only wow is the bill"; P.S. there's also a "great" bar upstairs and a basement nightclub.

Montpeliano ● S   18 | 17 | 19 | £38
13 Montpelier St., SW7 (Knightsbridge), 020-7589 0032
◪ "Useful" after shopping" at Harrods, this "comfortable" Traditional Italian spot in Knightsbridge is a "steady performer" with "versatile cooking" and staff with "lots of character"; the less-enthused say the "food is uninspired" and there's "room for improvement" on the service front; N.B. whilst there's rooftop seating, the garden is no longer.

Monza ●   21 | 14 | 17 | £34
6 Yeoman's Row, SW3 (Knightsbridge), 020-7591 0210; fax 020-7591 0210
◪ "Especially fun for Formula 1 lovers", this motor-racing themed "neighbourhood dream" is "relatively reasonably

priced for its location" in Knightsbridge, serving "huge portions" of "generally excellent" Modern Italian fare; a handful complain it's "fair at best", but they're in the minority; lunch is more "low-key" than the "noisy" evenings.

Moro 22 | 17 | 19 | £35
34-36 Exmouth Mkt., EC1 (Angel/Farringdon), 020-7833 8336; fax 020-7833 9338

■ "Gutsy" Moorish dishes ("terrific cooking influenced by Spain", North Africa and the Eastern Med) in "exciting" "combinations that work" are the main attraction at this "warm", "lively" Exmouth Market venue, staffed by "some of the hardest working" people; it's "still one of the most original" restaurants around, so "grab a pavement table in the summertime" and enjoy the "great people-watching"

Moshi Moshi Sushi 17 | 12 | 14 | £20
7-8 Limeburner Ln., EC4 (St. Paul's/Thames City), 020-7248 1808; fax 020-7248 1807
Unit 24, Liverpool St. Station, EC2 (Liverpool St.), 020-7247 3227 ●
Cabot Pl. East, level 2, E14 (Canary Wharf), 020-7512 9911; fax 020-7512 9201 ●

■ "Perfect for a quickie at lunchtime", these "hip" City spots "cater to the younger yuppie set" with "great fun conveyor belts" offering sushi and other "good Japanese staples"; "tasteless" "quasi-sushi" "spinning around" – "that's not how it should be" say knockers, but even they come round, agreeing these "efficient" places "serve a purpose."

MOSIMANN'S 26 | 25 | 25 | £57
Private club; inquiries: 020-7235 9625

■ "They pull out the stops" at Anton Mosimann's "classy" private club, a "superb church conversion" in Belgravia where the combination of "sumptuous" International fare and "courteous service" leave proponents purring "if I won the lottery I'd eat here every day"; it's a "place for celebration if your pocket can stand it", so "dig deep" – it's "worth the struggle to get a seat."

Motcomb's ⑤ 17 | 16 | 17 | £36
26 Motcomb St., SW1 (Knightsbridge/Sloane Sq.), 020-7235 6382; fax 020-7245 6351

■ "Steady, dependable" Modern British food and a "friendly welcome" can both be found at this "good central meeting point" in Belgravia, a "comfortable gentleman's eaterie" that's "improved since its revamp"; "nothing special" chime in a few, who also note "service can slip when it's busy."

Mr. Chow ●⑤ 20 | 17 | 18 | £43
151 Knightsbridge, SW1 (Knightsbridge), 020-7589 7347; fax 020-7584 5780

☑ "Still one of the great venues" for "scrummy Chinese with a '60s twist", this "haute" "haunt" in Knightsbridge "should keep going for many years yet"; it's "past its prime, but that's part of the charm" fawn fans, though critics lament it's "perhaps losing the plot a bit" and chafe at the "unexciting", "overpriced food" that isn't "all it's cracked up to be."

Mr. Kong ●S 20 | 10 | 14 | £21
21 Lisle St., WC2 (Leicester Sq.), 020-7437 7341
◪ Although the "shabby" "decor leaves something to be desired", this "noisy", "crowded" Chinatown venue is "well worth a visit" on account of "surprisingly friendly service" and "unfailingly excellent", "imaginative" "great-value" food – this is "how Cantonese cooking should be done"; one tip: "go straight for the specials" – "dishes not on the menu" are "finds."

Mr. Wing ●S 18 | 20 | 20 | £33
242-244 Old Brompton Rd., SW5 (Earl's Court), 020-7370 4450; fax 020-7565 4578
◪ "Sit amid lush foliage" in this "relaxed" Earl's Court Chinese, a "great lunchtime venue" that also comes into its own past dark, especially on live-music nights (Thursday–Sunday); if some go a bundle on the "good-quality" cooking, others bemoan "average", "woefully overpriced" fare; P.S "go see the fish" in the aquarium.

Mustards Smithfield Brasserie 14 | 13 | 16 | £28
60 Long Ln., EC1 (Barbican), 020-7796 4920; fax 020-7606 0720
◪ "Continues to be a cosy pit stop" exude enthusiasts who "enjoy" the "basic" French "bistro-style" Eclectic menu of "competent, pleasant" dishes at this venue overlooking Smithfield Market; it's "reliable, if unexciting", still it works for "lunchtime", "early meals" and "those late-night meetings", particularly if you happen to drop in on a jazz evening, when they play "interesting music while you eat."

MVH ●S – | – | – | E
5 White Hart Ln., SW13 (Kew Gardens), 020-8392 1111; fax 020-8878 1616
Bearing the initials of its namesake, chef-owner Michael Hruschka, formerly of the Birdcage (nka Archipelago), this intriguing Barnes eaterie tempts adventurous taste buds with a cultured, weekly changing International menu filled with exotic, unusual dishes (something of a MVH trademark); the decor is just as eye-opening, with a white, stylised dining area on the ground floor denoting heaven and a dark red bar and lounge upstairs denoting hell.

Myna Bird – | – | – | E
(fka Empire)
38 Lambs Conduit St., WC1 (Holborn/Russell Sq.), 020-7404 6835; fax 020-7404 5983
Iqbal Hussein, a chef who got his feet wet at Archipelago, hits a confident stride in this small, cleverly lit Bloomsbury

space, preparing "surprisingly consistent" Oriental-European fusion fare in audacious combinations; the call of the wild beckons with exotic eats such as crocodile dumplings, shark risotto and 24 ct. gold–plated scorpion.

Nahm ⓢ 20 | 17 | 19 | £54
Halkin Hotel, Halkin St., SW1 (Hyde Park Corner), 020-7333 1234; fax 020-7333 1100

◪ Australian chef David Thompson's high-profile arrival, intended to revitalise dining at this discreet Belgravia hotel, has polarised Londoners: enthusiasts extol the "absolutely sensational" Thai cooking that's "like heaven for taste buds", served amid "understated elegance" at this "powerful newcomer", whilst foes fume "praise is unwarranted", as the "peculiar" food is "not worth the fuss" and the room is stark and chilly"; N.B. the £18 prix fixe lunch has its devotees.

Naked Turtle ⓢ 18 | 17 | 18 | £28
505 Upper Richmond Rd. W., SW14 (Richmond), 020-8878 1995; fax 020-8392 1388

◪ The "singing waitresses" "make you feel at home" at this offbeat East Sheen eaterie, boasting "great atmosphere" and an "excellent" Eclectic menu that's "good for the adventurous who want to eat alligator and kangaroo"; live music makes for a "fun evening", and on Sundays there's even "magic with your meal", though the less spellbound posit "perhaps the magician should wave his wand over the kitchen", as "the dishes try hard" but they're "just average."

Nam Long Le Shaker ● 14 | 15 | 13 | £33
159 Old Brompton Rd., SW5 (Gloucester Rd./South Kensington), 020-7373 1926; fax 020-7373 6043

◪ "Stay at the bar" with your "big cocktail" to enjoy the "lively scene" at this South Kensington spot – unless you feel like "fighting your way through the crowd" of "trendy, young" things to dine on a "light menu" of "tasty, fresh" Vietnamese fare; "don't go for the food" most advise, go for the "liquid only", with a side of "people-watching."

Nautilus Fish 21 | 10 | 16 | £18
27-29 Fortune Green Rd., NW6 (West Hampstead), 020-7435 2532

■ Sure, the "kitsch decor" is "like sitting in an old aunt's tacky living room", but this "cramped" West Hampstead stalwart still has everyone crowing about some of "the best fish 'n' chips in the world", not to mention "excellent" seafood; "worth the trip", it's a "good experience" – but beware no reservations.

Neal Street Restaurant 20 | 17 | 18 | £42
26 Neal St., WC2 (Covent Garden), 020-7836 8368; fax 020-7240 3964

◪ "Love the 'shrooms" fawn fans of Antonio Carluccio's "fun", "pre-theatre favourite", a 30-year-old Traditional

| F | D | S | C |

Italian haunt in Covent Garden; the "usually stunning" food, including "yummy pasta dishes", is "first-rate" – "assuming you like mushrooms" – and the service is "efficient for a busy place"; detractors make digs at the "overpriced", "very disappointing" fare, concluding the funghi phenomenon is "not enough anymore."

New Culture Revolution S | 16 | 11 | 14 | £16
157-159 Notting Hill Gate, W11 (Notting Hill Gate), 020-7313 9688
442 Edgware Rd., W2 (Edgware Rd.), 020-7402 4841
305 King's Rd., SW3 (Sloane Sq.), 020-7352 9281
43 Parkway, NW1 (Camden Town), 020-7267 2700
42 Duncan St., N1 (Angel), 020-7833 9083

◪ "Great when you're on the go" say supporters of these "cheap" "fuelling stops" for "excellent noodles", dumplings and "tasty" Northern Chinese fare; it's "amazing value" and "healthy too", with "lovely food for vegetarians and others"; the unimpressed concur that whilst it "sounds like a good idea", "there's nothing here to make your heart beat faster."

New World ●S | 16 | 8 | 9 | £20
1 Gerrard Pl., W1 (Leicester Sq.), 020-7434 2508; fax 020-7287 8994

◪ "Dim sum from a trolley – it's the ultimate comfort" to see "those carts wheeled about" say admirers who head to this "reliable", "crowded" and mammoth-size Chinatown venue for "unpretentious, wholesome" Cantonese food and the "Hong Kong experience"; the disenchanted complain that the servers are "careless" and "rude."

Nicole's | 21 | 18 | 18 | £35
Nicole Farhi, 158 New Bond St., W1 (Green Park), 020-7499 8408; fax 020-7409 0381

■ "Stylish like the clothes", this "elegant", well-lit dining room in the basement of Nicole Fahri's store is "an oasis when shopping on Bond Street", plus the "delicious" Modern European–Med cooking is something of "a treat"; "Claudia Schiffer was there – what else can you say?" applaud celeb-spotters.

Nikita's ● | 14 | 17 | 16 | £32
65 Ifield Rd., SW10 (Earl's Court), 020-7352 6326; fax 020-7352 6969

◪ With a "deadly vodka selection" (over 35 to choose from) and private rooms concealed behind red curtains, this "cosy" Russian veteran on the Fulham-Chelsea border provides a "great" "alternative" dining experience; the "good combination of food, atmosphere" and strong spirits keeps many happy – particularly groups.

Noble Rot | 18 | 18 | 15 | £42
3-5 Mill St., W1 (Oxford Circus), 020-7629 8877; fax 020-7629 8878

◪ "Tucked away" near Regent Street, this late-night (open till 3 AM) glass-fronted eaterie offers "fantastic" Modern British cooking, an "equally good wine list" (FYI, noble rot is a mould that causes grapes to shrivel) and "good service";

| F | D | S | C |

the "fun bar" (ostensibly members only) is "even better", with live jazz and a "great atmosphere"; it's a "failed attempt to be special" sniff the unimpressed; N.B. a post-*Survey* post-fire redo may impact the above Decor rating.

NOBU ⓢ 27 | 21 | 20 | £56
Metropolitan Hotel, 19 Old Park Ln., W1 (Hyde Park Corner), 020-7447 4747; fax 020-7447 4749

■ Having wrested London's Most Popular spot away from The Ivy, this "achingly trendy", "lavishly expensive" Japanese–South American "eating paradise" inside Park Lane's Metropolitan Hotel "definitely deserves recognition"; "watch the beautiful people" and enjoy the "amazing electric atmosphere" – "if you're not too consumed" by the "ambrosial" food; whilst acolytes say "friendly staff" "help you navigate the menu", a handful huff they're "condescending" to "mere mortals."

Noor Jahan ●ⓢ 20 | 13 | 17 | £28
2A Bina Gardens, SW5 (South Kensington), 020-7373 6522

■ A "cut above the average Indian", this "dependable neighbourhood restaurant" in South Kensington blends "interesting flavours and spices" into "high-quality", "authentic" fare; "service is quick and friendly" – the "nerve-wrecking speed" with which the "very consistent" food is brought to table makes it a "favourite" "when in a hurry" and easier to overlook the "naff decor."

Noto 19 | 10 | 16 | £18
2-3 Bassishaw Highwalk, EC2 (Bank/Moorgate), 020-7256 9433; fax 020-7588 5656

■ "Never disappoints" say devotees who congregate at this "good, casual" City Japanese behind the Guildhall for "fantastic sushi"; "prices are reasonable" and the servers are "fast" and "cheerful" – indeed some say the "service is a dream"; no reservations are accepted at lunch, but it's "getting easier to book" at dinner; N.B. the Mansion House sibling closed due to building development.

Notting Grill ⓢ – | – | – | E
123A Clarendon Rd., W11 (Ladbroke Grove), 020-7229 1500

Another venture from irrepressible TV chef Antony Worrall Thompson, this first-floor Notting Hill grill, set in the space previously occupied by Wiz, specialises in British beef, supported by a wide range of seafood, lamb and organic chicken, as well as a "good wine list"; the comfortable setting is as straightforward as the unpretentious fare.

Notting Hill Brasserie ⓢ 18 | 20 | 17 | £36
92 Kensington Park Rd., W11 (Notting Hill Gate), 020-7229 4481; fax 020-7221 1246

☑ "You can dress up or head out in your jeans" to this "fun", "relaxed" Notting Hill venue that boasts an "elegant, pared-down rustic look", "very solid", "imaginative" Modern British cooking and "attentive" service; "standards have slipped after a promising opening" pout those put off by "food that is not up to snuff"; N.B. there's live jazz on Monday and Thursday nights.

Noura ●S 23 | 21 | 21 | £33
16 Hobart Pl., SW1 (Victoria), 020-7235 9444; fax 020-7235 9244

■ "A Lebanese that's just not like others", this "wonderful find" near Victoria Station offers "fantastic, refined" Middle Eastern cooking, including "great starters", "superb mezze" and "some very original dishes"; it's "excellent in every sense", with a "sleek", "generous space" that evokes a "feeling of intimacy", making it "good for a group" (little wonder it attracts a "smart" crowd); P.S. there's a "good home-delivery service" and a Paris branch to boot.

Oak, The S – | – | – | E
137 Westbourne Park Rd., W2 (Westbourne Park), 020-7221 3355

"The perfect" Modern European bi-level "eaterie around the corner", this "very relaxed" Westbourne Park newcomer, enhanced with antique furniture, "lofty" ceilings and chandeliers, offers a "graceful" setting for "impressive" meals; the "unpretentious" bar downstairs serves "basic but very good, simple" Eclectic fare suitable for "casual dining."

Odette's S 21 | 20 | 19 | £36
130 Regent's Park Rd., NW1 (Chalk Farm), 020-7586 5486; fax 020-7580 0508

◪ Adorned with gilt mirrors and alight with candles, this "super-romantic" venue is "still the jewel" in "Primrose Hill's crown"; the "beautifully executed", "bistro-style" Modern British dishes, "very good wine list" and "wonderful ambience never fail" to win over fans who advise "take the cue and join the queue"; grumblers gripe that the "food is bland" and "service can be lacklustre"; P.S there's also a wine bar downstairs and a "nice garden room" with a glass roof that opens up in summertime.

Odin's 21 | 21 | 21 | £42
27 Devonshire St., W1 (Baker St.), 020-7935 7296; fax 020-7493 8309

◪ "Still good after all these years" (35 and counting), this "charming" Marylebone standby has a "nice English feel", with art on the walls and "old-fashioned" Anglo-French cooking on offer; "an acquired taste – maybe" retort foes who feel that this "stuffy" spot has "seen better times"; N.B. new owners gave it a light refurb after taking over last year.

Oliveto ●S 18 | 13 | 15 | £28
49 Elizabeth St., SW1 (Sloane Sq./Victoria), 020-7730 0074; fax 020-7824 8190

◪ "The decor's a bit basic" at this "pleasant" Italian local in Belgravia, but the "brilliant pizzas, salads" and spaghetti make it "a place to come back to", especially as it's an "affordable" choice in an "expensive neighbourhood"; a handful of knockers grumble the "service is not as good as the pasta."

Olivo S | 21 | 15 | 17 | £34 |
21 Eccleston St., SW1 (Victoria), 020-7730 2505; fax 020-7824 8190

■ "Stuffed with Italians who know", this bright, "small" Victoria venue wins plaudits for its "really interesting", "vividly flavoured", "wonderful Sardinian food"; the "perfectly executed main courses are well above the norm", as are the "excellent" servers; admirers can't help but wonder whether "maybe it's underestimated by fans of other trendy Italians."

1 Lombard Street | 19 | 18 | 18 | £43 |
1 Lombard St., EC3 (Bank), 020-7929 6611; fax 020-7929 6622

■ More "upmarket" than its on-site sibling, Soren Jessen's "classic business restaurant" in the "heart of the City" showcases chef Herbert Berger's "superb" New French–Eclectic cooking in the "bright, airy" setting of a former bank; it's a "good expense-account location", especially for lunchtime "entertaining", though "vastly overpriced" per sceptics who also deem it as "loud as a market."

1 Lombard Street Brasserie | 19 | 16 | 15 | £36 |
1 Lombard St., EC3 (Bank), 020-7929 6611; fax 020-7929 6622

■ "Brightened by skylights and large windows", the more casual part of Soren Jessen's venture near the Bank of England provides a "very good option for eating well in the City" thanks to a "varied" menu of Modern European–International fare; it's an "overpriced, cookie-cutter expense-accounter" that's "convenient rather than distinctive" sound off cynics who insist the "noise detracts" from "any merits."

190, Downstairs at | 16 | 12 | 14 | £36 |
Gore Hotel, 190 Queens Gate, SW7 (Gloucester Rd.), 020-7581 5666; fax 020-7581 8172

■ Attracting a "trendy" crowd en route to Royal Albert Hall, this "good but pricey" seafooder set in the basement under Bistro 190 is popular for group functions and dancing; the few surveyors who know it find the service "completely disorganised" and the decor "nondescript, really."

192 ●S | – | – | – | E |
192 Kensington Park Rd., W11 (Ladbroke Grove/ Notting Hill Gate), 020-7229 0482; fax 020-7229 3300

Hasn't "changed in years" is no longer the story with this 20-year-old bi-level Notting Hill "hangout" thanks to a post-*Survey* revamp by new owners; the alteration, including a revised Modern British menu, has not been very dramatic, and most seem convinced it will remain a place "to be seen", with "showbiz stars" and other "trendy, youthful" folk.

				F	D	S	C

One-O-One ᴤ 22 | 19 | 21 | £46
Sheraton Park Tower, 101 William St., SW1 (Knightsbridge), 020-7290 7101; fax 020-7235 6196

■ "If you like fish", this "cool, spacious" New French–seafood "star" inside a Knightsbridge hotel is "arguably" one of "London's best"; the "elegantly presented" "superb combinations" are made with "inspired ingredients" and served by "impeccable" "top-notch staff" in a "marvellous", "lovely" setting; yes "it's very expensive at full price", but there's also an "incredible-value lunchtime" menu.

One-Seven-Nine ☽ ᴤ – | – | – | VE
(fka Conrad Gallahger)
179 Shaftesbury Ave., WC2 (Leicester Sq.), 020-7836 3111; fax 020-7836 3888

Vince Power's stylish, glass-fronted Theatreland venue has got off to a chequered start, with chef Steven Black and his "high-standard" New French–European cuisine replacing eponymous Conrad Gallagher and his Modern Irish menu, and the restaurant itself moving from the basement up to the ground floor; whilst the jury is still out, the prix fixe specials seem to be wooing back customers.

Ophim ᴤ – | – | – | E
139 Wardour St., W1 (Oxford Circus/Piccadilly Circus), 0207434 9899

Bright and "modern" with "friendly service", this Soho newcomer is "bowling over" fans with "deliciously complex Indian cooking" from chef Sitangsu Chakravarty of Red Fort fame; the small ground-floor cafe serves a tapas-style selection of "interesting" dishes, including unusual naan breads, while the bigger area below turns out larger, pricier portions of traditional and contemporary fare; P.S. the exotic, "deep red"–coloured Hareem bar serves an extensive selection of cocktails ("you must try the rose petal martini").

Oriel ᴤ 13 | 15 | 12 | £25
51 Sloane Sq., SW1 (Sloane Sq.), 020-7730 2804; fax 020-7730 7966

◪ A "cheerful Sloaney mainstay", this "buzzy" all-day eaterie is "among the best in its class" for "watching the world go by" while "lazing on a Sunday" or "after shopping in Sloane Square"; whilst some say the Mediterranean fare is "surprisingly good" "if you pick right", most find it's "reliable in a neighbourly fashion", advising "don't go for the food", go to "drink" and "people-watch."

Original Tagine ∇ 20 | 15 | 20 | £26
7A Dorset St., W1 (Baker St.), 020-7935 1545; fax 020-7925 8279

■ A "lovely little Moroccan" Marylebone "gem" with "really authentic" North African food and "friendly service", this "delightful" "well-kept secret" is worth a "try" say insiders; handmade tiled tables and Arabic hieroglyphics contribute to the "great atmosphere."

| F | D | S | C |

ORRERY 🆂   24 | 22 | 22 | £47
55-57 Marylebone High St., W1 (Baker St./Regent's Park), 020-7616 8000; fax 020-7616 8080

■ "Way out in front of other Conran" restaurants is the consensus on this "serene" Marylebone spot with a "lovely outdoor terrace" (offering a separate menu), "intuitive service" and "consistently delicious" New French cooking from chef Chris Galvin that "never lets you down"; a handful baulk at the "sky-high prices" and snipe that even this "class outfit" "has off days", but most consider it a "well-oiled machine" that deserves "top marks all-round."

Orsino ◐🆂   18 | 18 | 16 | £36
119 Portland Rd., W11 (Holland Park), 020-7221 3299; fax 020-7229 9414

◪ "Light, luscious and lovely – and that's just the food" fawn fans of this "cosy, welcoming" Modern Italian trattoria in Holland Park, Orso's younger sibling; it's "always good" report supporters who find the dishes "authentic" and "interesting" and the setting "laid-back"; critics carp it's "nothing special", with "forgettable" fare and "slow, albeit well-meaning, service."

Orso ◐🆂   19 | 16 | 18 | £36
27 Wellington St., WC2 (Covent Garden), 020-7240 5269; fax 020-7497 2148

◪ "Not as fashionable as it used to be, but better for it" say acolytes of this "noisy, crowded" "cosmopolitan cellar", a Modern "Italian restaurant with an English personality" in Covent Garden; the "unpretentious", "affordable" fare is "terrific après opera" or the theatre when "you can have what you want and it doesn't take forever"; disenchanted diners say it "seems tired" and feel it's "showing its age."

Oslo Court   22 | 13 | 23 | £39
Charlbert St., Prince Albert Rd., NW8 (St. John's Wood), 020-7722 8795

■ "Don't eat for a week before dining" at this "comfortable", "old-fashioned" St. John's Wood "institution" where people emerge "stuffed to the gills" thanks to "generous portions" of "terrific", "bourgeois" French cooking; "go for a long lunch" – it's an "astonishing anachronism", and yet it "still has great charm and service"; "restaurants come and go, but good old Court lives on – hurrah!"

Osteria Antica Bologna 🆂   19 | 16 | 18 | £27
23 Northcote Rd., SW11 (Clapham Junction B.R.), 020-7978 4771; fax 020-7978 4771

◪ "Friendly and snug", this "cheerful", busy Battersea spot serves "imaginative, authentic Italian" fare, with some dishes derived from ancient times – "classical Roman food, literally" – and all at "great-value" prices; it's "nothing special" retort foes who also report "muddled service" and "crammed" quarters.

www.zagat.com

			F	D	S	C

Osteria Basilico S
21 | 16 | 16 | £28

29 Kensington Park Rd., W11 (Ladbroke Grove), 020-7727 9957; fax 020-7229 7980

"If you're having Italy withdrawal", then this "youthful, bustling" Notting Hill trattoria is the "place to be"; the "lovely choice" of "affordable" Modern Italian dishes, "buzzy", "unpretentious" vibe and "great rustic" setting all contribute to that "transported to the Mediterranean" feeling; though it's a bit "too crowded and too hard to book" for some, it remains "a local favourite" of many; N.B. takeaway pizza is available.

Otto Dining Lounge S
▽ 17 | 22 | 16 | £39

215 Sutherland Ave., W9 (Maida Vale), 020-7266 3131

"Much needed in Maida Vale", this "sleek, sexy venue" draws locals to its "fresh, modern looking" dining room with "delicious, consistent" Modern European fare; it's a "nice", "lively early-evening place" boasting a "good bar" and a convenient "location between town and suburbia."

OXO TOWER S
19 | 23 | 17 | £44

Oxo Tower Wharf, Barge House St., SE1 (Blackfriars/Waterloo), 020-7803 3888; fax 020-7803 3838

"On a clear day you can see forever" exult enthusiasts of this "friendly", "inviting" top-floor South Bank landmark eatery that's "absolutely superb" for a "business meal or a romantic dinner"; it's "expensive, but worth every penny", as the "fantastic" Modern British–Pacific Rim fare "matches the stunning" vista; faultfinders retort "it's great to be up here, but the food and service disappoint" – "it's a lot of money for a view."

Oxo Tower Brasserie ◑ S
18 | 22 | 16 | £35

Oxo Tower Wharf, Barge House St., SE1 (Blackfriars/Waterloo), 020-7803 3888; fax 020-7803 3838

"Go in the summer and marvel" at the "panoramic views" overlooking the South Bank of the Thames whilst dining on "surprisingly good" Mediterranean–Pacific Rim cooking – that's "what makes it worthwhile" to visit the Oxo Tower's "modern, breezy", "lively little sister" along the eighth-floor corridor; "it still trades on its" location and the "food fails to live up to it" note knockers, still, even they concede it's a "great place" to "bring out-of-town visitors."

Ozer Restaurant & Bar ◑ S
19 | 19 | 17 | £31

5 Langham Pl., W1 (Oxford Circus), 020-7323 0505; fax 020-7323 0111

"Buzzing" and "lively", this "opulent" Modern Ottoman restaurant, owned by the Sofra group, makes a "useful addition to an otherwise bland area" near Oxford Street, serving "delicious" Turkish food including "good-quality mezze" at "stonking value", with "friendly", "attentive service" to boot; it's "ok, not incredible" impart a minority.

Pacific Oriental | 16 | 15 | 14 | £31 |
1 Bishopsgate, EC2 (Bank St.), 020-7621 9988; fax 020-7929 7227
◼ A "fine dining area" with "original Pacific Rim cuisine" and an on-site microbrewery, this Bishopsgate venue maintains a "good standard across the board", plus it boasts a downstairs bar and brasserie; it has "nothing new to offer" complain critics who also "write off" the "bland, businesslike decor"; N.B. closed on weekends.

Painted Heron, The S | – | – | – | E |
112 Cheyne Walk, SW10 (Sloane Sq.), 020-7351 5232
Spacious and simply decorated, this Chelsea riversider, set in the former Busabong Tree space, offers exciting, modern interpretations of traditional Indian cooking from ex-Tabla chef Yogesh Datta; the menu changes frequently, and there's a small, elegant garden at the rear for alfresco dining.

Palm Court S | ▽ 13 | 23 | 18 | £39 |
Le Meridien Waldorf, Aldwych, WC2 (Covent Garden), 020-7759 4001; fax 020-7240 9277
◼ "Reliable", versatile and "very" English, this "classy", all-day Modern British dining room in a famous Aldwych hotel is "like an old sweater that always fits"; but that doesn't mean it's always in style – if cream tea poured by "attentive servers" isn't exactly your cuppa "after a hard day's work", you may find the "bygone" experience "stuffy."

Parade S | ▽ 22 | 18 | 19 | £36 |
18-19 The Mall, W5 (Ealing Broadway), 020-8810 0202; fax 020-8810 0303
◾ "Believe me, it is" really "a terrific" spot in Ealing insist "locals" who consider this Modern British sibling of Sonny's and The Phoenix "outstanding"; impatient sorts pout that "slow service" and "parking in the next borough" add unwelcome minutes onto an otherwise "perfect experience."

Parisienne Chophouse S | 17 | 16 | 15 | £38 |
3 Yeoman's Row, SW3 (Knightsbridge), 020-7590 9999
◼ "Marco has done it again" fawn followers enamoured by Mr. Pierre White's newly "revived" Knightsbridge basement, serving "excellent, plain" French bistro fare; on the flip side, the less-convinced say it's "not MPW's best by a long way", citing "average food" and "inattentive staff with a blind spot to customers waving their arms"; still, some are grateful that it's "very accommodating to families with young children."

Parsee | ▽ 23 | 14 | 21 | £27 |
34 Highgate Hill, N19 (Archway), 020-7272 9091
◾ It's "my cup of chai" sums up how fans feel about this "super-friendly" "Highgate heaven", a newcomer where chef Cyrus Todiwala (of Café Spice Namaste fame) "scores again" with a "very interesting variant of Indian food" bearing "authentic", "distinctive" Persian influences; N.B. Parsees were followers of Zoarester in the 8th century A.D.

| F | D | S | C |

Pasha ●S
— — — M

1 Gloucester Rd., SW7 (Gloucester Rd.), 020-7589 7969

"You feel like you're in Casablanca" in the "amazing ambiance" of this "beautiful" South Kensington eaterie, and even if opinions on Moroccan offerings swing from "fabulous" to "anti-climactic" and the service is prone to be "slightly chaotic", most agree a meal amid decor straight out of "Aladdin's cave" makes for an "interesting experience."

Pasha ●S
— — — M

301 Upper St., N1 (Angel/Highbury & Islington), 020-7226 1454; fax 020-7226 1617

With a "fine array of well-executed dishes" at "excellent value", this "friendly" Islingtonian, which is "not related" to the same-named spot in SW7, is "a class above the average Turkish"; it's certainly a "relaxing place to dine", and a planned redo of the dining room could increase the comfort level even more.

Passione
22 15 18 £37

10 Charlotte St., W1 (Goodge St.), 020-7636 2833; fax 020-7636 2889

◪ "Repeat visitors" who dine here religiously say "God is in the details" of the "genuine", "home-cooked" meals at this "small, select" Modern Italian in Fitzrovia; the "delightful" dishes are "ideal for a special treat", making up for the "slightly bland surroundings" and "rather cramped" quarters.

Patara S
21 15 18 £31

3-7 Maddox St., W1 (Oxford Circus), 020-7499 6008; fax 020-7499 6007
9 Beauchamp Pl., SW3 (Knightsbridge/South Kensington), 020-7581 8820; fax 020-7581 2155
181 Fulham Rd., SW3 (South Kensington), 020-7351 5692; fax 020-7351 5692

◪ "Yuuumm!" rave friends of this "absolutely great" Thai trio in Knightsbridge, South Kensington and, newly, Mayfair; the "delicious", "delicate" selections are served in "no-frills" settings that can be "busy", "noisy" places, but "lovely staff", plus "reasonable prices", help diners "relax."

Patisserie Valerie S
19 14 14 £16

8 Russell St., WC2 (Covent Garden), 020-7240 0064; fax 020-7240 0064
105 Marylebone High St., W1 (Baker St./Bond St.), 020-7935 6240; fax 020-7734 6133
44 Old Compton St., W1 (Leicester Sq.), 020-7437 3466; fax 020-7935 6543
215 Brompton Rd., SW3 (Knightsbridge), 020-7823 9971; fax 020-7589 4993

■ "If you can't afford the fancy tea shops", these French bistro/patisseries present "a wonderful alternative" for a "cheap" "chill-out" "any time of day"; they're "a sweet-tooth's paradise" for "divine" desserts, while those with a

F | D | S | C

taste for savouries "go for scrambled eggs and salmon" and other "nice snacks"; service "can be surly" in the "cramped, smoke-filled rooms", so advocates of takeaway say "you can have your cake, but don't eat it there."

Peasant, The 17 | 13 | 13 | £25
240 St. John St., EC1 (Angel/Farringdon), 020-7336 7726; fax 020-7251 8525
◪ It's "homely", "cosy", "surly" and a "good value for your money" – in other words, it's "everything a gastro-pub should be"; this Victorian conversion in Clerkenwell is bustling downstairs and "more intimate" upstairs with a rooftop terrace, yet some peasants still revolt, griping that it "lacks atmosphere."

Pellicano S 20 | 17 | 20 | £33
19-21 Elystan St., SW3 (South Kensington), 020-7589 3718; fax 020-7584 1789
■ "Owner Marcello [Vargiu] continues to pamper regulars" at this "perfect neighbourhood" Italian near Chelsea Green, a "busy" spot that "tries hard" to deliver a "refreshing and reasonably priced" repast featuring "genuine Sardinian" treats; pavement tables make it a "good summer place", and though it can be "coldish in winter", a "decent" wine list and "most friendly staff" help keep customers warm.

People's Palace S 18 | 18 | 18 | £34
Royal Festival Hall, level 3, South Bank Ctr., SE1 (Charing Cross/Waterloo), 020-7928 9999; fax 020-7928 2355
◪ "Airy", with "spectacular views" of the Thames and "imaginative" Modern British–European cooking, this "spacious", "friendly place" inside the South Bank's Royal Festival Hall is the "ideal venue" for "concertgoers"; the "charming staff", "relaxed atmosphere" and "convenient", "perfect location on the river" add to its appeal; the "food is variable and service can be offhand" chide critics, but even they concede it can be "useful."

Pepper Tree S 20 | 12 | 15 | £17
19 Clapham Common Southside, SW4 (Clapham Common), 020-7622 1758; fax 020-7622 1758
■ You're "guaranteed a tasty feed" of "yummy" Thai food at this "no fuss" Clapham spot that's "brilliant for the money" and "perfect for a pit stop"; it's "noisy and crowded", with communal tables for "informal dining", and whilst it's "not a night out in itself, it's a good starting point."

Perseverance, The S – | – | – | M
63 Lambs Conduit St., WC1 (Holborn/Russell Sq.), 020-7405 8278; fax 020-7831 0031
This smartly revamped gastro-pub in Bloomsbury offers simple Modern European fare in the large ground-floor bar area at lunchtime, but come evening, food service moves upstairs whilst the downstairs room morphs into a popular

watering hole for an after-work crowd; pavement dining is also available in the summertime.

Pescatori 20 | 15 | 17 | £34
57 Charlotte St., W1 (Goodge St.), 020-7580 3289; fax 020-7580 0539
11 Dover St., W1 (Green Park), 020-7493 2652; fax 020-7499 3180
■ "You get what you pay for" at these Mediterranean seafooders in Fitzrovia ("very established" at over 40 years old) and Mayfair – "a great variety" of "simple", "delicious" "fish dishes" that "never fail", "keen service" and a "lively scene"; a few squawk that the bill can get a "bit pricey."

PÉTRUS 27 | 22 | 23 | £60
33 St. James's St., SW1 (Green Park), 020-7930 4272; fax 020-7930 9702
☒ "Suave" and "dignified", this "restaurant nirvana" in St. James's has fans purring over "course after course of perfectly prepared", "orgasmic" New French cooking from Gordon Ramsay's protégé, Marcus Wareing, as well as the "exceptional wine list" and "peerless staff"; the "sumptuous setting" heightens the "marvellous experience" – it's a "real treat every time" and "worth every penny"; but critics complain that it "doesn't live up to expectations" and are put off by the "stuffy, starchy" service and "stunning prices."

Pharmacy S 15 | 18 | 13 | £37
150 Notting Hill Gate, W11 (Notting Hill Gate), 020-7221 2442; fax 020-7243 2345
☒ A "cool concept", this Notting Hill "scene" "intrigues" visitors with its "funky interior" and "dangerous cocktails"; whilst fans find the Modern British fare some of the "tastiest 'medicine'" around, critics lament that it's "stylish but average", suggesting perhaps it's "better to drink" here; there's "no cure" for this "pretentious place" fume foes who quip "hasn't its prescription expired yet?"; N.B. the takeout shop next door is called Outpatients.

Philip Owens' Dining Room – | – | – | E
at Corney & Barrow
116 St. Martin's Ln., 1st fl., WC2 (Charing Cross/Leicester Sq.), 020 7655 9800
Chef Philip Owen, formerly of ICA, is establishing a new foothold for his Modern British dishes on the first floor above this Corney & Barrow Theatreland flagship, adding interesting twists to classic comfort fare, at reasonable prices; lending more food for thought, each selection is paired with a by-the-glass wine suggestion.

Phoenicia ●S 19 | 12 | 17 | £29
11-13 Abingdon Rd., W8 (High St. Kensington), 020-7937 0120; fax 020-7937 7668
☒ "Excellent-quality, authentic dishes", "warm hospitality" and "very courteous" staff are what make this "good, solid

Lebanese" a "favourite local haunt"; the "tired decor" is looking a "bit faded" say faultfinders, who also cite the service as "endearingly slapdash."

Phoenix Bar & Grill S | 19 | 19 | 18 | £32 |
162-164 Lower Richmond Rd., SW15 (Putney Bridge), 020-8780 3131; fax 020-8780 0019

■ "It's a hike, but boy is it worth it" exult enthusiasts of this bright Putney sibling of Sonny's; "loyal" fans "really like" the British-Italian cooking with a "modern twist" and "good-value" prices; nitpickers claim it's "expensive for a local" and "hit-or-miss on the service front", concluding it's "still a step away from the top"; N.B. retired, respected chef Franco Taruschio (ex Walnut Tree) is now a consultant.

PIED À TERRE | 25 | 18 | 22 | £52 |
34 Charlotte St., W1 (Goodge St.), 020-7636 1178; fax 020-7916 1171

■ "Fine and formal without the glitz" sums up this "smooth operation" in Fitzrovia, a "firm favourite" thanks to chef Shane Osborn's "genuinely original", "fabulously presented" New French cooking, a "spectacular" wine list boasting over 800 *vinos* and "cordial" "service that's a triumph"; the "intimate" "chic surroundings" feel like a "home away from home" (indeed a "recent refurbishment has done much to warm up the setting"); N.B. the prix fixe lunch is good value.

PIZZA EXPRESS ●S | 16 | 15 | 14 | £17 |
9-12 Bow St., WC2 (Covent Garden), 020-7240 3443; fax 020-7240 3443
137 Notting Hill Gate, W11 (Notting Hill Gate), 020-7229 6000
35 Earl's Court Rd., W8 (High St. Kensington), 020-7937 0761; fax 020-7938 4981
29 Wardour St., W1 (Leicester Sq.), 020-7437 7215; fax 020-7494 2582
46-54 Battersea Bridge Rd., SW11 (Earl's Court/Sloane Sq.), 020-7924 2774
363 Fulham Rd., SW10 (Fulham Broadway), 020-7352 5300
895-896 Fulham Rd., SW6 (Parsons Green), 020-7731 3117; fax 020-7371 7884
7 Beauchamp Pl., SW3 (Knightsbridge), 020-7589 2355; fax 020-7589 5159
The Pheasantry, 152-154 King's Rd., SW3 (Sloane Sq.), 020-7351 5031; fax 020-7349 9844
125 Alban Gate, London Wall, EC2 (Moorgate/St. Paul's), 020-7600 8880; fax 020-7600 8128
Additional locations throughout London

■ "The daddy of inexpensive dining", this "convenient" chain "gets it right year after year" with "tasty" pizza that's difficult to pass up and a "great selection" of pasta and Italian staples; even if some find the food "boring" and "predictable" and others quip "honey, someone shrunk my pizza", most say this outfit's "winning formula" "does exactly what it says on the tin."

		F	D	S	C

Pizza Metro S   24 | 12 | 18 | £23
64 Battersea Rise, SW11 (Clapham Common/Clapham Junction B.R.), 020-7228 3812; fax 020-7738 0987
■ "Conviviality is guaranteed" at this "fantastic example of a Neapolitan restaurant" in Battersea where the Italian "pastas and appetisers easily rival" the "legendary pizza and antipasti"; even if a handful gripe that it "lost some of its fun [vibe] since it expanded" a few years ago, the majority agree it's still "a great experience."

Pizza on the Park ◐S   16 | 16 | 15 | £22
11 Knightsbridge, SW1 (Hyde Park Corner), 020-7235 5273; fax 020-7236 6853
■ "Grab a bite" of "good Italian cuisine" upstairs in this "fun", "casual" Hyde Park Corner pizzeria owned by Pizza Express, then head downstairs for "excellent jazz evenings" in the basement Music Room; it's an "excellent place to combine simple food and great entertainment" – all in all, a "value"-packed evening out.

Pizza Organic S   16 | 12 | 13 | £16
100 Pitshanger Ln., W5 (Ealing Broadway), 020-8998 6878
20 Old Brompton Rd., SW7 (South Kensington), 020-7589 9613; fax 020-8397 5556 ◐
◪ "Good for casual pizzas" and Modern Italian eats, this functional duo in South Kensington and Ealing capitalises on the organic trend with healthful choices, all at "reasonable prices"; but bashers blast the "bland, forgettable" fare and "inattentive staff"; your call.

Pizza Pomodoro ◐   16 | 14 | 14 | £20
51 Beauchamp Pl., SW3 (Knightsbridge), 020-7589 1278; fax 020-7247 4001 S
7-8 Bishopsgate Churchyard, EC2 (Liverpool St.), 020-7920 9207; fax 020-7920 9206
■ "Anything goes" at this "hip" pizzeria pair in South Ken and the City where a "young, up-for-it" circle congregates for "fantastic" live music and dancing – perhaps the "best party in town"; for the record, the "food's not bad" either: "pizzas with a twist"; a few squawk it's "too noisy."

Pizzeria Castello   21 | 10 | 15 | £18
20 Walworth Rd., SE1 (Elephant & Castle), 020-7703 2556; fax 020-7703 0421
■ A "hidden gem in Elephant & Castle" that's "been there for ages", this "friendly" pizzeria satisfies customers with "tasty" portions of homemade Italian fare, all served by "friendly" staff; a handful say it's "not worth a detour."

PJ's Bar & Grill ◐S   15 | 16 | 15 | £27
52 Fulham Rd., SW3 (South Kensington), 020-7581 0025; fax 020-7581 0019
■ "Perfect for the homesick American", this "friendly", "Chelsea stalwart" gets "very crowded", not least on

Sundays thanks to its "great brunch"; it's a "comfortable place to eat and relax" and "good for people-watching" too, plus the service is "lovely", though a few gripe that it gets "too smoky."

PJ's Grill ●S   16 | 15 | 17 | £27

30 Wellington St., WC2 (Covent Garden), 020-7240 7529; fax 020-7836 3426

■ "Welcoming" and "civilised", this Covent Garden grill sports a "different" polo-themed setting and "better than expected" American-International cooking, "served with a smile"; it's "nice for lunch with work colleagues" and "useful for families."

Place Below   19 | 14 | 14 | £15

St. Mary-le-Bow Church, EC2 (St. Paul's), 020-7329 0789

■ It may be a "bit odd to eat cafeteria style in a [Norman] crypt", but it's definitely "something original" applaud admirers who tuck into this 11th-century church near St. Paul's for "good quality" Vegetarian lunch or breakfast fare; it's an "oasis of wholesome food in the City" that's not only "healthy" but "fun."

Planet Hollywood ●S   10 | 15 | 12 | £23

13 Coventry St., W1 (Leicester Sq./Piccadilly Circus), 020-7437 7639; fax 020-7734 0835

■ "Great fun for kids", this "rowdy" Piccadilly outpost of the international chain "makes for a loud experience", with "dreadful queues" outside and "fun Hollywood memorabilia" within; while some say the traditional American fare is "tasty", most advise "don't go for the food" – "go to enjoy the spectacle"; P.S. two "new additions" from family-man Marco Pierre White now grace the menu – seriously.

Poissonnerie de l'Avenue   23 | 18 | 20 | £45

82 Sloane Ave., SW3 (South Kensington), 020-7589 2457; fax 020-7581 3360

■ "A perfect place for winning business or a beloved's heart", this "charming" Brompton Cross Classic French–seafooder makes its "mostly older", "faithful clientele" feel "welcome and looked after"; it's a "reliable favourite", thanks to its "always excellent", "high-quality" fish and "elegant" setting that's "refreshingly not trendy"; a few find it "rather cramped" and baulk at the "fuddy-duddy decor."

Polygon Bar & Grill S   20 | 18 | 16 | £31

4 The Polygon, Clapham Old Town, SW4 (Clapham Common), 020-7622 1199; fax 020-7622 1166

■ "Delectable" Modern British–Pacific Rim cooking "with interesting flavours" and a "pleasant, busy atmosphere" draw "Thirty-something Claphamites" to this "fun location"; it's a "cool brunch place" and "enjoyable" for "whiling the evening away", but it doesn't always shape up that way for some critics, who deem it a "hit-or-miss affair."

F	D	S	C

Pomegranates ●   19 | 15 | 19 | £39
94 Grosvenor Rd., SW1 (Pimlico), 020-7828 6560;
fax 020-7828 2037
  ■ The "colourful", "entertaining" owner, Patrick Gwynne Jones, "has built a loyal clientele over many years" at this "old-fashioned" Pimlico stalwart that's "outlasted fads and fashions"; the "imaginative", "nicely prepared" Eclectic-International food and "attentive service" get the thumbs-up, but a strong lobby feel this "1970s time warp" basement "needs a face-lift."

Poons S   18 | 11 | 14 | £21
4 Leicester St., WC2 (Leicester Sq.), 020-7437 1528;
fax 020-8458 0968 ●
27 Lisle St., WC2 (Leicester Sq.), 020-7437 4549;
fax 020-8458 0968 ●
Royal National Hotel, 50 Woburn Pl., WC1 (Euston/Russell Sq.),
020-7580 1188; fax 020-8458 0968 ●
Whiteley's Shopping Ctr., 151 Queensway, W2
(Bayswater/Queensway), 020-7792 2884; fax 020-8458 0968
  ◪ "Good, cheap Chinese" is on the menu at this "busy" bunch of "nothing fancy" eateries – a Chinatown original with Bayswater, Bloomsbury and Covent Garden sibs – that fans call "reliably quick"-"grab-a-bite-before-a-movie" spots; pooh-poohers, though, put down the "standard fare", "indifferent staff" and practically "nonexistent decor."

Poons in the City   16 | 14 | 14 | £26
2 Minster Pavement, Minster Ct., Mincing Ln., EC3 (Monument/
Tower Hill), 020-7626 0126; fax 020-7626 1066
  ◪ "Functional" "but nothing great", this City venue in the basement of a office tower block serves "reasonable" and "filling" multiregional Chinese fare, including "good crispy duck"; some find it "pricey for what you get", though others opine that the midday "set menu is a good value"; those less than impressed with the service and decor consider it "a takeaway" first and foremost.

Pope's Eye ⌿   20 | 8 | 15 | £28
108 Blythe Rd., W14 (Olympia), 020-7610 4578
277 Upper Richmond Rd., SW15 (East Putney), 020-8788 7733
  ◪ When you "can't be bothered to grill your own", the "sublimely cooked meat and more meat" on offer at this "straightforward" duo in Putney and Olympia "works" so well, carnivores declare "who cares" that the "spartan" "decor could use upgrading"?; "they will even do vegetarian food" if ordered in advance, but sceptics still beef about "little choice" and feel the fare "should be much better."

Porters ●S   13 | 12 | 14 | £22
17 Henrietta St., WC2 (Covent Garden), 020-7836 6466;
fax 020-7379 4296
  ◪ Supporters say Lord Bradford's Covent Garden stalwart is "good for what it is" – an "inexpensive" "restaurant that's

representative of [Traditional] English cooking"; though some suggest that "other places would better suit the trendy and ambitious diner", this "noisy, outgoing" spot is perennially popular with "tourists and families", especially pre-theatre.

Portrait S | 16 | 22 | 16 | £28 |

The National Portrait Gallery, 2 St. Martin's Pl., WC2 (Charing Cross/Leicester Sq.), 020-7312 2490; fax 020-7925 0244

◪ From its "rooftop" perch, the National Portrait Gallery's "urbane" and "still undiscovered" restaurant/bar offers "minimalist decor" complemented by a "panoramic view" of Trafalgar Square and beyond; but diners are divided on its Modern British cooking (by caterer Searcy's): some say it's "sophisticated", while others call it "ordinary at best"; N.B. dinner served Thursdays and Fridays only.

Potemkin | 19 | 15 | 19 | £30 |

144 Clerkenwell Rd., EC1 (Farringdon), 020-7278 6661; fax 020-7278 5551

■ "A gastronomic curiosity", this "friendly" Clerkenwell eaterie named after Catherine the Great's legendary lover offers an "interesting" (albeit "short") menu of "delicious", "authentic" Russian "comfort food", accompanied by 120 "fantastic vodkas" and "unusual Russian beers" and presented by "lovely staff"; it's such a "different" experience that fans say it's "a shame it's not busier."

Prince Bonaparte S | 18 | 14 | 12 | £16 |

80 Chepstow Rd., W2 (Bayswater/Notting Hill Gate), 020-7313 9491; fax 020-7792 0911

■ "Hearty" Modern British cooking keeps fans "coming back" to this "better-than-most" "Notting Hill gastro-pub" off Westbourne Grove; you may have to "fight for a table" (they accept no reservations), but once ensconced expect a "laid-back", "trendy vibe" that's "well worth" the effort; P.S. the above Decor score may not reflect a recent refurb that regulars report "makes dining more enjoyable."

Princess Garden ●S | 19 | 17 | 17 | £38 |

8-10 N. Audley St., W1 (Bond St.), 020-7493 3223; fax 020-7629 3130

◪ "For a long time" (nearly two decades), this "worthwhile" Chinese has been serving "great", if "not extraordinary", multiregional fare – including "good vegetarian selections" – in an "upmarket" yet "comfy" environment; it's a "welcome escape" for "a quiet lunch", though wallet-watchers find it "unacceptable" that they "do not serve tap water, only bottled", and warn "be prepared to pay" "Mayfair prices."

Prism | 19 | 19 | 16 | £41 |

147 Leadenhall St., EC3 (Bank/Monument), 020-7256 3888; fax 020-7256 3883

◪ With a "stunning interior" and "complicated but pleasing" Modern British menu, this "airy" City spot (operated by

| F | D | S | C |

Harvey Nichols) in a former bank is a top "business" dining destination and a "good place to impress"; the unconvinced, though, claim the "prices are not justified" and find the "slightly pretentious" attitude of some servers as "lofty" as the "dining room's high ceilings."

Prospect Grill ◐ | 20 | 21 | 20 | £31 |
4-6 Garrick St., WC2 (Leicester Sq.), 020-7379 0412; fax 020-7836 3936
■ This "small gem hidden" "in the heart of Covent Garden" "impresses" many with its "comforting" environment (a cross between a "1940s cruise liner" and a "modern" "New York–style grill") and "excellent" menu of "delicious" Anglo-American grill dishes, including "great organic fare"; "attentive" staff ensure that "a wonderful time is had by all", whilst the prix fixe menu "pleases theatregoers."

Providores Rest./Tapa Room S | 22 | 19 | 18 | £34 |
109 Marylebone High St., W1 (Baker St/Bond St.), 020-7935 6175
■ "Newly established, and now a favourite", this bi-level Marylebone spot gives the "clever" "ex-Sugar Club team" of Peter Gordon and Anna Hansen a chance to showcase their "intelligently composed" Eclectic-International fare, a "fusion of [Asian, North African and Med] flavours"; the Tapa Room has communal tables and is "cheaper than upstairs", plus it's "great for breakfast."

Pucci Pizza ◐ S ≠ | 16 | 10 | 13 | £20 |
205 King's Rd., SW3 (Sloane Sq.), 020-7352 2134; fax 020-7352 0585
▲ "You can smell the pizzas baking a mile away from" this "entertaining" King's Road pizzeria, a "funky" spot where its "tasty" namesake and other "decent" Traditional Italian fare are served by "beautiful waitresses" to a "good-looking clientele"; mutineers mutter that the "forgettable" food is a "masterpiece of style over substance", plus the "painfully loud" "dance music" means "conversation is impossible."

Pug S | 21 | 18 | 18 | £29 |
66-68 Chiswick High Rd., W4 (Stamford Brook/Turnham Green), 020-8987 9988; fax 020-8987 9911
▲ "Snug booths", an "exciting" vibe and a "good choice" of "creative" "Modern [British] cuisine" fashioned from "fresh ingredients" make this spacious Chiswick "neighbourhood" haunt a "favourite" of many; those who object to the "buzzy atmosphere" (exacerbated by "terrible acoustics") of its "funky bar area" and "bustling" dining room can avail themselves of its "great outside seating."

Purple Sage | 16 | 15 | 14 | £28 |
92 Wigmore St., W1 (Bond St.), 020-7486 1912; fax 020-7481 1813
▲ "Run by the people who run Red Pepper", this "trendy pizzeria" near Oxford Street has fans who appreciate the "great atmosphere" and "light", "upmarket" Modern Italian

fare; it also has detractors, however, who call it "noisy" and "not particularly memorable"; either way, it's generally considered a "good lunch location" or somewhere "nice" for a "no-frills evening out."

Putney Bridge Restaurant S | 22 | 22 | 20 | £47 |

1 Embankment, Lower Richmond Rd., SW15 (Putney Bridge), 020-8780 1811; fax 020-8780 1211

"Every table has a lovely view of Putney Bridge and the Thames" at this "stunning venue" with "marvellous", "minimalist" decor, where Anthony Demetre's "tricksy but highly accomplished" New French cooking is a "revelation" to most, though "inconsistent" to a minority; similarly, views on the service range from "terrific" to "haughty", and some are put off by the "scary prices."

Qc S | ∇ 16 | 16 | 18 | £35 |

The Renaissance Hotel-Chancery Court Hotel, 252 High Holborn, WC1 (Holborn), 020-7829 7000; fax 020-7829 9889

Although not yet well known to surveyors, this dining room with "a little bit of history" (courtesy of its setting in a grandly restored Holborn hotel, formerly the Pearl Assurance company's headquarters) is "great for a business lunch" thanks to chef Jun Tanaka's "good" New French cooking and staff that "really try" to keep things "upbeat and lively."

QUAGLINO'S ●S | 18 | 20 | 16 | £39 |

16 Bury St., SW1 (Green Park), 020-7930 6767; fax 020-7839 2866

The "spectacle" of the Conran Group's "bustling", "mega-size" St. James's basement "brasserie" "still works" for those who find its "beautiful setting filled with vibrant people" and "remarkably good", seafood-focused Modern British fare, whereas detractors declare the "noisy" venue has "lost" its "cachet"; still, all agree it's "fun to make an entrance" "gliding down" the "grandest staircase in town."

Quality Chop House ●S | 20 | 15 | 16 | £31 |

94 Farringdon Rd., EC1 (Farringdon), 020-7837 5093; fax 020-7833 8748

"Hearty" "British dishes with a French twist" "come piping hot" to the "shared tables" of this "quirky", "quaint" "oasis in Farringdon Road"; nonetheless, comfort-cravers claim the "hip-to-hip seating" is "cramped" and complain the "church-pew" benches render "bums" "tender" ("please supply cushions"), whilst proletarians protest that "high prices" indicate this self-styled "workman's cafe" has "lost its original ethos."

Quilon | ∇ 23 | 19 | 23 | £35 |

Crowne Plaza London St. James, 41 Buckingham Gate, SW1 (St. James's Park/Victoria), 020-7821 1899; fax 020-7828 5802

Fans who "can't imagine a better Indian" restaurant "love" this "under-praised" Bombay Brasserie sib in the Crowne Plaza London St. James Hotel near Buckingham

Palace; it has "attentive service", "great decor" and "flabbergastingly tasty delicacies" including "lovely" coastal dishes of the Southwestern Kerala region – so "why is it so empty?"

Quod ● 16 | 17 | 15 | £25
57 Haymarket, SW1 (Piccadilly Circus), 020-7925 1234; fax 020-7839 4545

◪ With a "nice art display" and "relaxed" Tuscany-inspired interior, this "trendy" Haymarket newcomer "owned by Brown's" founder Jeremy Mogford is a "welcome addition to the area", with "good" Modern Italian cooking and "helpful staff"; still, dissenters declare the "menu is too ambitious" and report "nothing to write home about."

Quo Vadis ● 21 | 20 | 19 | £42
26-29 Dean St., W1 (Leicester Sq./Tottenham Court Rd.), 020-7437 9585; fax 020-7736 7593

◪ "Whilst glaring around before the tasty starters zoom to the table", "amuse yourself" with a peek at the "intriguing" creations on the walls of Marco Pierre White's "classy", "spacious" Soho eaterie; though the place is "worth a look" and the Modern Italian fare can be "excellent", service is "surprisingly amateur", leading Latin experts to wonder "just like the name, where is it going?"

Racine S – | – | – | E
239 Brompton Rd., SW3 (South Kensington), 020-7584 4477; fax 020-7584 4900

The pairing of respected chef Henry Harris (ex Hush), and the experienced Eric Garnier (ex Bank), who runs the front of house, bodes well for this promising, attractive French Knightsbridge newcomer; the robust menu is filled with satisfying classics, offset by a varied wine list, and the setting, an earthy mix of leather and wood, is just as pleasing.

Rainforest Cafe S 11 | 20 | 13 | £24
20 Shaftesbury Ave., W1 (Piccadilly Circus), 020-7434 3111; fax 020-7434 3222

◪ "If you have to take the kids out", the "jungle environment is great fun" at this "Disney-esque" eatery with an attached "tacky shop" in Piccadilly; some grown-ups might turn up their noses at the "fast food–quality" American fare and "slow" servers who seem to monkey around a bit much, grumbling that the "gimmicky" experience "makes you wish the rain forest would vanish already!"

Randall & Aubin S 18 | 18 | 16 | £30
14-16 Brewer St., W1 (Piccadilly Circus), 020-7287 4447; fax 020-7287 9317
329-331 Fulham Rd., SW10 (Fulham Broadway/ South Kensington), 020-7823 3515; fax 020-7823 3991

◪ "Every bit the happening Soho eaterie", Ed Baines' "relaxed" original in a "converted butcher's shop" is "excellent fun", with "great" seafood to satisfy "hungry punters", plus "window seats" so people-watchers can "see the world go by"; it's "noisy" inside and staff are rather "offhand", so those looking for less "crowd" and more "posh", as well as a wider Mediterranean menu, might try the newer branch in Chelsea.

Rani ▽ 20 | 12 | 17 | £22
7 Long Ln., N3 (Finchley Central), 020-8349 4386; fax 020-8349 4386
◪ "Light and delicious" Vegetarian dishes cooked in the Gujarti style make this family-run Indian "the local" for Finchley herbivores; "service is slow", so diners who don't want to wait through "all four seasons", or weather the stormy vibe, "tend to have takeaway."

Ransome's Dock S 20 | 16 | 19 | £38
35-37 Park Gate Rd., SW11 (Sloane Sq.), 020-7223 1611; fax 020-7924 2614
■ Respected chef-owner Martin Lam's "really interesting" Modern British "gem" overlooking a Battersea dock is "great on a summer's day"; though the "friendly, fast, fabulous, fun" "atmosphere suits a family celebration better than romance", "locals" seem to have fallen in love with the "delicious" seafood and "wonderful" "book they call a wine list" here.

Rasa S 23 | 16 | 20 | £27
6 Dering St., W1 (Bond St./Oxford Circus), 020-7629 1346; fax 020-7491 9540
5 Charlotte St., W1 (Tottenham Court Rd.), 020-7637 0222; fax 020-7637 0224
56 Stoke Newington Church St., N16 (Stoke Newington B.R.), 020-7249 1340; fax 020-7249 4692 ◓
55 Stoke Newington Church St., N16 (Stoke Newington B.R.), 020-7249 0344; fax 020-7249 4692
■ "Open up a whole new world of Keralan cuisine" with its "incredible multitude of flavours" at these "jolly", if modest-looking, Vegetarian-Indians in Stoke Newington and the West End; everything on the menu is so "light, fragrant, nourishing and delicious" that "returning guests" "could happily eat it all", and it's priced so "reasonably", you can pig out without having to "splash out"; N.B. the Charlotte Street branch also serves seafood.

Ravi Shankar S 17 | 9 | 13 | £16
133-135 Drummond St., NW1 (Euston), 020-7388 6458; fax 020-7388 2494
422 St. John St., EC1 (Angel), 020-7833 5849; fax 020-7388 2494
◪ They may not be as accomplished as the namesake musician, but you "can't knock" these Southern Indian siblings in Euston and St. John St. (the latter BYO) for "cheap vegetarian eats"; the "service and surroundings need improvement", sure, but those on a budget sing the praises of a "lunchtime buffet that's great."

| F | D | S | C |

Real Greek, The   22 | 18 | 18 | £33
15 Hoxton Mkt., N1 (Old St.), 020-7739 8212; fax 020-7739 4910
☒ "Discover very imaginative Greek cuisine and, surprise after surprise, get happy" at Hoxton's "hip", newly expanded "Hellenic gem" where Theodore Kyriakou's "gorgeous" "flavours just zip and sing" on plates large and small; "reasonable prices" and a "great wine list" make it "worth the trek", the "wait" and the "inexperienced staff"; N.B. there's a new mezze/wine bar next door called Mezedopolio.

Rebato's   ▽ 18 | 19 | 23 | £27
169 S. Lambeth Rd., SW8 (Stockwell), 020-7735 6388
☒ The "cosy" tapas bar of this Spaniard south of Vauxhall Bridge serves as an "introduction to a diverse country and its food" via "a little of this and that", whilst the "pleasant service" in the restaurant offers "enjoyable" regional dishes; N.B. a pianist provides "good family entertainment."

Red Cube Bar & Grill ◑   14 | 17 | 13 | £39
1 Leicester Pl., WC2 (Leicester Sq.), 020-7287 0101; fax 020-7851 0807
☒ Boasting a "bordello look", this "trendy" Leicester Square private members' club/restaurant attracts "mid-20s Hollyoaks extras" and "Essex boys and girls"; whilst admirers are taken with the "unexpectedly good" Modern British–International fare, foes see it from another angle, deeming it "nothing extraordinary", with "poor service" to boot.

Red Fort ◑   22 | 19 | 20 | £34
77 Dean St., W1 (Oxford Circus/Tottenham Court Rd.), 020-7437 2525
☒ "Comeback of the year" gush devotees of Amin Ali's revamped Soho Indian stalwart that "reopened and is as good as ever" after a fire closed it a few years ago; the "innovative" Mughal court cooking from Mohammed Rais and "great decor" make it a "classy choice", though the less enamoured find it "pleasant, but expensive"; N.B. the downstairs bar, Akbar, has a DJ on Saturdays.

Redmonds 🅢   ▽ 23 | 16 | 20 | £36
170 Upper Richmond Rd. W., SW14 (Mortlake B.R.), 020-8878 1922; fax 020-8878 1733
☒ A "local restaurant with London-quality food", this low-key East Sheen "favourite" shines thanks to "delicious" Modern British fare from "great chef" Redmond Hayward; "friendly" service helps ensure a "relaxing atmosphere", prompting regulars to return "again and again"; if a few find the "prices slightly high", fans retort it's "good value."

Red Pepper 🅢   20 | 11 | 15 | £25
8 Formosa St., W9 (Warwick Ave.), 020-7266 2708; fax 020-7266 5522
☒ "Delightful" pizzas and "simple, tasty" Modern Italian dishes lure diners to this "friendly", "fun", "informal"

Maida Vale outpost of the Red Pepper group – a "good local" spot "for the whole family"; but faultfinders fret that the "cramped" setting is "so tight" "you are packed in like sardines" and complain that "service has slipped a bit."

Reubens S | 15 | 11 | 12 | £24
79 Baker St., W1 (Baker St.), 020-7486 0035; fax 020-7486 7079

■ "For authentic Jewish deli food" head to this down-to-earth, "relaxed" Marylebone venue; "go hungry" to best enjoy the "classic salt beef" and "great tongue sandwiches" plus "tasty kosher" dishes, all served with wines from the Golan Heights; they do takeaway too.

Rhodes in the Square | 23 | 20 | 20 | £47
Dolphin Square Hotel, Dolphin Sq., Chichester St., SW1 (Pimlico), 020-7798 6767; fax 020-7798 5685

◪ The "rich blue" "nautical feel" of this "modern, yet elegant" dining room within Pimlico's Dolphin Square Hotel creates an "intimate, relaxing" setting for celebrity chef Gary Rhodes' "beautifully prepared", "marvellous" Modern British cooking; it's "ideal for a special meal or business lunch", plus the "wine list is exquisite"; foes prefer to set sail elsewhere, deeming the decor "too sterile" and the "food uninspiring."

Rib Room & Oyster Bar S | 23 | 21 | 20 | £48
Carlton Tower, 2 Cadogan Pl., SW1 (Knightsbridge/Sloane Sq.), 020-7858 7053; fax 020-7823 1708

◪ "As Oliver Twist would say, 'please sir, can I have more'", and so do fans with "vast appetites" tempted by the oyster bar, the "great rib roasts from the trolley" and the Traditional British fare at this plush dining room within the Carlton Tower hotel in Knightsbridge; the "attentive service" hits the mark, helping to make it as "good an experience as ever"; N.B. there has been a post-*Survey* change of chef, plus the hotel is now owned by Jumeirah International, which also houses the recently revamped Chinoiserie.

Riccardo's ●S | 19 | 11 | 16 | £27
126 Fulham Rd., SW3 (Gloucester Rd./South Kensington), 020-7370 6656; fax 020-7244 6401

■ A "perfect" Chelsea "spot for a lively local dinner", this Traditional Italian standby serves "small" but "nice-size servings" that "enable a lot" of "fresh", "original" "dishes to be sampled and shared"; fans appreciate that it's "not trying hard to be trendy" or "chichi" and give the "nice garden room in the front" (open throughout the year) a thumbs-up.

RICHARD CORRIGAN | 26 | 20 | 23 | £52
AT LINDSAY HOUSE
21 Romilly St., W1 (Leicester Sq./Piccadilly Circus), 020-7439 0450; fax 020-7437 7349

■ "A great place to treat overseas guests" – and "spoil yourself" – this "unpretentious", four-storey 1740s Soho

| F | D | S | C |

townhouse provides a "beautiful" backdrop for chef-patron Richard Corrigan's "flawless", "mouthwatering" Modern British–Irish fare; the "fantastic food" (which climbed three points since the last *Survey*), "coupled with a good wine list" and "thoughtful service", means a "delightfully unusual experience" that's "top-notch in all respects."

Richoux S 14 | 13 | 13 | £20

41A S. Audley St., W1 (Bond St.), 020-7629 5228; fax 020-7493 2204
172 Piccadilly, W1 (Green Park/Piccadilly Circus), 020-7493 2204; fax 020-7495 6658
86 Brompton Rd., SW3 (Knightsbridge), 020-7584 8300; fax 020-7589 8547 ◐
3 Circus Rd., NW8 (St. John's Wood), 020-7483 4001; fax 020-7483 3810

◪ "Whatever time of the day" you pop into these "twee" coffee shops in the West End and St. John's Wood, you'll find "quick", "dependable" British fare, including "fancy desserts" and "delicious pastries"; whilst some say they're "good for lunch" or a "light dinner", others claim "best for breakfast or tea" – either way, this franchise is "convenient"; "used to be much better" quibble those who also flinch at the "tourists [who] fill the place."

RITZ RESTAURANT ◐ S 24 | 27 | 25 | £58

Ritz Hotel, 150 Piccadilly, W1 (Green Park), 020-7300 2370; fax 020-7907 2681

■ Voted No. 1 for Decor in this *Survey*, this "magnificent" dining room in the world-renowned Ritz Hotel is "a must for a truly Edwardian experience", offering "extremely accomplished" Classic French–Traditional British food and "old-fashioned" service that "genuinely wants to please"; it's a "very impressive place" and a "wonderful", "romantic" dinner destination on Friday and Saturday nights when there's live entertainment and dancing; P.S. "if you want the opulence for a bit less cash, try it for breakfast."

Riva S 24 | 17 | 19 | £39

169 Church Rd., SW13 (Hammersmith), 020-8748 0434; fax 020-8748 0434

◪ The "unfussy surroundings" of this "storefront-style" Barnes eaterie belie the "sophisticated simplicity" of Andrea Riva's "fantastic Modern Italian food" that's "still excellent after all these years"; whilst some find "staff pleasant", grumblers gripe that "service is variable" and deem the "uninspired decor a letdown."

RIVER CAFE S 25 | 20 | 21 | £48

Thames Wharf, Rainville Rd., W6 (Hammersmith), 020-7386 4200; fax 020-7386 4201

◪ Offering "a plateful of pleasure every time", this "foodies' heaven" is "worth the trek to Hammersmith"; the Modern Italian cooking – "so simple you can enjoy the essence of each ingredient" – and the "elegant, modern setting" strike a "perfect balance of sophistication and informality" that "totally lives up to its reputation"; some surveyors say that it's "delectable but destroys your wallet", adding it's "overhyped" to boot, but far more throw bouquets, asserting it's "a privilege to eat here."

RK Stanley's | 17 | 15 | 16 | £21 |
6 Little Portland St., W1 (Oxford Circus), 020-7462 0099; fax 020-7462 0088

◪ Providing a "break from the norm", this "funky place" near Oxford Circus offers Traditional British fare such as "winter-warming bangers and mash" and other "comfort foods" that add up to a "yummy lunch"; it's "heaven if sausages are your thing", but dissenters can't quite make the link, opining it's "ok, but not very special."

Rocket | 19 | 19 | 16 | £24 |
4-6 Lancashire Ct., W1 (Bond St.), 020-7629 2889; fax 020-7629 2881

■ A "real little treasure", this "hard-to-find" "fun, groovy" bi-level venue on a "Mayfair back street" is a "favourite" for its "good Italian"-Med menu and "fantastic pizzas" at such "cheap" prices ("they're practically giving them away"); after a "quiet dinner upstairs", head to the "cosy bar" – it's usually "packed" with a "very well-heeled crowd."

Rodizio Rico ●S | 18 | 12 | 14 | £26 |
111 Westbourne Grove, W2 (Bayswater/Notting Hill Gate), 020-7792 4035; fax 020-7243 1401

◪ An "eat-as-much-as-you-can" "carnivore's delight", this Bayswater spot would "warm the cockles of Homer Simpson's heart" with its "inexpensive" Brazilian barbeque – but beware: the buffet of "salads and starters may tempt you to fill out" before the "much-awaited beef"; although "service can be unsmiling", all agree this "tasty concept works well" for a "group", as long as they're "not vegans!"

Rosmarino S | 21 | 18 | 19 | £37 |
1 Blenheim Terrace, NW8 (St. John's Wood), 020-7328 5014; fax 020-7625 2639

◪ "Moving away from the usual mould", this "popular St. John's Wood" Modern Italian offers "interesting recipes with first-class ingredients" and a "brilliant summer terrace" "filled with posh locals"; snipers snip it's "expensive for small portions" and say service can be "inattentive"; N.B. planned renovations should add seating inside and out.

ROUSSILLON | 24 | 21 | 22 | £48 |
16 St. Barnabas St., SW1 (Sloane Sq./Victoria), 020-7730 5550; fax 020-7824 8617

■ "As if a spaceship had picked up a top [New] French" eaterie "and dropped it" on a "backstreet" "in the heart of a boring neighbourhood", this Pimlico spot is a "fine-dining"

F | **D** | **S** | **C**

phenomenon; whilst its decor is "hardly exciting", a "mature crowd" is enthralled by chef Alex Gauthier's "great-value", "seasonal" dishes and set Vegetarian menu, which are "fresh, tasty and perfectly served."

Rowley's ●S   **16** | **14** | **16** | **£34**
113 Jermyn St., SW1 (Piccadilly Circus), 020-7930 2707; fax 020-7839 4240
◪ "Unlimited chips with the house steak specialty" is the "same old formula" that makes this "reliable, unpretentious" St. James's veteran "a favourite" "for the boys" or "before a show"; those unenchanted by the "not cheap", "simple" Traditional British fare and "slapdash service" just don't deign to "darken its doors."

ROYAL CHINA S   **23** | **14** | **15** | **£26**
13 Queensway, W2 (Queensway), 020-7221 2535; fax 020-7792 5752
40 Baker St., W1 (Baker St./Bond St.), 020-7487 4688; fax 020-7935 7893
68 Queen's Grove, NW8 (St. John's Wood), 020-7586 4280; fax 020-7722 0750
30 Westferry Circus, E14 (Canary Wharf), 020-7719 0888; fax 020-7719 0889
◪ The "hilarious black-and-gold nightclub-style surrounds" are simply part of the "experience" at this Chinese quartet of "kitsch palaces" around town where "truly outstanding dim sum" and other "delicious" Cantonese dishes are "as good as anything to be had in Hong Kong"; although "monstrous queues" and "abrupt", "pushy waiters" don't "make for a leisurely" meal, Canary Wharf has a "calmer atmosphere" than its siblings and "a nice view to boot" "overlooking the river."

R.S.J.   **22** | **15** | **21** | **£33**
13A Coin St., SE1 (Waterloo), 020-7928 4554; fax 020-7401 2455
■ "Another tried-and-tested favourite", this "earthy jewel" down a "Waterloo side street" may not have "much atmosphere", but it wins over many with "absolutely lovely" Modern British food that's "now very good" and "super-friendly, unpretentious service"; it's a "great place for fans of Loire Valley wines", with a "wonderful", "novel list" focused on that region.

Rudland Stubbs   **18** | **16** | **17** | **£32**
35-37 Green Hill Rents, Cowcross St., EC1 (Farringdon), 020-7253 0148; fax 020-7253 1534
◪ How "fish can taste so fresh so far off the coast" is anyone's guess, but "it does" at this "very friendly and relaxed", "traditional" seafooder on the edge of Smithfield Market; whilst a few see it as a "boring" venue that "could be so much better", plenty of fin fans "still frequent" it, since they maintain "excellent" standards.

| F | D | S | C |

RULES ●S   21 | 22 | 20 | £42
35 Maiden Ln., WC2 (Covent Garden), 020-7836 5314; fax 020-7497 1081

◪ For "a lovely welcome" to bonny olde Britain, "tourists" "must do" a "classic" English meal at this seemingly "timeless", yet actually 205-year-old, Covent Garden landmark; the "perfect British experience" includes "thoroughy enjoyable" "pheasant and Yorkshire pudding" in "attractive", "Dickensian" "rooms"; cynics claim "huge portions don't make up for the lacklustre fare", still there's a "sense of occasion" about this "characterful" place.

Sabbia ●S   ▽ 19 | 18 | 20 | £45
103 Walton St., SW3 (South Kensington), 020-7589 6008

■ From the team behind nearby Scalini and Signor Sassi, this "lovely" "new discovery" in the Chelsea digs formerly occupied by San Martino offers a daily changing menu of "great" Traditional Italian dishes served by well-liked staff in a relaxed atmosphere; surveyors agree it's "not bad at all."

Saga S   ▽ 24 | 17 | 23 | £37
43 South Molton St., W1 (Bond St.), 020-7408 2236; fax 020-7629 7507

■ At 28 years and counting, this "plain"-looking stalwart near Bond Street is still a "fave Japanese place" with "great service" and a "good variety" of "quality" food at affordable prix fixe "values"; champions challenge "I defy anyone to come here and still claim they don't like sushi."

Saigon ●   19 | 13 | 15 | £28
45 Frith St., W1 (Leicester Sq./Piccadilly Circus), 020-7437 7109; fax 020-7734 1668

◪ "Good" Vietnamese cooking ("you must try the aromatic crispy duck") and "reasonable" prices are the hallmarks of this "authentic", "charming" Soho venue according to fans; gripers grouse that the "food's fine but rather run-of-the-mill" and lash out that the "service is erratic" and the decor is "overdue for a refurbishment."

Sale e Pepe ●   19 | 16 | 20 | £35
9-15 Pavilion Rd., SW1 (Knightsbridge), 020-7235 0098

◪ "There's more elbow space in a sardine tin" than at this "noisy" Knightsbridge veteran "down the street from Harrods" that serves "surprisingly hearty [Traditional] Italian food" and "has not changed in years"; whether the "loud" "singing" "waiters are entertaining" or "over the top" and "out of tune" is a matter of taste, but either way, "expect a lot of attention [from them] if you're female."

Salisbury Tavern, The S   – | – | – | M
21 Sherbrooke Rd., SW6 (Fulham Broadway/Parsons Green), 0207381 4005

"Dedicated chef" Micky O'Connor, a former Marco Pierre White pupil, produces "exciting" Modern European cooking

| | | | F | D | S | C |

that's easy on the wallet at this laid-back Fulham "sister to the Admiral Cod"; Nina Campbell is the designer behind the smart gastro-pub setting, whilst Berry Bros & Rudd is the name behind the good-value wine list.

Salloos ◐ — 22 | 16 | 19 | £39
62-64 Kinnerton St., SW1 (Hyde Park Corner/Knightsbridge), 020-7235 4444; fax 020-7259 5703

■ "Any curry tour would be incomplete without a visit" to this "quiet", "well-established" venue with "old-fashioned service" and "first-class", "reasonably priced" Pakistani-Indian food that "melts in your mouth"; though its "out-of-the-way location" in Knightsbridge mews may make it "hard to find", this "excellent change of pace" is "worth the effort."

Salt House S — 17 | 14 | 16 | £26
63 Abbey Rd., NW8 (St. John's Wood), 020-7328 6636; fax 020-7625 9168

◪ Admirers attest that this "original gastro-pub" in St. John's Wood "has established itself well" and "found its niche" with an "always interesting" Modern British menu, a "comfy" setting and a "lively vibe"; if the "disappointed" feel it's "let down by the smoky atmosphere" and "bland" fare that's "pricey for what you get", at least "staff are as pretty as the stained-glass decor."

Salusbury Pub & Dining Room S — 17 | 14 | 15 | £25
50-52 Salusbury Rd., NW6 (Queen's Park), 020-7328 3286

■ "Without a reservation" for the dining room, there's "no chance to enjoy" the "surprisingly good" Modern Italian "comfort food" (an "excellent value for the money") at this "cool", "busy" Queen's Park "restaurant-cum-bar" that's "one of the youngest but one of the best gastro-pubs", even if it's too "noisy and smoky" for some tastes; N.B. they also run a deli next door that delivers.

Sambuca ◐ — 19 | 16 | 19 | £37
62 Lower Sloane St., SW1 (Sloane Sq.), 020-7730 6571; fax 020-7225 1210

■ The "friendly" staffers "treat clients like old friends" at this "old-fashioned" and "unpretentious" venue near Sloane Square that supporters "recommend" as a "good local" "standby" for "nice meals" of "enjoyable" Traditional Italian fare; picky patrons are also pleased that they'll "provide off-menu [items] without complaining", making for "pleasant lunchtimes" and "jolly evenings."

Sand Bar & Restaurant ◐S — – | – | – | M
156 Clapham Park Rd., SW4 (Clapham Common), 020-7622 3022; fax 020-7498 4651

A buzzy, local crowd have latched onto this Clapham late-night hangout, comprised of a subtly lit restaurant serving straightforward Modern European fare at dinnertime and a bar area where you can kick back on leather sofas, challenge your partner to a round of backgammon or dance to the DJ who spins on weekends.

Sandrini S
▽ 19 | 16 | 17 | £37

260 Brompton Rd., SW3 (South Kensington), 020-7584 1724; fax 020-7225 1210

■ With popular pavement tables looking out on Brompton Cross, "this is one of" those "great locations" for "outside" dining on "a hot summer evening", and whilst most agree the "reliable" Traditional Italian cooking, "warm welcome" and "attentive service" make it a "good" "fallback", others knock it as "expensive."

San Frediano ● S
17 | 17 | 18 | £40

62-64 Fulham Rd., SW3 (South Kensington), 020-7589 2232; fax 020-7225 2982

■ It's "a port in a storm" thanks to "much improved" Modern Italian cooking (including "decently priced" prix fixe menus) and "extremely welcoming staff", but some say that the "latest incarnation" of this famous, recently expanded South Kensington '60s hangout is still "needing [more of] a revival" before it's back to its heyday.

San Lorenzo ● ⌀
19 | 18 | 18 | £46

22 Beauchamp Pl., SW3 (Knightsbridge), 020-7584 1074; fax 020-7584 1142

■ After 40 "vibrant" years, the "same old formula works" at this "casually chic" and "romantic" Knightsbridge "classic" that "deserves its popularity" thanks to "consistently high-quality [Traditional] Italian" cooking and "attentive service"; though foes "cannot understand all the fuss" and claim it's "not the star it was", the "celebrities", "pop singers and famous people turning heads" keep things "fun."

San Lorenzo Fuoriporta S
▽ 17 | 17 | 15 | £39

38 Wimbledon Hill Rd., SW19 (Wimbledon), 020-8946 8463; fax 020-8947 9810

■ "More relaxed than its sister", San Lorenzo (and run by the sons of its owners, Mara and Lorenzo Berni), this attractive Wimbledon veteran has *amici* who appreciate its "good" Modern Italian food and "nice service"; a handful think staff "need a kick up the bum", but either way, it's the hottest place in town during the tennis championships.

Santa Fe S
14 | 14 | 14 | £24

75 Upper St., N1 (Angel), 020-7288 2288; fax 020-7288 2287

■ "For a lively night" ("if you don't mind queuing" on a Saturday), most say this "comfy restaurant" with a "loud, Islington rah-rah atmosphere" does not disappoint with its "good selection" of "consistently above-average", "basic American" Southwestern "standbys" served in "large portions" and accompanied by "bracing margaritas"; P.S. fans of the "great men's toilet" hope that its recently stolen "barbed-wire seat" will be promptly replaced.

		F	D	S	C

Santini ●S
29 Ebury St., SW1 (Victoria), 020-7730 4094;
fax 020-7730 0544

| 19 | 17 | 19 | £47 |

"Solid, dependable and pricey" sums up views on the Modern Italian cooking at this well-established Belgravia eaterie near Victoria Station that attracts an "older crowd"; a post-*Survey* refurbishment of the previously "dated", "dull" digs, including an expansion of a private dining space and the opening of a 40-seat front terrace, may impact the above Decor score.

Sarkhel's S
197-199 Replingham Rd., SW18 (Southfields), 020-8870 1483;
fax 020-8874 6603

| 24 | 15 | 21 | £28 |

"Even for North Londoners", this unprepossessing venue in Southfields is "worth travelling to" according to fans who say its "superb" dishes are not only "great value" but "open up a whole new world of Indian cuisine"; true, the setting is "not atmospheric, but the food makes up for it"; P.S. "the delicious express lunch is a well-kept secret."

Sartoria ●S
20 Savile Row, W1 (Oxford Circus/Piccadilly Circus), 020-7534 7000; fax 020-7534 7070

| 19 | 19 | 18 | £42 |

"Stroll down Savile Row" to this "quiet, serene" Mayfair venue "full of [sartorial] paraphernalia" where, supporters say, "the Conran formula works" thanks to "highly reliable" Modern Italian cooking and staffers who "try hard"; still, opponents are "not impressed" with what they call "forgettable food" (especially "at this price level") and the "stuffy" "attitude" of some servers; N.B. a live pianist plays on Friday and Saturday nights.

Satsuma ●S
56 Wardour St., W1 (Leicester Sq./Piccadilly Circus), 020-7437 8338; fax 020-7437 3389

| 19 | 14 | 14 | £19 |

"For a quick bite in Soho", those "in a hurry" "go early" to this "lively place" that "fills up fast" at lunch with folks hungry for "tasty" and "nutritious" Japanese food at "reasonable prices", including "good sushi" and a "wide" "variety of noodle and rice dishes"; "no-nonsense" service makes it "not a place to linger", and "communal tables" mean "you must gossip quietly", but it's nevertheless "fun."

Savoy Grill
Savoy Hotel, The Strand, WC2 (Covent Garden/Embankment), 020-7420 2065; fax 020-7420 2450

| 23 | 22 | 23 | £50 |

The "epitome of business" dining (expect "many suits"), this "dignified" hotel dining room on The Strand attracts a "power" crowd with "impeccable service" and "hearty" food that's "up there with the best Traditional" British fare; whilst the somewhat "stodgy", "old-world charm" isn't everyone's cuppa and the "high prices" make some wince, it "rarely disappoints" as a "great place to see and be seen."

| F | D | S | C |

Savoy River Restaurant ●S 22 | 24 | 23 | £51
Savoy Hotel, The Strand, WC2 (Covent Garden/Embankment), 020-7420 2698; fax 020-7420 2450

◪ "Wonderful wining and dining" win many over at this "grand", "self-assured" Strand Hotel dining room with a "booming view over" the Thames (try to "secure a window table"), "upbeat" service and a Traditional British menu that's "kept up with modern tastes"; P.S. there's "fantastic dancing" to a live band on Fridays and Saturdays – "good times are guaranteed."

Scalini ●S 20 | 16 | 19 | £42
1-3 Walton St., SW3 (Knightsbridge/South Kensington), 020-7225 2301; fax 020-7225 3953

◪ "You forget you're in London" at this "fun" Chelsea spot that's "still rocking after all these years" thanks to a "lively" cosmopolitan atmosphere, a "tasty" Traditional Italian menu with "loads of variety" and "professional" yet "friendly staff"; though some say it's "a bit too expensive", "cramped" and "noisy", those with "no complaints" say you "can't blame Scalini" for the ruckus – "it's the patrons!"

Scotts S 20 | 19 | 18 | £43
20 Mount St., W1 (Bond St./Green Park), 020-7629 5248; fax 020-7499 8246

◪ With more than a century and a half under its belt, this "great old seafooder" is a "tried-and-true" "favourite" of many for "high-quality", "fresh" fish dishes served in a "beautiful", bright room that attracts a "mature set"; snipers may snip that the "patchy service" and "not innovative" "food selection could be improved", but the "interesting entertainment" in the downstairs jazz bar ensures "more buzz than normal in this part of Mayfair"; N.B. at press time the restaurant was being sold to private owners.

Searcy's at the Barbican 17 | 15 | 17 | £32
Barbican Ctr., Silk St., level 2, EC2 (Barbican/Moorgate), 020-7588 3008; fax 020-3822 7247

◪ Many Barbican concertgoers claim it's "worth arriving early to take advantage" of this "quiet venue" on level 2, "a haven" in the local "wilderness" thanks to "well-presented" Modern British cooking; whilst excitement seekers sigh that it's "boring in every respect", at least it makes a "discreet" City "business" haunt "away from braying bankers"; N.B. the refurbished bar area has comfy sofas.

Seashell 17 | 9 | 14 | £20
49-51 Lisson Grove, NW1 (Marylebone), 020-7224 9000; fax 020-7724 9071

◪ "The bait" at this "no-frills" Marylebone seafooder is "honest fish 'n' chips" served in "large portions" in a "jolly atmosphere"; it's "good, but not legendary" shun some surveyors, whilst nostalgic diners wax wistful about "the old days"; P.S. "wonderful takeaway" is available next door.

| F | D | S | C |

Shepherd's 22 | 19 | 21 | £37
Marsham Ct., Marsham St., SW1 (Pimlico/St. James's Park), 020-7834 9552; fax 020-7233 6047

■ "If you don't mind the odd MP sitting by you", this "great clubby" "Westminster institution" is "an inviting place" for "fine", "classic" Traditional British food that's also "reasonably priced", with "pleasant service" thrown in for good measure; one tip: "don't order 'trendy' food, stick to the old-school favourites!"

Shogun S 23 | 19 | 19 | £44
Millennium Mayfair Hotel, Adam's Row, W1 (Bond St.), 020-7493 1255; fax 020-7493 1255

■ "Genuine Japanese" fare, including "amazing sushi" and teriyaki, can be found in this "nice cave-like setting" located in the basement of the Millennium Mayfair, a Georgian-style hotel that dates back to the 18th century; "private, but not excessively snobby", this dinner-only venue also "attracts celebrities"; N.B. closed Mondays.

Signor Sassi 20 | 17 | 18 | £37
14 Knightsbridge Green, SW1 (Knightsbridge), 020-7584 2277; fax 020-7225 3953

■ The "Signor is sassy" applaud admirers of this "fun", "lively", "upmarket" Knightsbridge "gem" with "good, wholesome" Traditional Italian food and "friendly" service – perhaps that's why fans "want to come back again and again"; the "relaxed but noisy atmosphere" makes it a "great place to take the kids for Saturday lunch" and "ideal" for "celebrating a birthday" "with a crowd."

Signor Zilli ● 20 | 14 | 15 | £32
41 Dean St., W1 (Leicester Sq./Tottenham Court Rd.), 020-7734 3924; fax 020-7734 7786

◪ "Buzzy" and "pleasant", this "small" Soho trattoria is "sometimes graced by [chef-patron] Aldo Zilli" – "what a character!" – who oversees the "very good", "affordably priced" Traditional Italian cooking; "this man knows about seafood" exult enthusiasts who also pine for "pasta done the way it should be"; the "food is unpredictable" retort diners who report "a few disappointments."

Silks & Spice 18 | 13 | 14 | £23
95 Chiswick High Rd., W4 (Turnham Green), 020-8995 7991; fax 020-8994 7773 S
23 Foley St., W1 (Goodge St./Oxford Circus), 020-7636 2718; fax 020-7323 1927 ● S
28 Chalk Farm Rd., NW1 (Camden Town/Chalk Farm), 020-7267 5751 S
Temple Ct., 11 Queen Victoria St., EC4 (Bank/Mansion House), 020-7248 7878; fax 020-7248 9595

◪ This "cheerful" Thai-Malaysian chain around town is appreciated for its "excellent variety" of "imaginative", "authentic" dishes – the "seasoning leaves a glow", and the "well-presented" food "offers good value"; the less-enthused are put off by the "chaotic service" and "loud music" in the bar areas, which can create an "office party atmosphere"; N.B. the Clerkenwell and Fulham branches are now closed.

Simply Nico | 18 | 14 | 16 | £35 |
48A Rochester Row, SW1 (St. James's Park/Victoria), 020-7630 8061; fax 020-7828 8541
12 Sloane Sq., SW1 (Sloane Sq.), 020-7896 9909; fax 020-7896 9908
London Bridge Hotel, 10 London Bridge St., SE1 (London Bridge), 020-7407 4536; fax 020-7407 4554
"Simply good" New French food at "fair prices" is the main attraction at this "quiet" trio (no longer associated with the original owner, Nico Ladenis), including a couple of "excellent pre-theatre" spots; foes are "not impressed", by the "bland", "overpriced" menu, concluding it's "average in all respects"; N.B. the Blackfriars branch is now closed.

Simpson's-in-The-Strand/ Grand Divan | 18 | 20 | 20 | £41 |
100 The Strand, WC2 (Charing Cross), 020-7836 9112; fax 020-7836 1381
A "quintessentially English" setting "straight out of *Upstairs Downstairs*", this "nostalgic" Strand dining room is most appreciated for its "magnificent roast beef", "carved at your table", along with other "good, if not sophisticated", Traditional British cooking; the less-enamoured report "unappetising" food, "ponderous" service and "busloads of tourists" soaking up the "Victorian club atmosphere."

Simpson's-in-The-Strand/ Simply Simpson's | 19 | 19 | 17 | £41 |
100 The Strand, WC2 (Charing Cross), 020-7836 9112; fax 020-7836 1381
"Perfect for old-school" enthusiasts, this "quietly formal" first-floor Strand dining room above the Grand Divan "keeps [many] happy" with "solid" Traditional British food and a "nice" comfortable cocktail bar offering "good piano music"; whilst most enjoy this "visit to the past", others dismiss it as too "predictable" and find the "service very slow."

Singapore Garden | 20 | 12 | 16 | £24 |
83/83a Fairfax Rd., NW6 (Swiss Cottage), 020-7328 5314; fax 020-7624 2656
"If you're in the [Swiss Cottage] area, you would miss out not to visit" this "popular" Chinese restaurant featuring an "authentic" multiregional menu that includes "really unusual Singaporean" and Malaysian dishes amongst the "house specialities"; "it's all about good food and good service" – that's what makes it a "local favourite"; still, a handful think staff need "sorting out."

| F | D | S | C |

Singapura 17 | 14 | 15 | £30
1-2 Limeburner Ln., EC4 (Blackfriars/St. Paul's), 020-7329 1133; fax 020-7236 2325
78-79 Leadenhall St., EC3 (Aldgate/Tower Hill), 020-7929 0089
An "efficient", straightforward City duo, this Southeast Asian outfit offers "interesting set menus" from £8.50 and a "good variety" of "authentic" fare; there's "no special excitement" here, but it's a "reasonable place for both food and cost"; P.S. delivery is available for those who would rather not "eat in."

Sir Charles Napier S 22 | 22 | 20 | £38
Spriggs Alley, Chinnor, Oxfordshire, 01494 48 3011; fax 01494 48 5311
"Divine in winter, sublime in summer", this "relaxed", casual 18th-century inn situated in Oxfordshire's Chiltern Hills is a "favourite" of many who say the "honest [Modern British] food at honest value" "hasn't disappointed yet"; the "service remains impeccable" and the "atmosphere friendly" – "if only it were closer" say the wistful wishful.

Six-13 S 19 | 16 | 17 | £40
19 Wigmore St., W1 (Bond St./Oxford Circus), 020-7629 6133; fax 020-7629 6135
"The crème de la crème of kosher" Fusion cooking, say fans who find this "very stylish" Marylebone destination an "interesting experience", complete with a "nice ambience" and "attentive service"; the less-enthused complain that it "should be better for the price"; N.B. opening times change according to Jewish law, and at press time plans were underway to open a more casual brasserie downstairs.

Smiths of Smithfield – Dining Room 20 | 19 | 18 | £31
67-77 Charterhouse St., EC1 (Farringdon), 020-7251 7950; fax 020-7236 5666
"Finally, some space" sigh the "Clerkenwell trendies" who fill this "fun and funky" multi-level Smithfield Market warehouse that's a study in "industrial chic"; the "hearty" Modern British cooking is "fresh" and "interesting", and what's more, it's a "groovy place for brunch after a heavy night out"; a few quibble "what's all the hype about", but for most it's "just sooo cool."

Smiths of Smithfield-Top Floor S 22 | 21 | 19 | £42
67-77 Charterhouse St., EC1 (Farringdon), 020-7251 7950; fax 020-7236 5666
An "amazing rooftop paradise for meat lovers" is one spin on this "pleasantly airy" top-floor venue that boasts "inventive" Modern British food and an "awesome view" over Smithfield Market; even if foes point to "indifferent" service and "overpriced", "uninspired" fare that "doesn't blow you away", most agree it's a "safe bet for a business lunch" – and "perfect in summer."

| F | D | S | C |

Smollensky's on the Strand   14 | 14 | 14 | £28
105 The Strand, WC2 (Charing Cross/Covent Garden), 020-7497 2101; fax 020-7836 3270 S
Bradmore House, Bradmore Sq., W6 (Hammersmith), 020-8741 8124; fax 020-8741 5695
O₂ Ctr., 255 Finchley Rd., NW3 (Finchley Rd.), 020-7431 5007; fax 020-7431 7533 S
Mash Court, EC1 (Canary Wharf), 020-7719 0101; fax 020-7719 0060
Hermitage Wharf, 22 Wapping High St., E1 (Tower Bridge/ Wapping High St.), 020-7680 1818; fax 020-7680 1787 S

"Reliable, if unoriginal", American food is the common thread at this rapidly expanding chain that's "fun when you're in the mood for a U.S. fix" or need somewhere "good for children's parties"; those who find the Strand original "touristy" and "formulaic" may be tempted by the much smarter "new Wapping restaurant" with views of Tower Bridge; N.B. the new Canary Wharf venue opened post-*Survey*.

Snows on the Green S   20 | 17 | 19 | £32
166 Shepherd's Bush Rd., W6 (Hammersmith), 020-7603 2142; fax 020-7602 7553

■ "Always a good choice" is the reassuring view of Sebastian Snow's "small, individual" Shepherd's Bush "oasis" where locals gather for "imaginative", "carefully prepared" Modern British food; after a dozen years, this "good neighbourhood place" "still produces" the goods.

Sofra ●S   18 | 13 | 15 | £21
36 Tavistock St., WC2 (Covent Garden), 020-7240 3773; fax 020-7836 6633
1 St. Christopher's Pl., W1 (Bond St.), 020-7224 4080; fax 020-7224 0022
18 Shepherd St., W1 (Green Park), 020-7493 3320; fax 020-7499 8282

■ "Great for that Turkish fix", these "reliable, welcoming" "standbys" in prime West End locations are "great pre- or post-theatre options", offering "generous portions" of "delicious", "quality" Middle Eastern fare and "excellent mezze-type meals"; whilst a few gripe that they feel a bit "squeezed" by "tables that are too close" together, fans don't seem to mind, especially on "summer evenings, when you can sit outside"; N.B. a new branch is scheduled to open this autumn in Exmouth Market.

Soho House ●S   18 | 18 | 16 | £33
Private club; inquiries: 020-7734 5188

It's "great" to dine on "imaginative" Modern British fare "alongside stars" in this "casual", "cosy and friendly" private club, a "quiet sanctuary in the chaos of Soho" with "lots of smaller rooms" filled with "big old furniture"; although fans say "it's a privilege to be a member", foes beg to differ: "loves itself but shouldn't."

www.zagat.com

| F | D | S | C |

Soho Spice ◐ S   16 | 14 | 13 | £23
124-126 Wardour St., W1 (Leicester Sq./Tottenham Court Rd.), 020-7434 0808; fax 020-7434 0799

■ "Colourful" and "lively", this "great value" Indian in Soho offers a "nice presentation" of "spicy and delicious" fare that's a "bit different" from the usual, plus a bar that's a "good place to meet after work"; detractors, however, find it "disappointing", citing "bland food" and "scatty service"; N.B. there's a DJ on Friday and Saturday nights.

Solly's S   17 | 11 | 12 | £23
148A Golders Green Rd., NW11 (Golders Green), 020-8455 2121

■ It "redefines falafel and schwarma" proclaim lovers of this "noisy" kosher Middle Eastern destination in Golders Green with a casual ground-floor room and "superbly" decorated upscale upstairs restaurant; sceptics find the menu "uninspiring" and the food "simple and bland."

Sonny's S   22 | 18 | 19 | £33
94 Church Rd., SW13 (Hammersmith), 020-8748 0393; fax 020-8748 2698

■ One of the "best by far in Barnes", this "very cheery", "great all-rounder" attracts its "quotient of Putney mums" and other local folk with "simple" yet "innovative" Modern British cooking that's "surprisingly consistent"; "very cooperative, lovely staff" also get a thumbs-up, solidifying its status as a "friendly neighbourhood" spot that's "got its act together."

Sophie's Steakhouse & Bar ◐ S   – | – | – | M
311-313 Fulham Rd., SW10 (South Kensington), 020-7352 0088

Named after co-owner Sophie Mogford, daughter of Browns chain founder Jeremy Mogford, this unpretentious Fulham Road newcomer with a Manhattan warehouse feel serves up American chophouse fare; formerly the home of All Bar One, the setting has been transformed with exposed-brick walls and light bulbs, oak tables and leather banquettes and also boasts a buzzy after-work/pre-cinema bar.

Souk ◐ S   18 | 23 | 17 | £23
27 Litchfield St., WC2 (Leicester Sq.), 020-7240 1796

■ "For that Moroccan feeling" come to this "transporting" "party place" in Theatreland with a "magical" atmosphere, "charming" staff and "tasty" North African cooking; "get a table downstairs where you can sit on cushions on the floor", listen to "great music" and watch the belly dancers; a few find it "a bit squashed" with "woeful service", but most are seduced by this "wonderful underground haven."

Spago ◐ S   17 | 12 | 14 | £22
183 Lavender Hill, SW11 (Clapham Junction), 020-7228 2660
6 Glendower Pl., SW7 (South Kensington), 020-7225 2407

■ "When they crank up the music and provided you're in the mood, it's a blast" say fans of these "fun" pizzerias in South

| F | D | S | C |

Kensington and Lavender Hill; "watch Italian football on TV" or just dig into the "good" house specialty, plus seafood and pasta, at this "more than ordinary" spot that's "good for a quick bite" say fans; it's "nothing remarkable" – "just another pizza place" sigh the blasé.

Spiga S
18 | 15 | 15 | £25

84-86 Wardour St., W1 (Leicester Sq./Piccadilly Circus), 020-7734 3444; fax 020-7734 3332
312-314 King's Rd., SW3 (Sloane Sq.), 020-7351 0101; fax 020-7349 1488

Offering "robust" Modern Italian fare and "fantastic" wood-fired pizzas, these "lively" Italians set in "one of the handiest Soho settings" and a "pleasant" bi-level King's Road location are "nice with children"; they're "too noisy" and not "terribly special, though affordable" opine others.

Spighetta S
18 | 12 | 15 | £26

43 Blandford St., W1 (Baker St.), 020-7486 7340; fax 020-7486 7340

"Phenomenal pizza" from a wood-fired oven and a Traditional Italian menu offset by "interesting specials" lure fans to this "informal", bright "contemporary" basement setting "off-the-beaten-track" near Baker Street; service splits opinions: "charming" vs. "exceptionally slow."

Spoon+ at Sanderson S
16 | 21 | 15 | £50

Sanderson Hotel, 50 Berners St., W1 (Goodge St./Oxford Circus), 020-7300 1444; fax 020-7300 1479

You "can't help being swept away" by Ian Schrager's "cool" hotel near Oxford Street, the backdrop for this "see-and-be-seen" Modern European–International offshoot of Alain Ducasse's Parisian concept; the "mix-and-match" menu features "inventive" fare, but the "food is incidental" to the "hip bar scene" full of "eye candy"; "give me a knife and fork" quip quibblers who find the "high concept low on execution", still it's "worth experiencing once."

SQUARE, THE S
26 | 22 | 24 | £58

6-10 Bruton St., W1 (Bond St./Green Park), 020-7495 7100; fax 020-7495 7150

"Sophisticated in all respects", this "outstanding hot spot" in Mayfair may be "eye-wateringly expensive", "but boy" do "they pull out all the stops" with "cutting-edge" New French cooking from celebrated chef/co-owner Philip Howard, "impeccable service" that "goes the extra mile" and a "lovely setting" with a "luxurious" feel; this "top-drawer" "splurge is worth every penny" – and much "like a Mercedes limo, it's slick, unshowy and utterly reliable."

Sri Siam S
19 | 15 | 17 | £26

16 Old Compton St., W1 (Leicester Sq./Tottenham Court Rd.), 020-7434 3544; fax 020-7287 1311

"A pearl" in Soho, this "nice setting" offers "charming service" and a "great choice" of "consistent quality" Thai

| F | D | S | C |

food, including "very good vegetarian options"; the less convinced, however, deem it "nothing special", declaring there are "no surprises" here.

Sri Siam City ● | 19 | 15 | 16 | £30 |
85 London Wall, EC2 (Liverpool St.), 020-7628 5772
◼ "Popular with suits" "on expenses", this "understated" Sri Siam original offers a "dependable formula" of "quality" Thai cooking in a "plum [City] location"; even if sceptics feel the servers "don't seem to try too hard" and find it a "bit pricey for the fare", the "queue to get in at lunchtime" suggests they're doing something right.

Sri Thai ● | 19 | 16 | 16 | £30 |
3 Queen Victoria St., EC4 (Bank), 020-7827 0202; fax 020-7827 0200
◼ "Convenient for a business dinner" or a "reliable lunch", this "useful place in the City" offers "surprisingly good Thai food" and "pleasant service"; observers who find it "boring" and "a tad expensive" by day see it in a different light at night when a "raucous" after-work crowd stops by "for bar snacks."

Star of India ● S | 20 | 15 | 17 | £32 |
154 Old Brompton Rd., SW5 (Gloucester Rd./South Kensington), 020-7373 2901; fax 020-7373 5664
◼ With its "wild", "entertaining owner", Reza Mahammad, and "bizarre rococo decor", this "friendly" cramped South Ken Indian has its followers who "love the place and like" the "lovely food", deeming it "great for family get-togethers"; naysayers, however, cite "somewhat surly service" and "disappointing food" that's "sometimes variable."

Stepping Stone | ▽ 20 | 17 | 20 | £35 |
123 Queenstown Rd., SW8 (Clapham Common), 020-7622 0555; fax 020-7622 4230
◼ "Brilliance in Battersea" awaits at Gary Levy's "friendly", "unassuming" eatery declare boosters of the "limited [yet] classy choice" of Modern British dishes and "good all-round service"; whilst a few think it "lacks character" and can be "a little unpredictable", all "the basics are there" to make it "worth a trip"; N.B. "it's a shame they no longer do [Sunday] lunch – are they mad?!"

Sticky Fingers ● S | 14 | 14 | 14 | £23 |
1A Phillimore Gardens, W8 (High St. Kensington), 020-7938 5338; fax 020-7937 0145
◼ With "plenty of memorabilia" on the walls, Bill Wyman's "noisy" Kensington "shrine" to Mick and the boys is "great for teenagers and those who were teenagers when the Stones were young"; whilst fans spend the night together with "juicy hamburgers" and other "American-style diner" fare, foes paint the cooking as "predictable", jesting that "the place should be renamed 'sticky tables'!"

F | D | S | C

St. John
21 | 16 | 19 | £35
26 St. John St., EC1 (Farringdon), 020-7251 0848; fax 020-7251 4090
■ "Committed carnivores" clamour for this "unusual" eaterie in an old Smithfield smokehouse that does "intriguing things with dead animals", using every part "from snout to tail" to create an "adventurous" British menu of "offally good", "fancy food"; whilst many feel the "bleak" decor "could be softened" and baulk at the "inflated prices", most consider this "strangely wonderful" place, with its "charming service", "a real treat" – but it's definitely "not for the squeamish."

Strada S
18 | 16 | 16 | £21
Market Pl. 9-10, W1 (Oxford Circus), 020-7580 4644; fax 020-7580 7877
15-16 New Burlington St., W1 (Oxford Circus), 020-7287 5967; fax 020-7287 7607
91 Wimbledon High St., SW19 (Wimbledon), 020-8946 4363
11-13 Battersea Rise, SW11 (Clapham Junction), 020-7801 0794; fax 020-7801 0754
175 New King's Rd., SW6 (Parsons Green), 020-7731 6404; fax 020-7731 1431
237 Earl's Court Rd., SW5 (Earl's Court), 020-7835 1180; fax 020-7835 2093
102 Clapham High St., SW4 (Clapham North), 020-7627 4847; fax 020-7720 2153
105-106 Upper St., N1 (Angel), 020-7226 9742; fax 020-7226 9187 ◐
8-10 Exmouth Mkt., EC1 (Farringdon), 020-7278 0800; fax 020-7278 6907
■ "Keep it up" urge fans of this growing group of "everyday Italian" eateries serving "pizzas with a difference" (as well as other "really good, simple" fare) at "reasonable prices"; even if some feel "rushed service lets down" the side, most say these "welcome additions" to the ranks of London purveyors "deserve to be packed every night – which they are"; P.S. you "cannot book in advance."

Stratford's S
∇ **21 | 15 | 19 | £32**
7 Stratford Rd., W8 (High St. Kensington), 020-7937 6388; fax 020-7938 3435
■ The few who know this "lovely", "cosy" Kensington townhouse call it a "special place" and "go often" for its "consistently" "tasty" and "fresh" French seafood dishes (especially the "excellent-value pre–7 PM" menu) offered "in an unfussy manner" by "attentive but not intrusive" staff that "make [you feel] welcome"; P.S. "having a table upstairs" affords a garden view.

Stream, Bubble & Shell
∇ **19 | 13 | 17 | £28**
50-52 Long Ln., EC1 (Barbican/Farringdon), 020-7796 0070; fax 020-7796 0069
◪ Visitors to this bright, easygoing Smithfield restaurant/bar "come for the seafood", including an "excellent lobster

| F | D | S | C |

[shellfish] platter" that rivals many "this side of Sydney"; some say its glass frontage makes the experience "too much like being in a goldfish bowl", whilst others report its "best decor is actually in the toilets", which feature tanks of color-coded fish – blue in the gents, pink in the ladies.

SUGAR CLUB S | 23 | 19 | 20 | £42 |
21 Warwick St., W1 (Piccadilly Circus), 020-7437 7776; fax 020-7437 7778

☑ The "beautiful blending of seemingly opposing flavours" "keeps the taste buds guessing" at this "happening" Soho eaterie where it's almost as "interesting to look around" and "spot celebs", "poseurs" and other "in-crowd" types as it is to study the "exotic", "exciting" Pacific Rim menu; "terrible acoustics" and "indifferent service" sour some, but it's a "regular favourite" of those sweet on sampling the "fabulously unusual."

Sugar Hut ●S | – | – | – | E |
374 North End Rd., SW6 (Fulham Broadway), 020-7386 8950

Ambient music, intriguing art and dramatic artefacts from India, China, Thailand, Indonesia and Morocco greet arrivals at this opulent Fulham newcomer; the intimate restaurant serves a wide variety of Western-influenced Thai fare (dinner only) whilst the stylish bar pours exotic cocktails.

Sugar Reef ● | 14 | 16 | 13 | £36 |
41-44 Great Windmill St., W1 (Piccadilly Circus), 020-7851 0800; fax 020-7851 0807

☑ "Meet a footballer", loads of "Essex boys" and "hen nights" in full flight at this large, multi-level restaurant-cum-"nightclub" near Piccadilly Circus with "trendy, modern decor" and "pretty average" Asian-International cooking; those "not impressed" by the "surly staff", "overpriced food" and "way-too-noisy tables" conclude it's somewhere "to be seen, not served"; N.B. 3 AM license.

Sumosan ● | – | – | – | VE |
266 Albemarle St., W1 (Green Park), 020-7495 5999

Formerly the site of Coast, and more recently Mash, this Mayfair offshoot of a Moscow-based chainlet offers a sleek, modern, East-meets-West, neutral-coloured setting for dining on high-end classical and contemporary Japanese dishes; visitors can also descend the walnut staircase to the hip, plush J Bar for drinks, sushi and Asian tapas.

Suntory S | 24 | 17 | 20 | £53 |
72-73 St. James's St., SW1 (Green Park), 020-7409 0201; fax 020-7499 0208

☑ "One of the excellent Japanese" restaurants "in town for corporate" "entertaining" or "for socialising", this "formal" but "comfortable" St. James's outpost of an international chain serves "wonderful" "traditional" fare ("especially the teppanyaki") that's a bit "pricey"; some say

| F | D | S | C |

the "smart" interior offers "little atmosphere", but the "friendly and attentive service" helps make amends.

Sushi Wong S ▽ 14 | 10 | 14 | £23
38C-D Kensington Church St., W8 (High St. Kensington), 020-7937 5007; fax 020-7937 0670

☒ You "don't go for the decor" at this bi-level Kensington Japanese, but to "enjoy" "consistent sushi" (including some "inventive rolls") "and more", all "at decent value"; nevertheless, naysayers say it's "taken a turn for the worse", complaining of "plebian" fare, and even fans advise you to "eat downstairs, away from the harsh lighting upstairs", which is for speedy dining.

Sweetings 22 | 14 | 18 | £34
39 Queen Victoria St., EC4 (Mansion House), 020-7248 3062

■ "Step into the past" at this "never-changing" City seafooder circa 1889, a "surprisingly relaxed and lively" lunch-only venue where "a magic formula" of "good, fresh fish" dishes ("no fusion rubbish!") and "charming service" "proves that some institutions are worth keeping"; regulars applaud the recent "change in ownership" ("keep up the good work"), though some hope a revamp of the "not-very-comfortable", "faded decor" will follow.

Tabla ▽ 21 | 15 | 18 | £30
Dockmaster's House, Hertsmere Rd., E14 (Canary Wharf), 020-7345 0345; fax 020-7363 1013

☒ Fans report "delicious and different" Indian fare seasoned with "subtle spices" and served by "knowledgeable staff" at this little known two-year-old; even detractors say it has "potential", though some wish the "nice-enough dining room" was as "impressive" as the Georgian Docklands building at West India Quay that houses it and warn that prices are "higher than you might expect."

Tamarind ●S 23 | 20 | 21 | £40
20 Queen St., W1 (Green Park), 020-7629 3561; fax 020-7499 5034

■ "In a city known for great Indian food", this "top-flight" Mayfair option "stands out" on account of "sublime, sexy [Northern] food" made with "vibrant seasonings" and "helpful service"; true, a meal in this "nicely appointed" and "comfortable basement" is "expensive, but the ethos, ambience and menu make up for the prices"; P.S. the "great vegetarian choices" are also appreciated.

Tandoori of Chelsea ●S 19 | 15 | 19 | £30
153 Fulham Rd., SW3 (South Kensington), 020-7589 7617; fax 020-7584 3168

■ Since opening its doors in 1964, this veteran Chelsea Indian has been a "reliable" spot that fans say "deserves much greater recognition for its good service and food", including a selection of dishes from the Northwest Frontier

F	D	S	C

Tartuf S
| 17 | 12 | 17 | £17 |

169 Clapham High St., SW4 (Clapham Common), 020-7622 8169; fax 020-7622 3087 ◐
88 Upper St., N1 (Angel), 020-7288 0954; fax 020-7288 0957

■ "Bringing Alsace to London", this "friendly" Islingtonian and its new Clapham sibling put a "different spin on Alsatian food" with their house specialty – "yummy", "inventive pizzas" (in both "savoury" and "dessert" varieties) called "*tartes flambées*" whose "thin" crusts are covered with "different toppings"; whilst "not very classy" looking, these "sociable eateries" are "fun for a group", and the "cheap" prices make for "great value."

Tas ◐ S
| 21 | 17 | 18 | £21 |

33 The Cut, SE1 (Southwark), 020-7928 1444

■ Devotees dub this "great discovery" near Waterloo the "first chic Turk in London", for though folks certainly "enjoy" its "good-size portions" of "fabulous mezze" and other "zesty" fare, it's "the buzz" of its "cheerful" atmosphere that "keeps [them] coming back" to this "popular" spot.

Tate Gallery Restaurant S
| 18 | 20 | 16 | £27 |

Tate Britain, Millbank, SW1 (Pimlico), 020-7887 8825; fax 020-7887 8902

☑ "A good mix of culture and food" and a "nice break from the art" await at this "delightful place" in the Tate Britain on Millbank with a "good", "wholesome" Modern British menu that may be "limited in range" but is "a cut above most museum food"; some suggest the "chief attractions" are its "innovative wine list" (400 strong) and the "wonderful [Rex] Whistler mural" that graces its "lovely room."

TATSUSO
| 25 | 18 | 23 | £56 |

32 Broadgate Circle, EC1 (Liverpool St.), 020-7638 5863; fax 020-7638 5864

■ A "real Japanese experience" can be found at this Broadgate Circle venue known for "immaculate food" offered with "great service" on two levels – "wonderful teppanyaki" is "beautifully cooked" on the ground floor, whilst "mouthwateringly fresh" sushi and sashimi is sliced below (where the decor is more "basic"); "it's so expensive", though, that wallet-watchers call it "perfect for when someone else is paying."

Teatro ◐
| 19 | 18 | 17 | £39 |

93-107 Shaftesbury Ave., W1 (Leicester Sq.), 020-7494 3040; fax 020-7494 3050

☑ To many, Lee Chapman and Lesley Ash's "oddly" shaped Theatrelander serving "good" Modern European cooking is "excellent for business" and "particularly enjoyable after

| F | D | S | C |

the theatre", though some cite "mixed experiences"; either way, expect a few "B-list celebrities" (like "Sky News presenters") among the "beautiful people with big wallets" "getting plastered on bubbly."

TECA   23 | 19 | 19 | £42
54 Brooks Mews, W1 (Bond St.), 020-7495 4774; fax 020-7491 3545
Given its "fantastic" wine list and "graceful" Modern Italian cooking that "goes from strength to strength", this "stylish", slightly "quirky", "very Mayfair" eaterie owned by A to Z Restaurants (Aubergine, Zafferano) has supporters "surprised that it isn't full up" all of the time; if a few find it "nothing special" and complain of "slow service", all agree it's a plus that "you can always get a table."

TENTAZIONI   24 | 18 | 21 | £40
Lloyd's Wharf, 2 Mill St., SE1 (London Bridge/Tower Hill), 020-7237 1100; fax 020-7237 1100
"Too bad it's so far away from things" lament lovers of this "quiet" "gem" "tucked away" in a converted warehouse behind Butler's Wharf, which receives raves for its monthly changing menu of "creative" Modern Italian fare employing the "highest-quality ingredients"; "personal service" from an "enthusiastic", "knowledgeable" staff is a further factor in its favour; N.B. a post-*Survey* refurbishment may impact the above Decor rating.

Tenth Restaurant & Bar, The   ▽ 20 | 24 | 21 | £41
Royal Garden Hotel, 2-24 Kensington High St., 10th fl., W8 (High St. Kensington), 020-7361 1910; fax 020-7361 1921
Possibly "London's best-kept secret" for "unbelievable views" across Kensington Gardens and the skyline beyond, this Modern British dining room on the Royal Garden Hotel's 10th floor makes a smart choice for a business meal, offering several prix fixe and degustation options; things get livelier on 'Manhattan nights', when there's "great entertainment" (dancing to live jazz, on the last Saturday of each month); P.S. it also has a full bar complete with a "great cigar selection."

Terminus S   16 | 14 | 14 | £30
Great Eastern Hotel, Liverpool St., EC2 (Liverpool St.), 020-7618 7400; fax 020-7618 7401
An "upbeat atmosphere" marks the Conran Group's "busy", train-themed Modern British brasserie in the Great Eastern Hotel by Liverpool Street Station, which supporters consider "a must" for "business breakfasts" and lunches; "should be called Terminal" joke peeved passengers "let down" by "iffy service" and "dull" tucker, but even critics concede its bar is "convenient" for "after-work drinks."

Terrace, The S   19 | 15 | 18 | £37
33C Holland St., W8 (High St. Kensington), 020-7937 3224
It may be "just a quiet little neighbourhood restaurant", but this "totally charming", "intimate spot" "hidden" on a

| F | D | S | C |

Kensington backstreet is quite "popular" thanks to its "very good" Modern British food and "personal attention" from "friendly" staff; despite sometimes "cramped" conditions, most vote it "wonderful in every way."

Terrace, The ⑤ ▽ 20 | 21 | 20 | £39
Le Meridien Piccadilly, 21 Piccadilly, W1 (Green Park/ Piccadilly Circus), 020-7851 3085; fax 020-7851 3090
■ There's a "very calm atmosphere" at this spacious, first-floor conservatory in the Le Meridien Piccadilly, a favoured business destination that's "nice when the sun shines" (and a bit gloomy when it's "pouring with rain"); the kitchen's French cuisine, supervised by Michel Rostang, "matches the lovely room", as does the "knowledgeable" service.

Texas Embassy Cantina ⑤ 14 | 15 | 14 | £22
1 Cockspur St., SW1 (Charing Cross/Piccadilly Circus), 020-7925 0077; fax 020-7925 0444
☑ "For a shot of Americana", try this "loud, brassy" "theme" joint off Trafalgar Square boasting "huge portions" of Tex-Mex vittles, margaritas deemed "reasonably close to the real thing" and "that can-do American service"; but whilst it might be "lots of fun" for "groups", "kids" and "homesick" expats, critics find it rather "rough and ready" for their liking, citing "greasy" grub and "touristy" tendencies.

T.G.I. Friday's ●⑤ 12 | 12 | 14 | £21
6 Bedford St., WC2 (Charing Cross/Covent Garden), 020-7379 0585; fax 020-7240 3239
96-98 Bishop's Bridge Rd., W2 (Bayswater/Royal Oak), 020-7229 8600; fax 020-7727 4150
25-29 Coventry St., W1 (Piccadilly Circus), 020-7839 6262; fax 020-7839 6296
☑ "If you can cope with the must-be-happy environment" and "'80s decor", these "loud" and "lively" chain links around town have a simple formula of "enthusiastic staff" and "basic" "American fast food" (burgers, fajitas and the like) that "kids love"; "fantastic cocktails [from] entertaining barmen" also ensure a steady stream of "office parties."

Thai on the River ⑤ 19 | 17 | 17 | £34
4 Chelsea Wharf, 15 Lots Rd., SW10 (Fulham Broadway/ Sloane Sq.), 020-7351 1151; fax 020-7823 3390
☑ "London needs more Thai restaurants like this" declare enthusiasts of this "wonderful" Thamesider near Chelsea Harbour with "lovely [terrace] views" and "surprisingly good food"; those who find the regular menu "expensive" might consider the bargain buffet that's "perfect for Sunday lunch."

Thai Pavilion ●◑⑤ 18 | 16 | 17 | £30
42 Rupert St., W1 (Leicester Sq./Piccadilly Circus), 020-7287 6333; fax 020-7587 0484
☑ "There's something for every Thai taste" at this tri-level Soho eaterie where the menu is long enough to "read like

| F | D | S | C |

a book"; those who find it "fun to sit on the floor while eating" suggest "be sure to ask for" the Sawasdee Room, with its "traditional" cushion seating.

Thai Square
| 19 | 20 | 17 | £28 |

21-24 Cockspur St., SW1 (Charing Cross/Piccadilly Circus), 020-7839 4000 ● S
347-349 Upper St., N1 (Angel Station), 020-7704 2000 S
136-138 Minories, EC3 (Tower Hill), 020 7680 1111; fax 020-7680 1112

◪ "Glitzy Thai jewel boxes" with "attentive" ("if kooky") staff, these "prime" Trafalgar Square and Tower Hill locations stir up "authentic" cooking that "blossoms on the taste buds"; still, there are a few grumbles about "over-the-top decor with prices to match"; P.S. a huge City sibling based on the same formula opened recently and is off to a "very good start" (closed weekends).

Thierry's S
| 17 | 13 | 16 | £32 |

342 King's Rd., SW3 (Sloane Sq.), 020-7352 3365; fax 020-7352 3365

◪ "Perfect for a quiet " meal, "romantic or otherwise", this "warm, cosy" French bistro in Chelsea offers "good, traditional" fare with the promise of occasional "celebrity-spotting" amongst "all the locals who dine here"; whilst admirers gush there's "no room for improvement", cynics claim it's merely "resting on its history."

Thyme
| – | – | – | E |

14 Clapham Park Rd., SW4 (Clapham Common), 020-7627 2468; fax 020-7627 2424

An "innovative menu" of starter-size Modern British dishes "executed to high standards" helps make this Clapham newcomer (on the former site of Moxon's) a "great neighborhood restaurant"; the "service is young, knowledgeable and enthusiastic", much like chefs Adam Byatt and Adam Oates, both formerly of The Square, and the setting is cosy and welcoming, with a large, striking painting of a blue nude dominating the room.

Tiger Lil's S
| 14 | 13 | 13 | £19 |

75 Bishop's Bridge Rd., W2 (Bayswater/Queensway), 020-7221 2622
16A Southside Clapham Common, SW4 (Clapham Common), 020-7720 5433 ●
270 Upper St., N1 (Highbury & Islington), 020-7226 1118 ●

◪ "You only have yourself to blame for poor dishes" at this Asian trio based on a "fantastic" concept: diners choose their "own ingredients for flaming stir-fries", which the cooks "prepare in front of" them; although "the environment is fun and cheerful" (especially for "groups"") and there's "special consideration for vegetarians", doubters wonder "why pay so much for something anyone can cook at home?"; N.B. the Chelsea branch has closed.

| F | D | S | C |

Timo ⑤ — | — | — | E
343 Kensington High St., W8 (High St./Kensington), 020-7603 3888; fax 020-7603 8111
Chef Valerio Daros, who formerly cooked with Andrew Needham at sibling restaurant Zafferano, turns out refined, flavourful Modern Italian fare, complemented by a well-priced wine list, at this buzzy, smartly decorated Kensington newcomer; the efficient front-of-house staff works hard to please, as reservations are already hard to come by.

Toast ◐⑤ 15 | 16 | 13 | £27
50 Hampstead High St., NW3 (Hampstead), 020-7431 2244; fax 020-7794 2333
◪ Still a "northern outpost for the 'in' crowd" (even if snobs sniff it's "had its day"), this "small, but swish" eaterie located directly above the Hampstead tube station radiates an "urban lounge feel"; whilst some consider it "better as a bar", especially considering its "fab cocktails", others say its "simple menu" of "pleasant" Modern European fare is the "trendiest" in the area; N.B. lunch served only on weekends.

Tokyo Diner ◐⑤ 17 | 11 | 16 | £17
2 Newport Pl., WC2 (Leicester Sq.), 020-7287 8777; fax 020-7434 1415
■ This "cheap, cheerful and consistent" Chinatown Japanese is appreciated for its "yummy" sushi, bento boxes and other "efficiently" served classics, which are particularly "good when you're in a hurry"; however, few would disagree that its decidedly "unimposing" decor could stand a "painting."

Tom's Delicatessen ⑤ 19 | 14 | 13 | £17
226 Westbourne Grove, W11 (Notting Hill Gate), 020-7221 8818; fax 020-7221 7717
■ "Trendy mums with toddlers eating ciabatta" are all part of the scene at Tom Conran's "tiny", "fashionable" all-day Notting Hill deli/diner where it "can be a crush" to get a table, especially on weekends; "top-quality" Eclectic snacks (like "terrific salads and sandwiches") are what draw the throngs that happily overlook any service shortcomings for "some of the best coffee" in town.

Tootsies ⑤ 14 | 11 | 14 | £19
120 Holland Park Ave., W11 (Holland Park), 020-7229 8567
35 Haven Green, W5 (Ealing Broadway), 020-8566 8200
148 Chiswick High Rd., W4 (Turnham Green), 020-8747 1869 ◐
35 James St., W1 (Bond St.), 020-7486 1611
48 High St., SW19 (Wimbledon), 020-8946 4135
147 Church Rd., SW13 (Hammersmith), 020-8748 3630
107 Old Brompton Rd., SW7 (South Kensington), 020-7581 8942 ◐
177 New King's Rd., SW6 (Parsons Green), 020-7736 4023
36-38 Abbeville Rd, SW4 (Clapham South), 020-8772 6646; fax 020-8772 0672

| F | D | S | C |

(continued)
Tootsies
196-198 Haverstock Hill, NW3 (Belsize Park), 020-7431 3812 ☻
Additional locations throughout London
◪ "Does the job" say supporters of this long-established American-style diner chain that "remains popular" for its "simple, wholesome" food (like "comfort burgers and chips" and "all-day breakfasts"); if the less-impressed shrug "nothing special", "kids love it" and parents give "cheap" prices the thumbs-up.

Toto's ☻S 21 | 19 | 20 | £45
Walton House, Walton St., SW3 (Knightsbridge), 020-7589 2062; fax 020-7581 9668
◪ The fact that it's "not hard to get a table" at this "stylish" yet "old-fashioned" Chelsea eaterie surprises those enamoured by its "consistently" "delicious" Modern Italian cooking, "great wine list" (plus a wide grappa selection) and "warmest" service; the "wonderful outside" seating area (at lunch only) adds to the appeal of this "very nice place"; P.S. remember, bring a "fat wallet."

Tramp 15 | 16 | 17 | £44
Private club; inquiries: 020-7734 0565
◪ With it's "very noisy", "crowded dance floor", this perennially in vogue St. James's private nightclub is "still rolling along"; whilst some appreciate the Traditional British cooking and "attentive service" on offer in the darkened dining area, more critical members find the "food is still the weak link" at this stalwart.

Troubadour, The ☻S 17 | 20 | 16 | £15
265 Old Brompton Rd., SW5 (Earl's Court), 020-7370 1434; fax 020-7370 0029
■ "Will expansion spoil it?" wonder worriers about the recent "upmarket" renovations at this "quirky" Earl's Court coffeehouse, which has earned its spurs over nearly 50 years as a "truly wonderful place"; virtually "anything goes" here, including "poetry readings" and "spontaneous jam sessions", and the no-frills Modern British menu is one of the "best values" around; N.B. the above Decor score predates the refurbishment.

Truc Vert S 21 | 14 | 15 | £23
42 North Audley St., W1 (Bond St.), 020-7491 9988; fax 020-7491 7717
■ "There's always something yummy on the menu" at this "lovely addition to Mayfair", a "refreshingly unfussy" restaurant-cum-food shop serving a daily changing roster of "homemade", "healthy" French bistro fare "at fair prices"; it's no surprise, then, that it "can be very noisy" and a bit "slow" service-wise; P.S. there are "lots of goodies to buy on the way out", like pâtés, cheeses and wine.

www.zagat.com

| F | D | S | C |

Tsunami ⑤   20 | 18 | 17 | £31
5-7 Voltaire Rd., SW4 (Clapham North), 020-7978 1610
■ Boasting the skills of former Nobu chef Singi Nakamura as well as "great staff", this spacious Clapham yearling with "lots of atmosphere" is making waves by bringing "magnificent sushi and sashimi" to "an area with no Japanese" options of note; it's a "real find" fawn fans, though a few note that it's "promising" but "needs some time to settle down."

Tuk Tuk Thai ⑤   16 | 11 | 15 | £21
330 Upper St., N1 (Angel), 020-7226 0837
■ A "trustworthy Islington fixture", this "cheerful and cheap" family-owned "favourite" is all about "good-value, wholesome Thai cooking"; it's "nothing fancy", but it's "authentic, reliable" and "interesting enough."

Tuscan Steak ●   19 | 18 | 16 | £43
St. Martins Lane Hotel, 45 St. Martins Ln., WC2 (Leicester Sq.), 020-7300 5500; fax 020-7300 5501
◪ "Quieter than Asia de Cuba" though located in the same Ian Schrager hotel, this Theatreland offshoot of the Italian steakhouse chain offers "fab portions" of "lovely food" that's "not messed about with"; admirers adore the "excellent sharing idea" and deem it a "fun night out on an expense account"; critics chide that flying "to Florence is cheaper", still they're hopeful that it "may get better" in time; N.B. afternoon tea includes a selection of unusual cocktails.

Tuttons Brasserie ●⑤   14 | 14 | 14 | £26
11-12 Russell St., WC2 (Covent Garden), 020-7836 4141; fax 020-7379 9979
◪ A "good pit stop while shopping on a Saturday", this "busy, convenient" Covent Garden brasserie offers browsers a "relaxing" respite with "unassumingly good", if "uneventful", Modern British dishes; it's a "nice people-watching" perch from which you can see "the world go by", especially "in the summertime when you can eat outside."

Two Brothers Fish   21 | 9 | 15 | £20
297-303 Regent's Park Rd., N3 (Finchley Central), 020-8346 0469; fax 020-8343 1978
■ "If you like fish 'n' chips", it's "worth the schlep" to this Finchley seafooder; acolytes go ape for the "outstanding quality" of the "good down-to-earth food" – it's the "freshest ever and worth a repeat visit"; thanks to a recent renovation it's "not so cramped anymore", still, it's "nothing fancy"; N.B. reservations taken for lunch only.

UBON   26 | 21 | 20 | £50
34 Westferry Circus, E14 (Canary Wharf), 020-7719 7800; fax 020-7719 7801
■ "When you want a quieter, easier-to-get-into Nobu", head to "Nobu's little sister" in Canary Wharf, a "wow" spot with

an "astonishing view" of the Thames that offers the same "unique", "expensive" Japanese–South American fusion fare (including the signature "melt-in-your-mouth black cod"); inevitably it has "less atmosphere" than its famous sib and a few find the "service variable", but for most this "delightful" destination is "as good as the real thing."

Union Cafe | 17 | 11 | 14 | £28 |
96 Marylebone Ln., W1 (Bond St.), 020-7486 4860; fax 020-7486 4860

■ "If you're in the mood for simple [Modern British] dishes, don't hesitate" to try John Brinkley's "friendly" Marylebone haunt, a "nice, relaxed venue" that also boasts a "brilliant", "well-priced wine list"; some sceptics suggest the "so-so" menu "could do with a tune-up", but most say it "still rates."

Upstairs at The Savoy ● | 21 | 18 | 21 | £34 |
Savoy Hotel, The Strand, WC2 (Covent Garden/Embankment), 020-7836 4343; fax 020-7420 2450

■ A "lovely, uplifting" "hideaway with a good view of arrivals" getting "out of the Rolls", the Savoy Hotel's more "casual" first-floor bar/cafe on The Strand is also "handy" for a "quick" "pre- or post-theatre meal" of "wonderfully reliable" seafood with an "imaginative" "Asian twist"; it's also "ideal for a ladies' lunch" and "great for a late-night dessert", and whilst it's "expensive", most feel it's "worth it."

Vale, The S | ▽ 17 | 14 | 17 | £28 |
99 Chippenham Rd., W9 (Maida Vale), 020-7266 0990; fax 020-7286 7224

■ "Every neighbourhood should have" one say followers "who are so honoured to have this little" Modern British spot as their Maida Vale "local"; admirers praise the "innovative", "constantly changing" menu of "jolly good tucker" as well as the "cheerful", "lovely staff"; the "not terribly memorable" dishes are "sadly inconsistent" counter a couple of critics, but for most it's "reliably good."

VAMA ● S | 25 | 19 | 18 | £33 |
438 King's Rd., SW10 (Sloane Sq.), 020-7565 8500; fax 020-7565 8501

■ A "completely transcendental experience", this "utterly civilised" World's Ender "just quietly gets on with the business of creating wonderful", "unique" Northwest Punjabi dishes imbued with "magical" Indian flavours, all brought to table in a "beautiful" setting; whilst some find "impeccable" "staff knowledgeable", a few gripe that the "slow" "service could be improved to match the food."

Vasco & Piero's Pavilion | 21 | 17 | 22 | £35 |
15 Poland St., W1 (Oxford Circus), 020-7437 8774; fax 020-7437 0467

■ Its "big reputation is deserved" opine supporters of this "potential star-spotting venue" in Soho that gets "very

| F | D | S | C |

crowded" thanks to "warm", "personal" service, a "well-chosen wine list" and "great" Italian food that's "sensibly priced"; if a minority find the "room a bit plain", the "buzzy atmosphere" more than compensates.

Veeraswamy ●S 20 | 18 | 18 | £33
Victory House, 99 Regent St., W1 (Piccadilly Circus), 020-7734 1401; fax 020-7439 8434
◾ "Light years ahead of traditional Indian" fare, the "subtle cooking" at this "upmarket" Piccadilly standby is so "stylish" it just might "convert unbelievers"; "love the contemporary decor" applaud aesthetes – the "modern" refurbishment a few years ago belies that it's "London's oldest" (it turns 75 this autumn) of its kind; "they survive off their reputation" claim the "underwhelmed" who label it "a bit touristy", but most are grateful it's "still going strong."

Vegia Zena S ▽ 19 | 15 | 17 | £29
17 Princess Rd., NW1 (Camden Town/Chalk Farm), 020-7483 0192; fax 020-7483 0192
◾ It's "variable, but it has moments of modest bliss" say the few surveyors who have found their way to this unassuming-looking Italian with a "lovely garden" located "by the zoo" in Primrose Hill; it's "disappointing" retort detractors who report "indifferent meals."

Verbanella ●S 15 | 13 | 18 | £31
30 Beauchamp Pl., SW3 (Knightsbridge), 020-7584 1107; fax 020-7589 9662
◾ "Still reliable" after 35-plus years, this "somewhat cramped standby" in Knightsbridge "serves up" "good solid" Traditional Italian food at "reasonable prices"; it's an "undistinguished eaterie" gripe grumblers who lament that it's "inconsistent."

Viet Hoa ●S 21 | 6 | 13 | £15
70-72 Kingsland Rd., E2 (Old St.), 020-7729 8293; fax 020-7729 8293
◾ Never mind the "canteen-style surroundings" at this "no atmosphere" "nice dive" – just concentrate on the "fab" "authentic Vietnamese" offered "at really reasonable prices"; it's favoured more for "just a quick bite" than "a night out", still, it "crowds quickly", and whilst some find the servers "warm", others snipe about "surly service."

Villandry S 19 | 15 | 15 | £31
170 Great Portland St., W1 (Great Portland St.), 020-7631 3131; fax 020-7631 3030
◾ Pass through the "grocery store that awakens the taste buds better than any starter" on your way to the Modern British "foodie heaven" that awaits at this "sparsely" decorated dining room on Great Portland Street; the "fantastically fresh", "well-executed dishes" "change with the seasons", revealing a "gently pleasurable" kind of

| F | D | S | C |

"innovation"; whilst a few find it "too noisy and crowded", most feel it's a "cool place to be"; P.S. the all-day bar next door gets "very busy" during weekday lunches.

Vine, The S ▽ | 15 | 16 | 14 | £27 |
86 Highgate Rd., NW5 (Kentish Town B.R.), 020-7209 0038; fax 020-7209 3161

■ The few fans who know about this "unpretentious" gastro-pub "hangout" in Kentish Town dote on the "nice atmosphere" and "good" Modern British–European tucker; but a handful of others may need more time to grow fond, claiming they "liked it better before" the recent change of ownership; N.B. there's a large covered terrace at the back.

Vineyard at Stockcross S | 23 | 22 | 23 | £54 |
Vineyard at Stockcross, Stockcross, Newbury, Berkshire, 01635 528770; fax 01635 528398

■ You "really couldn't ask for more" than this "incredibly accommodating" Berkshire hotel restaurant say surveyors swept away by the "superb" Modern British–Classic French fare and "amazingly detailed" "to-die-for wine list" of international and "super California" selections featuring vinos from owner Sir Peter Michael's Sonoma County winery; naysayers have a different take, suggesting it's "overrated" and "not really worth driving out there for."

Vingt-Quatre ●S | 13 | 11 | 12 | £20 |
325 Fulham Rd., SW10 (South Kensington), 020-7376 7224

■ A "stop-off for those hungry at unearthly times of night", this 24-hour Chelsea haunt is "perfect" for "basic" Modern British–Eclectic fare (like "good American-style breakfast") "after a pub/club" night; on the downside, it's "cramped" and "smoky", with "mediocre food", but it has that one trump card: "it's always open."

VONG ●S | 23 | 20 | 19 | £49 |
Berkeley Hotel, Wilton Pl., SW1 (Hyde Park Corner), 020-7235 1010; fax 020-7235 1011

■ Celeb chef Jean-Georges Vongerichten's "luscious", "well-presented" New French–Thai "combinations taste so wonderful you'll swear East and West should never be separated again" say fans who fill this Berkeley Hotel basement venue in Hyde Park Corner; the "stylish" servers offer "good advice" with the "unusual", "diverse menu", helping to make it an "all-round experience"; it's "anti-climatic" after visiting the "brilliant New York" branch gripe grumblers who claim it's "not worth the hype."

Vrisaki ▽ | 22 | 12 | 21 | £24 |
73 Myddelton Rd., N22 (Bounds Green/Wood Green), 020-8889 8760; fax 020-8889 0103

■ You "must have the mezze" – the "amazing food" plates just keep "arriving" applaud the smattering of surveyors who frequent this traditional Greek taverna in Wood Green;

| F | D | S | C |

"wish it was near home" wax the wishful, still it's "very much worth the drive."

WAGAMAMA | 18 | 14 | 15 | £16 |

14A Irving St., WC2 (Leicester Sq.), 020-7930 7587 S
1 Tavistock St., WC2 (Charing Cross/Covent Garden), 020-7836 3330; fax 020-7240 8846 S
4A Streatham St., WC1 (Tottenham Court Rd.), 020-7323 9223; fax 020-7323 9224 S
26A Kensington High St., W8 (High St. Kensington), 020-7376 1717; fax 020-7376 1552 S
10A Lexington St., W1 (Piccadilly Circus), 020-7292 0990; fax 020-7734 1815 S
101A Wigmore St., W1 (Bond St./Marble Arch), 020-7409 0111; fax 020-7409 0088 S
Harvey Nichols, 109-125 Knightsbridge, SW1 (Knightsbridge), 020-7201 8000; fax 020-7201 8080 S
8 Norris St., SW1 (Piccadilly Circus), 020-7321 2755; fax 020-7839 5827 S
11 Jamestown Rd., NW1 (Camden Town), 020-7428 0800; fax 020-7482 4887 S
1A Ropemaker St., EC2 (Moorgate), 020-7588 2688
109 Fleet St., EC4 (Blackfriars/Chancery Ln.), 020-7583 7889; fax 020-7583 7867

■ A "quick crowd-pleaser" with "communal tables", this "no-frills" chain of "ultra-funky Japanese" "pleasant filling stations" around town is a "must for noodle lovers" "of all ages", offering "low-priced" "wholesome" dishes all "served with a smile"; a few feel this "casual" outfit has "lost its flair", but the faithful fawn the "novelty never wears off" – it "still hits the spot"; N.B. a new City branch opened post-*Survey*.

Wapping Food S | 20 | 22 | 18 | £30 |

Wapping Hydraulic Power Station, Wapping Wall, E1 (Wapping), 020-7680 2080; fax 020-7680 2081

◪ A Modern British "oasis in a culinary desert", this "really interesting" Wapping "space and concept" set in a former generating station looks like a "mini Tate Modern", with "surroundings that range from industrial machinery to art exhibitions"; it's a "sophisticated eating experience" rave acolytes who praise the "adventurous, daily changing menu", "superb Aussie wine list" and "staff that hit just the right note"; knockers quibble that the "food is so-so and service an afterthought."

Waterloo Fire Station S | 14 | 13 | 12 | £23 |

150 Waterloo Rd., SE1 (Waterloo), 020-7620 2226; fax 020-7633 9161

◪ The "simply served" Modern British "grub" is "fine as long as you can stand the noise" from the "lively bar" at this "huge" Waterloo gastro-pub set in a converted fire station; foes fume at the "undistinguished" fare ("go for a drink, not a meal"), nevertheless this "very popular" spot "certainly has its fan club."

WATERSIDE INN 🇸 | 26 | 25 | 26 | £71 |
Waterside Inn, Ferry Rd., Bray-on-Thames, Berkshire, 01628 620691; fax 01628 784710

■ It "all comes together like a well-rehearsed orchestra" at this "sophisticated" yet "not at all stuffy" inn in Berkshire, with "wonderful rooms" and a "lovely view" of the Thames; it's a "must for romantic dates", enhanced by Michel Roux's "high-calibre" French cooking and "impeccable service" ("as my napkin hit the floor, I was handed a replacement!"); alas, the "best things in life are not necessarily free", though even diners daunted by the "breathtaking prices" claim it's "worth every penny."

Waterstones Red Room | 14 | 14 | 12 | £26 |
Waterstones, 203-206 Piccadilly, W1 (Piccadilly Circus), 020-7851 2464; fax 020-7851 2469

■ "Good" for a "quick, value lunch" of Modern British fare say fans of this "basement" in-store eaterie at Waterstones bookstore in Piccadilly; still, the majority write it off as "hit-or-miss", with food that's as "uninteresting" as a "bad novel" and "indifferent service"; N.B. the fifth-floor cafe also serves a light menu.

Westbourne, The 🇸 | 16 | 17 | 12 | £21 |
101 Westbourne Park Villas, W2 (Royal Oak/Westbourne Park), 020-7221 1332; fax 020-7243 8081

■ With its "simple", "wholesome" Eclectic fare and "fun", "lively" atmosphere, this "friendly", "laid-back" Notting Hill gastro-pub attracts a "wide variety of people of all ages and professions"; the "lovely outside" terrace is "particularly comfortable" – and "the place to be seen if the sun comes out in London"; critics, however, are "put off" by the "unexceptional food" and "rude staff."

West Street ● | 20 | 18 | 19 | £42 |
13-15 West St., WC2 (Leicester Sq.), 020-7010 8600; fax 020-7010 8601

■ It's "improving all the time" is the loyalists' view of this "interesting" Theatreland newcomer, a "pleasant, minimalist" two-floor venue serving Modern British–Italian fare and wood-fired pizzas; "given the pedigree of the kitchen" (it's run by Rowley Leigh of Kensington Place fame), some say the "food is a letdown", but most agree the "excellent bar downstairs" is worth checking out – that's where "all the action" is.

Wheeler's, St. James's | – | – | – | E |
12A Duke of York St., SW1 (Piccadilly Circus), 020-7930 2460
Revitalized with a glossy makeover and an upscale, classy Modern British seafood menu, this 50-year-old St. James's eaterie is the only link in the stalwart seafood chain to

| F | D | S | C |

reopen after being sold last year to Marco Pierre White and Robert Earl (of Planet Hollywood); plans are underway to roll out a number of similar venues in the months to come.

Wilton's S 23 | 21 | 22 | £52
55 Jermyn St., SW1 (Green Park/Piccadilly Circus), 020-7629 9955; fax 020-7495 6233
■ A Traditional British "old-school treat" that requires a jacket and tie, this "clubby" St. James's "institution", dating back to 1742, offers the "perfect classical dining experience"; the "kitchen seems rejuvenated" purr acolytes who adore the "wonderful seafood" as well as the "very high standards of service"; whilst a few say it's "rather too grand", most find its "immense charm" "reassuring"; N.B. the above Food rating may be impacted by the post-*Survey* arrival of chef Jerome Ponchelle, formerly of The Connaught.

Windows on the World S 18 | 22 | 18 | £45
Hilton Park Lane, 22 Park Ln., W1 (Hyde Park Corner), 020-7208 4021; fax 020-7208 4144
☒ "The view is spectacular" from this 28th-floor restaurant/bar atop the Park Lane Hilton ooh and ah admirers who suggest you use the "fabulous", "romantic" setting to "impress your date"; whilst some say the Classic French fare is "good", others say "never mind the inconsistent food" – just make sure you "get a table by the window."

Wòdka ●S 18 | 15 | 18 | £30
12 St. Albans Grove, W8 (High St. Kensington), 020-7937 6513; fax 020-7937 8621
☒ "Forget all your prejudices about Polish fare – this "slightly decadent" Kensington "novelty" is "ace", with "models as waitresses" serving "interesting", "hearty" Eastern European dishes; the "amazing choice of vodkas" (thus the name) may lead you on a "journey into the land of euphoria" ("having tested the drinks menu, I can't recall much about the food"), so "beware of between-course" shots – or at least "have a taxi waiting!"

Wok Wok S 14 | 12 | 13 | £18
7 Kensington High St., W8 (High St. Kensington), 020-7938 1221; fax 020-7938 3330
140 Fulham Rd., SW10 (Fulham Broadway/South Kensington), 020-7370 5355; fax 020-7244 0600
30 Hill St. (Richmond), Richmond, 020-8332 2646; fax 020-8332 9171
☒ "Always busy and bustling", this "congenial", "casual" noodle-bar chain is "great for a quick bite" of "fresh", "yummy" "Asian food at reasonable tabs"; it's "surprisingly tasty" – "much better than you would expect" – and "good value" too; foes suggest this "once promising" outfit is "not as good as it used to be", citing "slapdash service" and "uninteresting food" that "lacks character"; N.B. the Chiswick and Angel branches have closed.

| F | D | S | C |

Wong Kei ●🅂⇗ | 12 | 6 | 5 | £13 |
41-43 Wardour St., W1 (Leicester Sq./Piccadilly Circus), 020-7437 8408

◩ "No one believes quite how rude they can be" at this Chinatown "masochist's paradise" where the "scary" service is an "integral part of the experience"; as for the Chinese cooking, opinions are mixed: the inarguably "cheap" fare strikes some as "surprisingly good" and others as "so bad, it makes you crave a sandwich."

Yas 🅂 | ▽ | 19 | 11 | 16 | £23 |
31-33 Sussex Pl., W2 (Paddington), 020-7706 2633
7 Hammersmith Rd., W14 (Olympia), 020-7603 9148 ●

■ "Don't be fooled by its humble location" near Olympia, because the clientele at this "authentic" Persian stalwart includes "real Iranians" and other "beautiful people" sporting "diamond Rolexes"; the "tasty", traditional dishes are all the better when paired with flatbread from "a special oven"; N.B. a Marylebone branch opened post-*Survey*.

Yatra 🅂 | ▽ | 16 | 18 | 17 | £32 |
34 Dover St., W1 (Green Park), 020-7493 0200; fax 020-7493 4228

◩ "Fab-looking" decor (including a waterfall in the dining room) makes a "pleasing" backdrop for the "unusual blend" of traditional and contemporary Indian dishes at this "enjoyable" Mayfair eaterie; there's also live music and dancing in the downstairs club, Bar Bollywood.

Yellow River Cafe | 15 | 14 | 13 | £22 |
12 Chiswick High Rd., W4 (Stamford Brook), 020-8987 9791 🅂
206 Upper St., N1 (Highbury & Islington), 020-7354 8833 🅂
10 Cabot Sq., E14 (Canary Wharf), 020-7715 9515;
fax 020-7715 9528

◩ With branches from Chiswick to Canary Wharf, this "clever", "handy and cheap" Pan-Asian chain has won many fans with its "hearty", "surprisingly interesting" meals; however, vocal foes claim the offerings are "neither comforting nor outstanding" and implore "more variety, please"; N.B. the St. John's Wood branch has closed.

Ye Olde Cheshire Cheese 🅂 | 13 | 20 | 15 | £21 |
145 Fleet St., EC4 (Blackfriars), 020-7353 6170; fax 020-7353 0845

◩ There's a "terrific Dickensian ambience" at this nearly "400-year-old" Fleet Street pub that may be a tad "corny" but remains "a must for tourists" wanting a taste of "very olde London"; as for the "cheap and cheerful grub", some think "what they do, they do very well", whilst others suggest "go right for the port and Stilton."

Yoshino | 23 | 18 | 19 | £27 |
3 Piccadilly Pl., W1 (Piccadilly Circus), 020-7287 6622;
fax 020-7254 6751

■ A welcome "change from the conveyor-belt restaurants", this "unpretentious" "treasure hidden" away in a Piccadilly

www.zagat.com

alley offers "well-presented", "superb" sushi, sashimi and other "authentic Japanese victuals" amid a "relaxed dining atmosphere"; there are also "good values" to be found here, including a prix fixe lunch for £5.80.

Yo! Sushi S | 15 | 13 | 13 | £20

11-13 Bayley St., WC1 (Goodge St./Tottenham Court Rd.), 020-7636 0076
52 Poland St., W1 (Oxford Circus), 020-7287 0443 ●
Selfridges, 400 Oxford St., W1 (Bond St.), 020-7318 3944; fax 020-7318 3885
Harvey Nichols, Knightsbridge, 5th fl., SW1 (Knightsbridge), 020-7201 8641
O₂ Ctr., 255 Finchley Rd., NW3 (Finchley Rd.), 020-7431 4499
95 Farringdon Rd., EC1 (Farringdon), 020-7841 0785
Unit 2, N1 Centre, Parkfield St., N1 (Angel Station), 020-7359 3507

"What a sushi bar should be", this "cute, kitschy" chain follows a "very modern" formula of "decent"-quality "little morsels" served via conveyor belt and "robot waiter" in a "bright", "futuristic" setting; if for a few it's "lost its attraction" ("uneven", "expensive for what it is"), most "love" the "sheer fun" of it, especially "in a group" or when a "serious craving" hits; a new Islington branch opened post-*Survey*.

Yum Yum Thai S | ▽ 20 | 14 | 16 | £25

30 Stoke Newington Church St., N16 (Seven Sisters), 020-7254 6751; fax 020-7241 3857

This "great local" Stoke Newington Thai offers "all you want in a neighbourhood restaurant": traditional cuisine that's both "good and cheap" as well as truly "friendly service" ("that's what hospitality is all about"); better yet, cognoscenti consider their rice dishes "a tried-and-true hangover cure" that really "works"!

ZAFFERANO S | 25 | 20 | 21 | £47

15 Lowndes St., SW1 (Knightsbridge), 020-7235 5800

"Beg for a table" urge devotees of this "intimate", "secluded" Belgravia establishment that "ranks amongst the finest" (once again it's rated the *Survey*'s No. 1 Italian) thanks to Andrew Needham's "impeccable" cooking that "scales the heights", as does the "truly professional" service and "excellent wine list"; if a disgruntled few "can't see why it's so hard to get in" ("over-hyped"), that cuts no ice with fans who say it's simply "*magnifico.*"

Zaika S | 23 | 20 | 19 | £41

1 Kensington High St., W8 (High St. Kensington), 020-7795 6533; fax 020-7937 8854

Diners are divided as to whether "the move to new premises" has been an improvement for Claudio Pulze's "upscale" Indian in a "spacious" former Kensington bank, but there is widespread applause for Vineet Bhatia's "imaginative", "subtle" cuisine that reflects a "remarkable blending of flavours"; if there are a few whispers that the kitchen "has slipped a bit", as far as most are concerned this "joy and delight" still deserves its accolade as one of "London's best."

Zaika Bazaar 20 | 17 | 18 | £28

2A Pond Pl., SW3 (South Kensington), 020-7584 6655; fax 020-7584 6755

☑ "Eat and shop simultaneously" at this "informal" Zaika offshoot in a "pleasant" Chelsea "basement", where the "delicious" Modern Indian bites are "promptly served" at "extremely reasonable prices"; there's also the added attraction of being able to purchase the "beautiful" native artefacts that adorn the premises.

Zamoyski S ▽ 20 | 15 | 20 | £23

85 Fleet Rd., NW3 (Belsize Park), 020-7794 4792

☑ It's got the "right mix of everything" applaud admirers of the "fantastic Polish home cooking" and "great vodka" list at this "naff, but cosy" Belsize Park place; insiders suggest you "go on a Friday or Saturday night" to hear performances of Eastern European folk songs.

Zen Central ●S 20 | 18 | 18 | £36

20 Queen St., W1 (Green Park), 020-7629 8089; fax 020-7493 6181

☑ "Terrific" "reliable" multiregional Chinese fare and "friendly service" make this "upscale" Mayfair Zen sib the "pick of the chain" for some enlightened surveyors; others fail to see the light, claiming it's a "yawn", as "nothing stands out" on the "rather pricey" menu; your call.

Zen Chelsea ●S 18 | 14 | 15 | £34

Chelsea Cloisters, 85 Sloane Ave., SW3 (South Kensington), 020-7589 1781; fax 020-7584 0596

☑ Surveyors seeking "above-average Chinese" dishes (including "good-value dim sum") and "attentive service" head to the Zen group's "well-established" original venue in Chelsea; less-enthused diners claim it "needs reviving" – the "disappointing food" has "lost its charm."

ZeNW3 S 18 | 14 | 15 | £31

83-84 Hampstead High St., NW3 (Hampstead), 020-7794 7863; fax 020-7794 6956

☑ Still a "favourite family restaurant", this Hampstead Zen outpost has its devotees who appreciate the "lovely", "high-class" Chinese fare, "nice atmosphere" and "efficient staff"; "what a comedown" fume foes, claiming the "food is not good enough to compensate" for the "heavy bill."

Ziani ●S 21 | 15 | 20 | £34

45 Radnor Walk, SW3 (Sloane Sq.), 020-7351 5297; fax 020-7244 8387

■ "You are seated close, so no secrets should be shared" at this "nice neighbourhood place" in Chelsea where the

F | D | S | C

"excellent" Italian "food is good enough to overlook the cramped quarters"; "service can be over-effusive", but it's all part of the "welcoming trattoria" experience.

Zilli S
20 | 15 | 16 | £31

210 Kensington Park Rd., W11 (Ladbroke Grove), 020-7792 1066; fax 020-7734 7786

■ "Young, old, fashion crowds, families – all seem welcome at" celeb chef Aldo Zilli's "vibrant" Notting Hill offshoot, a "bustling atmosphere" for dining on "wonderful" Modern Italian dishes (from a Sardinian chef) including "great seafood"; it's "good, but not individual enough" baulk bashers who deem it "nothing special" and "very noisy."

Zilli Fish ☻
20 | 16 | 17 | £33

8-18 Wild St., WC2 (Covent Garden/Holborn), 020-7240 0011
36-40 Brewer St., W1 (Piccadilly Circus), 020-7734 8649; fax 020-7734 7786

◪ The "well-presented", "fantastic", "fresh fish" dishes are "creatively dealt with" at Aldo Zilli's "buzzy", "comfy" and "very friendly" Soho Italian seafooder and its "excellent" sibling, a Covent Garden yearling; faultfinders feel the "service is not great" and find it "overpriced"; N.B. the Wild Street site also has a wood-burning pizza oven.

Zinc Bar & Grill
15 | 15 | 14 | £31

21 Heddon St., W1 (Oxford Circus/Piccadilly Circus), 020-7255 8899; fax 020-7255 8888

◪ "Hearty" Modern British fare and "moderately priced wines" are "courteously" served in a "pretty convincing brasserie atmosphere" at this "casual Conran venue" just off Regent Street that's "typical of its kind but good" for a "fun night out"; gripers, however, complain it's "starting to look tired" and find the "service surly."

Zizzi S
17 | 15 | 15 | £20

20 Bow St., WC2 (Holborn), 020-7836 6101
73-75 The Strand, WC2 (Charing Cross), 020-7240 1717; fax 020-7379 9753 ☻
231 Chiswick High Rd., W4 (Chiswick), 020-8747 9400
35-38 Paddington St., W1 (Baker St.), 020-7224 1450 ☻
35-37 Battersea Rd., SW11 (Clapham South), 020-7924 7311 ☻
87 Allitsen Rd., NW8 (St. John's Wood), 020-7722 7296

■ "Surprisingly good for a chain", these "homey", "family"-oriented places about town offer wood-fired pizzas plus Modern Italian fare that's "fine" for a "casual supper"; "staff retain good humour" even when the place is "full of children", though some quip that "service can be slow."

Zucca S
17 | 16 | 15 | £28

188 Westbourne Grove, W11 (Notting Hill Gate), 020-7727 0060; fax 020-7726 0069

◪ "Tasty" Modern Italian food, including "consistently fresh and perfectly cooked fish dishes", and "proper service" make this "pleasant" Notting Hill spot a "favourite local" that most seem to "like more and more"; a smattering squawk that staff "could be much better."

Zuccato | 19 | 15 | 15 | £22 |

O₂ Ctr., 255 Finchley Rd., NW3 (Finchley Rd.), 020-7431 1799; fax 020-7431 7198 ●🅂
41 Bow Ln., EC4 (Mansion House), 020-7329 6364
■ With "interesting", "well-prepared" Modern Italian fare that's "great for casual outings, whether business or family", this "lively and enjoyable" Finchley and City duo seems to have its "excellent formula" down; whilst a few feel the food can be "very mixed", they're in the minority – most simply "love coming here."

Zuma 🅂 | – | – | – | E |

5 Raphael St., SW7 (Knightsbridge), 020-7584 1010; fax 020-7584 5005
Attracting a glam crowd, this sophisticated, modern-looking Knightsbridge newcomer is making a big splash on the scene due to its interesting take on authentic Japanese fare, with a vast variety offered under one roof; the large space features a fully equipped sushi bar, traditional robata grill and chef's table, plus there's a sake bar where you can sample over 25 different varieties.

Indexes

CUISINES
LOCATIONS
SPECIAL FEATURES

Indexes list the best of many within each category.

Cuisine Index

CUISINES

Argentinean
El Gaucho (multi. loc.)
Gaucho Grill (multi. loc.)

Asian
Asia de Cuba (WC2)
Champor-Champor (SE1)
Cicada (EC1)
E&O (W11)
itsu (SW3)
Jim Thompson's Wok (multi. loc.)
Singapura (multi. loc.)
Sugar Reef (W1)
Tiger Lil's (multi. loc.)
Upstairs/Savoy (WC2)
Wok Wok (multi. loc.)
Yellow River Cafe (multi. loc.)

Bangladesh
Ginger (W2)

Barbecue
Arkansas Cafe (E1)

Belgian
Belgo Centraal (WC2)
Belgo Noord (NW1)
Belgo Zuid (W10)
Bierodrome (multi. loc.)

Brasseries
Balans (multi. loc.)
Bluebird (SW3)
Brasserie/Sans Culottes (WC2)
Brasserie St. Quentin (SW3)
Browns Rest. (multi. loc.)
Café des Amis du Vin (WC2)
Cafe Rouge (multi. loc.)
Camden Brasserie (NW1)
Cantina Vinopolis (SE1)
Chez Gérard (multi. loc.)
Elena's l'Etoile (W1)
House/Rosslyn Hill (NW3)
La Brasserie (SW3)
Langan's Brasserie (W1)
Le Metro (SW3)
Le Palais du Jardin (WC2)
L'Estaminet (WC2)
Mustards Smithfield (EC1)
Notting Hill Brasserie (W11)
1 Lombard St. Brass. (EC3)
Oxo Tower Brasserie (SE1)
Pacific Oriental (EC2)
Quaglino's (SW1)
Randall & Aubin (multi. loc.)
Tuttons Brasserie (WC2)

Union Cafe (W1)
Zinc B&G (W1)

Brazilian
Rodizio Rico (W2)

British (Modern)
Alastair Little (W1)
Alastair Little/Lancaster Rd. (W11)
Anglesea Arms (W6)
Atlantic B&G (W1)
Axis (WC2)
Balans (multi. loc.)
Bankside (SE1)
Belvedere (W8)
Bistrot 190 (SW7)
Bradley's (NW3)
Brinkley's (SW10)
Browns Rest. (multi. loc.)
Builders Arms (SW3)
Cafe at Sotheby's (W1)
Cafe, Level Seven (SE1)
Catch (SW5)
Che (SW1)
Chez Bruce (SW17)
Chiswick, The (W4)
Circus (W1)
City Rhodes (EC4)
Clarke's (W8)
Clerkenwell Din. Rm./Bar (EC1)
Clock (W7)
Cotto (W14)
Cow, The (W2)
Creelers (SW3)
Crescent (W1)
Cucina (NW3)
Dan's (SW3)
Dibbens (EC1)
Duke of Cambridge (N1)
Engineer (NW1)
English Garden (SW3)
Fifth Floor (SW1)
First Floor (W11)
Fishmarket (EC2)
Frederick's (N1)
Gladwins (EC3)
Glaister's Garden (multi. loc.)
Glasshouse (Kew)
Globe (NW3)
Gravetye Manor (W. Sus)
Greenhouse (W1)
Harry's Social Club (W2)
Hartwell House (Bucks)
Havelock Tavern (W14)
Honest Cabbage (SE1)

Cuisine Index

Hush (W1)
Ifield (SW10)
Indigo (WC2)
Ivy (WC2)
Joe's (SW3)
Joe's Rest. Bar (SW1)
Julie's (W11)
Just St. James's (SW1)
Kensington Place (W8)
Lansdowne (NW1)
Launceston Place (W8)
Le Cafe du Jardin (WC2)
Le Caprice (SW1)
Le Metro (SW3)
Mesclun (N16)
Motcomb's (SW1)
Noble Rot (W1)
Notting Hill Brasserie (W11)
Odette's (NW1)
192 (W11)
Oxo Tower (SE1)
Palm Court (WC2)
Parade (W5)
People's Palace (SE1)
Pharmacy (W11)
Philip Owens' (WC2)
Phoenix B&G (SW15)
Polygon B&G (SW4)
Portrait (WC2)
Prince Bonaparte (W2)
Prism (EC3)
Prospect Grill (WC2)
Pug (W4)
Quaglino's (SW1)
Ransome's Dock (SW11)
Red Cube B&G (WC2)
Redmonds (SW14)
Rhodes in the Square (SW1)
Richard Corrigan/Lindsay (W1)
R.S.J. (SE1)
Salt House (NW8)
Scotts (W1)
Searcy's/Barbican (EC2)
Sir Charles Napier (Oxon)
Smiths of Smithfield - Din. (EC1)
Smiths of Smithfield-Top (EC1)
Snows on the Green (W6)
Sonny's (SW13)
Stepping Stone (SW8)
St. John (EC1)
Tate Gallery Rest. (SW1)
Tenth (W8)
Terminus (EC2)
Terrace (W8)
Thyme (SW4)
Troubadour (SW5)
Tuttons Brasserie (WC2)

Union Cafe (W1)
Vale (W9)
Villandry (W1)
Vine (NW5)
Vineyard/Stockcross (Berks)
Vingt-Quatre (SW10)
Wapping Food (E1)
Waterloo Fire Station (SE1)
Waterstones Red Rm. (W1)
West Street (WC2)
Wheeler's, St. James's (SW1)
Zinc B&G (W1)

British (Traditional)
Bentley's (W1)
Boisdale (multi. loc.)
Bug-Bar, Rest. & Lounge (SW2)
Butlers Wharf Chop Hse. (SE1)
Chelsea Bun (multi. loc.)
Cow, The (W2)
Dorchester, Grill Rm. (W1)
ffiona's (W8)
Fish! (multi. loc.)
Fortnum's Fountain (W1)
French Horn (Berks)
George Bar (EC2)
Goring Dining Rm. (SW1)
Greens (SW1)
Grenadier (SW1)
Grumbles (SW1)
Hartwell House (Bucks)
Honest Cabbage (SE1)
Langan's Brasserie (W1)
Langan's Coq d'Or (SW5)
Maggie Jones's (W8)
Monkeys (SW3)
Odin's (W1)
Porters (WC2)
Quality Chop Hse. (EC1)
Rib Room/Oyster Bar (SW1)
Richoux (multi. loc.)
Ritz (W1)
RK Stanley's (W1)
Rowley's (SW1)
Rules (WC2)
Savoy Grill (WC2)
Savoy River (WC2)
Scotts (W1)
Shepherd's (SW1)
Simpson's/Strand/Grand (WC2)
Simpson's/Strand/Simply (WC2)
St. John (EC1)
Wilton's (SW1)
Ye Olde Cheshire Cheese (EC4)

Burmese
Mandalay (W2)

www.zagat.com 173

Cuisine Index

Chinese
Aroma Chinese (multi. loc.)
Bayee House (multi. loc.)
China Dream (NW3)
China House (W1)
Chuen Cheng Ku (W1)
Dorchester, Oriental (W1)
East One (EC1)
ECapital (W1)
Feng Shang Floating Rest. (NW1)
Four Regions (SE1)
Four Seasons Chinese (W2)
Fung Shing (WC2)
Golden Dragon (W1)
Good Earth (multi. loc.)
Green Cottage (NW3)
Gung-Ho (NW6)
Hakkasan (W1)
Harbour City (W1)
Hunan (SW1)
Imperial City (EC3)
Jade Garden (W1)
Jen Hong Kong (W1)
Joy King Lau (WC2)
Kai (W1)
Kaifeng (NW4)
Lee Fook (W2)
Lee Ho Fook (W1)
Mandarin Kitchen (W2)
Mao Tai (multi. loc.)
Memories of China (multi. loc.)
Mr. Chow (SW1)
Mr. Kong (WC2)
Mr. Wing (SW5)
New Culture Rev. (multi. loc.)
New World (W1)
Poons (multi. loc.)
Poons in the City (EC3)
Princess Garden (W1)
Royal China (multi. loc.)
Singapore Garden (NW6)
Wong Kei (W1)
Zen Central (W1)
Zen Chelsea (SW3)
ZeNW3 (NW3)

Chophouses
Black & Blue (W8)
Butlers Wharf Chop Hse. (SE1)
Christopher's (multi. loc.)
Criterion Grill (W1)
El Gaucho (multi. loc.)
Gaucho Grill (multi. loc.)
Notting Grill (W11)
Parisienne Chophse. (SW3)
Pope's Eye (multi. loc.)
Quality Chop Hse. (EC1)
Rib Room/Oyster Bar (SW1)
Rules (WC2)
Smiths of Smithfield - Din. (EC1)
Smiths of Smithfield-Top (EC1)
Sophie's Steakhse. (SW10)
Tuscan Steak (WC2)

Cuban
Asia de Cuba (WC2)

Danish
Lundum's (SW7)

Dim Sum
China Dream (NW3)
China House (W1)
Chuen Cheng Ku (W1)
Dorchester, Oriental (W1)
Golden Dragon (W1)
Hakkasan (W1)
Harbour City (W1)
Jade Garden (W1)
Joy King Lau (WC2)
Lee Ho Fook (W1)
Mr. Wing (SW5)
New World (W1)
Royal China (multi. loc.)
Zen Chelsea (SW3)

Eclectic/International
Andrew Edmunds (W1)
Archipelago (W1)
Aurora (EC2)
Axis (WC2)
Balans (multi. loc.)
Bankside (SE1)
Bibendum (SW3)
Bibendum Oyster Bar (SW3)
Bistrot 190 (SW7)
Blakes Hotel (SW7)
Blue Print Cafe (SE1)
Books for Cooks (W11)
Brinkley's (SW10)
Browns Rest. (multi. loc.)
Bug-Bar, Rest. & Lounge (SW2)
Cafe Med (multi. loc.)
Cantina Vinopolis (SE1)
Caviar Kaspia (W1)
Che (SW1)
Chez Moi (W11)
Cinnamon Cay (SW11)
Collection (SW3)
Ebury Wine Bar (SW1)
Engineer (NW1)
Enterprise (SW3)
Fifth Floor Cafe (SW1)
First Floor (W11)
Fish Hoek (W4)

Cuisine Index

Food for Thought (WC2)
Four Seasons, Lanes (W1)
Gate (multi. loc.)
Giraffe (multi. loc.)
Granita (N1)
Ifield (SW10)
Just the Bridge (EC4)
Kettners (W1)
Lanesborough (SW1)
Lansdowne (NW1)
Le Cafe du Jardin (WC2)
Livebait (multi. loc.)
Manor (W11)
Mustards Smithfield (EC1)
MVH (SW13)
Myna Bird (WC1)
Naked Turtle (SW14)
1 Lombard St. Brass. (EC3)
190, Downstairs (SW7)
Otto Dining Lounge (W9)
PJ's Bar & Grill (SW3)
PJ's Grill (WC2)
Pomegranates (SW1)
Prospect Grill (WC2)
Providores/Tapa Rm. (W1)
Red Cube B&G (WC2)
Spoon+ at Sanderson (W1)
Sugar Club (W1)
Sugar Reef (W1)
Tenth (W8)
Terminus (EC2)
T.G.I. Friday's (multi. loc.)
Toast (NW3)
Tom's Deli (W11)
Villandry (W1)
Vingt-Quatre (SW10)
Wapping Food (E1)
Westbourne (W2)

Fish 'n' Chips

Fish! (multi. loc.)
Geale's Fish (W8)
George Bar (EC2)
Livebait (multi. loc.)
Nautilus Fish (NW6)
Rudland Stubbs (EC1)
Seashell (NW1)
Sweetings (EC4)
Two Brothers Fish (N3)

French (Bistro)

Bibendum Oyster Bar (SW3)
Café Boheme (W1)
Café des Amis du Vin (WC2)
Cafe Rouge (multi. loc.)
Chez Gérard (multi. loc.)
Elena's l'Etoile (W1)
Glaister's Garden (multi. loc.)
Grumbles (SW1)
Incognico (WC2)
La Bouchée (SW7)
Langan's Bistro (W1)
Langan's Coq d'Or (SW5)
La Poule au Pot (SW1)
La Trouvaille (W1)
L'Aventure (NW8)
Le Boudin Blanc (W1)
Le Café du Marché (EC1)
Le Mercury (N1)
L'Escargot (W1)
Monsieur Max (Hampton Hill)
Parisienne Chophse. (SW3)
Patisserie Valerie (multi. loc.)
Quality Chop Hse. (EC1)
Tartuf (N1)
Thierry's (SW3)
Truc Vert (W1)

French (Classic)

Almeida (N1)
Aubergine (SW10)
Beoty's (WC2)
Brasserie Roux (SW1)
Brasserie/Sans Culottes (WC2)
Brasserie St. Quentin (SW3)
Chez Bruce (SW17)
Chez Gérard (multi. loc.)
Chez Max (SW10)
Club Gascon (EC1)
Coq d'Argent (EC2)
Drones (SW1)
Elena's l'Etoile (W1)
Embassy (W1)
Foliage (SW1)
French House (W1)
John Burton-Race (NW1)
La Bouchée (SW7)
La Brasserie (SW3)
Langan's Brasserie (W1)
La Poule au Pot (SW1)
La Tante Claire (SW1)
L'Aventure (NW8)
Le Boudin Blanc (W1)
Le Café du Marché (EC1)
Le Colombier (SW3)
Le Gavroche (W1)
Le Palais du Jardin (WC2)
L'Escargot (W1)
L'Estaminet (WC2)
Les Trois Garcons (E1)
Le Suquet (SW3)
Lobster Pot (SE11)
L'Oranger (SW1)
Lou Pescadou (SW5)
Mirabelle (W1)

Cuisine Index

Monkeys (SW3)
Mon Plaisir (WC2)
Monsieur Max (Hampton Hill)
Odin's (W1)
Oslo Court (NW8)
Parisienne Chophse. (SW3)
Poissonnerie de l'Avenue (SW3)
Racine (SW3)
Ritz (W1)
Simply Nico (multi. loc.)
Stratford's (W8)
Vineyard/Stockcross (Berks)
Waterside Inn (Berks)
Windows on the World (W1)

French (New)

Admiralty (WC2)
Aubergine (SW10)
Bam-Bou (W1)
Belair House (SE21)
Belvedere (W8)
Bibendum (SW3)
Bleeding Heart (multi. loc.)
Bush Bar & Grill (W12)
Capital (SW3)
Caviar Kaspia (W1)
Cellar Gascon (EC1)
Chez Moi (W11)
Chinon (W14)
Cliveden, Waldo's (Berks)
Club Gascon (EC1)
Coq d'Argent (EC2)
Crivelli's Garden (WC2)
Deca (W1)
Don, The (EC4)
Drones (SW1)
Fat Duck (Berks)
Foliage (SW1)
Gordon Ramsay/Claridge's (W1)
Gordon Ramsay/68 Royal (SW3)
Incognico (WC2)
John Burton-Race (NW1)
La Cage Imaginaire (NW3)
La Trompette (W4)
Le Cabanon (W1)
Le Manoir/Quat'Saisons (Oxon)
L'Escargot (W1)
Le Soufflé (W1)
LMNT (E8)
L'Oranger (SW1)
Maison Novelli (EC1)
Maquis (W6)
Mirabelle (W1)
Mon Plaisir (WC2)
1 Lombard St. (EC3)
One-O-One (SW1)
One-Seven-Nine (WC2)

Orrery (W1)
Pétrus (SW1)
Pied à Terre (W1)
Putney Bridge (SW15)
QC (WC1)
Roussillon (SW1)
Simply Nico (multi. loc.)
Square (W1)
Terrace (W1)
Vong (SW1)
Waterside Inn (Berks)

Greek

Beoty's (WC2)
Costa's Grill (W8)
Daphne (NW1)
Greek Valley (NW8)
Halepi (multi. loc.)
Kalamaras Taverna (W2)
Lemonia (NW1)
Real Greek (N1)
Vrisaki (N22)

Hamburgers

Arkansas Cafe (E1)
Big Easy (SW3)
Black & Blue (W8)
Ed's Easy Diner (multi. loc.)
Hard Rock Cafe (W1)
Joe Allen (WC2)
Kettners (W1)
Maxwell's (multi. loc.)
PJ's Bar & Grill (SW3)
PJ's Grill (WC2)
Planet Hollywood (W1)
Sticky Fingers (W8)
T.G.I. Friday's (multi. loc.)
Tootsies (multi. loc.)
Vingt-Quatre (SW10)

Hungarian

Gay Hussar (W1)

Indian

Bengal Clipper (SE1)
Bombay Bicycle Club (SW12)
Bombay Brasserie (SW7)
Cafe Lazeez (multi. loc.)
Cafe Spice Namaste (multi. loc.)
Chor Bizarre (W1)
Chutney Mary (SW10)
Chutney's (NW1)
Cinnamon Club (SW1)
Gopal's of Soho (W1)
Great Nepalese (NW1)
Kastoori (SW17)
Khan's (W2)
Khan's of Kensington (SW7)

Cuisine Index

Lahore Kebab Hse. (E1)
La Porte des Indes (W1)
Ma Goa (SW15)
Malabar (W8)
Malabar Junction (WC1)
Masala Zone (W1)
Mela (WC2)
Memories of India (multi. loc.)
Noor Jahan (SW5)
Ophim (W1)
Painted Heron (SW10)
Parsee (N19)
Quilon (SW1)
Rani (N3)
Rasa (multi. loc.)
Ravi Shankar (multi. loc.)
Red Fort (W1)
Salloos (SW1)
Sarkhel's (SW18)
Soho Spice (W1)
Star of India (SW5)
Tabla (E14)
Tamarind (W1)
Tandoori of Chelsea (SW3)
Vama (SW10)
Veeraswamy (W1)
Yatra (W1)
Zaika (W8)
Zaika Bazaar (SW3)

Irish
Richard Corrigan/Lindsay (W1)

Italian (Contemporary)
Alba (EC1)
Al Duca (SW1)
Al San Vincenzo (W2)
Aperitivo (W1)
Arancia (SE16)
Ark (W8)
Artigiano (NW3)
Bertorelli (multi. loc.)
Bice (W1)
Black Truffle (NW1)
Buona Sera at the Jam (SW3)
Calzone (multi. loc.)
Caraffini (SW1)
Caravaggio (EC3)
Carpaccio (SW3)
Casale Franco (N1)
Cibo (W14)
Como Lario (SW1)
Daphne's (SW3)
De Cecco (SW6)
Diverso (W1)
Eco (SW4)
Emporio Armani Caffe (SW3)
Enoteca Turi (SW15)

Floriana (SW3)
Florians (N8)
Formula Veneta (SW10)
Four Seasons, Quadrato (E14)
Getti (multi. loc.)
Great Eastern Dining Rm. (EC2)
Green Olive (W9)
Grissini (SW1)
Ibla (W1)
Il Convivio (SW1)
Il Forno (W1)
Il Posto (W11)
Innecto (W1)
Isola (SW1)
Kettners (W1)
L'Accento Italiano (W2)
Light House (SW19)
L'Incontro (SW1)
Little Italy (W1)
Locanda Locatelli (W1)
Luigi's (WC2)
Mediterraneo (W11)
Metrogusto (multi. loc.)
Monza (SW3)
Oliveto (SW1)
Olivo (SW1)
Orsino (W11)
Orso (WC2)
Osteria Antica Bologna (SW11)
Osteria Basilico (W11)
Passione (W1)
Phoenix B&G (SW15)
Pizza Express (multi. loc.)
Pizza Organic (multi. loc.)
Pizza Pomodoro (SW3)
Pizzeria Castello (SE1)
Purple Sage (W1)
Quod (SW1)
Quo Vadis (W1)
Red Pepper (W9)
Riva (SW13)
River Cafe (W6)
Rosmarino (NW8)
Salusbury Pub (NW6)
San Frediano (SW3)
San Lorenzo Fuoriporta (SW19)
Santini (SW1)
Sartoria (W1)
Spago (SW11)
Spiga (multi. loc.)
Strada (W1)
TECA (W1)
Tentazioni (SE1)
Timo (W8)
Toto's (SW3)
Tuscan Steak (WC2)
Vasco & Piero's (W1)

Cuisine Index

Vegia Zena (NW1)
Zafferano (SW1)
Ziani (SW3)
Zilli (W1)
Zilli Fish (multi. loc.)
Zizzi (multi. loc.)
Zucca (W11)
Zuccato (multi. loc.)

Italian (Traditional)

Alloro (W1)
Ask Pizza (multi. loc.)
Assaggi (W2)
Bertorelli (multi. loc.)
Buona Sera (SW11)
Cantinetta Venegazzu (SW11)
Caraffini (SW1)
Carluccio's Caffe (multi. loc.)
Cecconi's (W1)
Condotti (W1)
De Cecco (SW6)
Del Buongustaio (SW15)
Diverso (W1)
Elistano (SW3)
Friends (SW10)
Getti (multi. loc.)
Il Falconiere (SW7)
La Famiglia (SW10)
La Fontana (SW1)
Little Italy (W1)
Luigi's (WC2)
Made in Italy (SW3)
Mimmo d'Ischia (SW1)
Montpeliano (SW7)
Neal Street (WC2)
Osteria Antica Bologna (SW11)
Pellicano (SW3)
Pizza Express (multi. loc.)
Pizza Metro (SW11)
Pucci Pizza (SW3)
Riccardo's (SW3)
Sabbia (SW3)
Sale e Pepe (SW1)
Sambuca (SW1)
Sandrini (SW3)
San Lorenzo (SW3)
Scalini (SW3)
Signor Sassi (SW1)
Signor Zilli (W1)
Spago (multi. loc.)
Spighetta (W1)
Strada (multi. loc.)
Tuscan Steak (WC2)
Vegia Zena (NW1)
Verbanella (SW3)
Ziani (SW3)
Zizzi (NW8)

Japanese

Aykoku-Kaku (EC4)
Benihana (multi. loc.)
Cafe Japan (NW11)
City Miyama (EC4)
Defune (W1)
Hi Sushi (W1)
Ikeda (W1)
Ikkyu (multi. loc.)
itsu (multi. loc.)
Jin Kichi (NW3)
Koi (W8)
Kulu Kulu Sushi (multi. loc.)
Matsuri (SW1)
Mitsukoshi (SW1)
Miyama (W1)
Mju (SW1)
Moshi Moshi Sushi (multi. loc.)
Nobu (W1)
Noto (EC2)
Saga (W1)
Satsuma (W1)
Shogun (W1)
Sumosan (W1)
Suntory (SW1)
Sushi Wong (W8)
Tatsuso (EC1)
Tokyo Diner (WC2)
Tsunami (SW4)
Ubon (E14)
Wagamama (multi. loc.)
Yoshino (W1)
Yo! Sushi (multi. loc.)
Zuma (SW7)

Jewish

Bloom's (NW11)
Reubens (W1)
Solly's (NW11)

Kosher

Bloom's (NW11)
Kaifeng (NW4)
Reubens (W1)
Six-13 (W1)
Solly's (NW11)

Malaysian/Indonesian

Champor-Champor (SE1)
Melati (W1)
Silks & Spice (multi. loc.)
Singapore Garden (NW6)
Singapura (multi. loc.)

Mediterranean

Café Grand Prix (W1)
Cafe Med (multi. loc.)
Camden Brasserie (NW1)

Cuisine Index

Cantaloupe (EC2)
Cantina del Ponte (SE1)
Cantina Vinopolis (SE1)
Crivelli's Garden (WC2)
Duke of Cambridge (N1)
Eagle (EC1)
Fifth Floor Cafe (SW1)
Julono (NW3)
Levant (W1)
Little Bay (multi. loc.)
Moro (EC1)
Nicole's (W1)
Oriel (SW1)
Oxo Tower Brasserie (SE1)
Peasant (EC1)
Pescatori (multi. loc.)
Rocket (W1)

Mexican/Tex-Mex/SW

Cactus Blue (SW3)
Cafe Pacifico (WC2)
Canyon (Richmond)
Dakota (W11)
La Perla B&G (multi. loc.)
Montana (SW6)
Texas Embassy Cantina (SW1)

Middle Eastern

Al Bustan (SW7)
Al Hamra (W1)
Alounak (multi. loc.)
Al Sultan (W1)
Al Waha (W2)
Beiteddine (SW1)
Fairuz (multi. loc.)
Fakhreldine (multi. loc.)
Ishbilia (SW1)
Iznik (N5)
Levant (W1)
Maroush (multi. loc.)
Noura (SW1)
Ozer Rest. & Bar (W1)
Pasha (N1)
Phoenicia (W8)
Sofra (multi. loc.)
Solly's (NW11)
Tas (SE1)
Yas (W2)

Modern European

Abingdon (W8)
Admiral Codrington (SW3)
Andrew Edmunds (W1)
Atlantic B&G (W1)
Aurora (EC2)
Avenue (SW1)
Babylon (W8)
Bank Aldwych (WC2)

Bank Westminster/Zander (SW1)
Blandford Street (W1)
Bluebird (SW3)
Blue Print Cafe (SE1)
Brackenbury (W6)
Brown's Hotel, 1837 (W1)
Byron's (NW3)
Cantina Vinopolis (SE1)
Chives (SW10)
Connaught (W1)
County Hall (SE1)
Cow, The (W2)
Crescent (W1)
Dan's (SW3)
Don, The (EC4)
Electric Brasserie (W11)
English Garden (SW3)
Enterprise (SW3)
Four Seasons, Lanes (W1)
Granita (N1)
House/Rosslyn Hill (NW3)
Ifield (SW10)
Independence (N1)
Ivy (WC2)
J. Sheekey (WC2)
Kennington Lane (SE11)
Le Caprice (SW1)
Le Deuxieme (WC2)
Le Pont de la Tour (SE1)
Lola's (N1)
Mash (W1)
Mezzo (W1)
Nicole's (W1)
Noble Rot (W1)
Oak, The (W2)
1 Lombard St. Brass. (EC3)
One-Seven-Nine (WC2)
Otto Dining Lounge (W9)
People's Palace (SE1)
Perseverance (WC1)
Quo Vadis (W1)
Salisbury Tavern (SW6)
Sand Bar (SW4)
Spoon+ at Sanderson (W1)
Teatro (W1)
Toast (NW3)
Vine (NW5)

Moroccan

Ayoush (W1)
Julono (NW3)
Momo (W1)
Original Tagine (W1)
Pasha (SW7)
Souk (WC2)

Nepalese

Great Nepalese (NW1)

Cuisine Index

North African
Ayoush (W1)
Laurent (NW2)
Levant (W1)
Momo (W1)
Original Tagine (W1)
Pasha (SW7)
Souk (WC2)

North American
Arkansas Cafe (E1)
Big Easy (SW3)
Cactus Blue (SW3)
Canyon (Richmond)
Chelsea Bun (multi. loc.)
Christopher's (multi. loc.)
Dakota (W11)
Ed's Easy Diner (multi. loc.)
Hard Rock Cafe (W1)
Joe Allen (WC2)
Lucky Seven (W2)
Maxwell's (multi. loc.)
Montana (SW6)
PJ's Bar & Grill (SW3)
PJ's Grill (WC2)
Planet Hollywood (W1)
Prospect Grill (WC2)
Rainforest Cafe (W1)
Reubens (W1)
Santa Fe (N1)
Smollensky's/Strand (multi. loc.)
Sophie's Steakhse. (SW10)
Sticky Fingers (W8)
Texas Embassy Cantina (SW1)
T.G.I. Friday's (multi. loc.)
Tootsies (multi. loc.)

Pacific Rim
Blakes Hotel (SW7)
Cinnamon Cay (SW11)
I-Thai (W2)
Oxo Tower (SE1)
Oxo Tower Brasserie (SE1)
Pacific Oriental (EC2)
Polygon B&G (SW4)
Sugar Club (W1)
Yellow River Cafe (multi. loc.)

Persian
Alounak (multi. loc.)
Kandoo (W2)
Yas (W14)

Peruvian
Fina Estampa (SE1)

Pizza
Ask Pizza (multi. loc.)
Buona Sera (SW11)
Calzone (multi. loc.)
Cantina del Ponte (SE1)
Casale Franco (N1)
Condotti (W1)
Eco (multi. loc.)
Friends (SW10)
Il Forno (W1)
Kettners (W1)
La Porchetta Pizzeria (multi. loc.)
Made in Italy (SW3)
Oliveto (SW1)
Orso (WC2)
Pizza Express (multi. loc.)
Pizza Metro (SW11)
Pizza on the Park (SW1)
Pizza Organic (multi. loc.)
Pizza Pomodoro (multi. loc.)
Pizzeria Castello (SE1)
Pucci Pizza (SW3)
Red Pepper (W9)
Rocket (W1)
Spago (SW11)
Spiga (multi. loc.)
Spighetta (W1)
Strada (multi. loc.)
West Street (WC2)
Zizzi (multi. loc.)
Zucca (W11)

Polish
Baltic (SE1)
Daquise (SW7)
Wòdka (W8)
Zamoyski (NW3)

Russian
Caviar Kaspia (W1)
Nikita's (SW10)
Potemkin (EC1)

Scottish
Boisdale (SW1)
Creelers (SW3)

Seafood
Belgo Centraal (WC2)
Belgo Noord (NW1)
Belgo Zuid (W10)
Bentley's (W1)
Bibendum Oyster Bar (SW3)
Bluebird (SW3)
Cafe Fish (W1)
Catch (SW5)
Chamberlain's (EC3)
Creelers (SW3)

Cuisine Index

Fish! (multi. loc.)
Fish Hoek (W4)
Fishmarket (EC2)
Geale's Fish (W8)
Greens (SW1)
Jason's (W9)
J. Sheekey (WC2)
Le Suquet (SW3)
Livebait (multi. loc.)
Lobster Pot (SE11)
Lou Pescadou (SW5)
Manzi's (WC2)
Notting Grill (W11)
190, Downstairs (SW7)
One-O-One (SW1)
Pescatori (multi. loc.)
Poissonnerie de l'Avenue (SW3)
Quaglino's (SW1)
Randall & Aubin (multi. loc.)
Rudland Stubbs (EC1)
Scotts (W1)
Seashell (NW1)
Stratford's (W8)
Stream, Bubble & Shell (EC1)
Sweetings (EC4)
Two Brothers Fish (N3)
Upstairs/Savoy (WC2)
Wheeler's, St. James's (SW1)
Wilton's (SW1)
Zilli Fish (multi. loc.)

South African
Dumela (W4)

South American
La Piragua (N1)

Spanish
Cambio de Tercio (SW5)
Cigala (WC1)
El Blason (SW3)
Eyre Brothers (EC2)
Galicia (W10)
Gaudí (EC1)
La Rueda (multi. loc.)
Lomo (SW10)
Meson Don Felipe (SE1)
Moro (EC1)
Rebato's (SW8)

Sudanese
Mandola (W11)

Swedish/Scandinavian
Garbo's (W1)
Lundum's (SW7)

Thai
Bangkok (SW7)
Ben's Thai (multi. loc.)
Blue Elephant (SW6)
Blue Jade (SW1)
Busaba Eathai (W1)
Busabong Too (SW10)
Chiang Mai (W1)
Churchill Arms (W8)
Esarn Kheaw (W12)
I-Thai (W2)
Lan Na Thai (SW11)
Mango Tree (SW1)
Mezzonine (W1)
Nahm (SW1)
Patara (multi. loc.)
Pepper Tree (SW4)
Silks & Spice (multi. loc.)
Sri Siam (W1)
Sri Siam City (EC2)
Sri Thai (EC4)
Sugar Hut (SW6)
Thai on the River (SW10)
Thai Pavilion (W1)
Thai Square (multi. loc.)
Tuk Tuk Thai (N1)
Vong (SW1)
Yum Yum Thai (N16)

Turkish
Efes Kebab (multi. loc.)
Gallipoli (multi. loc.)
Iznik (N5)
Ozer Rest. & Bar (W1)
Sofra (multi. loc.)
Tas (SE1)

Vegetarian
Bam-Bou (W1)
Blah! Blah! Blah! (W12)
Bug-Bar, Rest. & Lounge (SW2)
Chutney's (NW1)
Food for Thought (WC2)
Gate (multi. loc.)
Kastoori (SW17)
Mildreds (W1)
Place Below (EC2)
Rani (N3)
Rasa (multi. loc.)
Ravi Shankar (multi. loc.)
Roussillon (SW1)

Vietnamese
Bam-Bou (W1)
Nam Long Le Shaker (SW5)
Saigon (W1)
Viet Hoa (E2)

www.zagat.com

Location Index

LOCATIONS

CENTRAL LONDON

Belgravia
Beiteddine
Drones
Ebury Wine Bar
Grenadier
Grissini
Il Convivio
Ishbilia
Lanesborough
La Tante Claire
Memories of China
Mimmo d'Ischia
Motcomb's
Nahm
Oliveto
One-O-One
Pizza on the Park
Rib Room/Oyster Bar
Salloos
Santini
Vong
Zafferano

Bloomsbury
Archipelago
Ask Pizza
Bam-Bou
Bertorelli
Carluccio's Caffe
Chez Gérard
Cigala
Efes Kebab
Elena's l'Etoile
Hakkasan
Ikkyu
La Perla B&G
Le Cabanon
Malabar Junction
Mash
Myna Bird
Passione
Perseverance
Pescatori
Pied à Terre
Poons
Rasa
RK Stanley's
Silks & Spice
Spoon+ at Sanderson
Villandry
Wagamama
Yo! Sushi

Chinatown
Aroma Chinese
Chuen Cheng Ku
ECapital
Fung Shing
Golden Dragon
Harbour City
Ikkyu
itsu
Jade Garden
Jen Hong Kong
Lee Ho Fook
Manzi's
Mr. Kong
New World
Poons
Tokyo Diner
Wong Kei

Covent Garden
Admiralty
Asia de Cuba
Axis
Bank Aldwych
Belgo Centraal
Beoty's
Bertorelli
Bierodrome
Brasserie/Sans Culottes
Browns Rest.
Café des Amis du Vin
Cafe Pacifico
Cafe Rouge
Chez Gérard
Christopher's
Food for Thought
Indigo
Ivy
Joe Allen
J. Sheekey
La Perla B&G
Le Cafe du Jardin
Le Deuxieme
Le Palais du Jardin
L'Estaminet
Livebait
Luigi's
Maxwell's
Mon Plaisir
Neal Street
One-Seven-Nine
Orso

Location Index

Palm Court
Patisserie Valerie
Philip Owens'
Pizza Express
PJ's Grill
Poons
Porters
Prospect Grill
Rules
Savoy Grill
Savoy River
Simpson's/Strand/Grand
Simpson's/Strand/Simply
Smollensky's/Strand
Sofra
T.G.I. Friday's
Tuscan Steak
Tuttons Brasserie
Upstairs/Savoy
Wagamama
West Street
Zilli Fish
Zizzi

Knightsbridge
Brasserie St. Quentin
Cafe Rouge
Capital
Emporio Armani Caffe
Fifth Floor
Fifth Floor Cafe
Floriana
Foliage
Good Earth
Isola
Joe's Rest. Bar
Le Metro
Maroush
Mju
Montpeliano
Monza
Mr. Chow
Parisienne Chophse.
Patara
Patisserie Valerie
Pizza Express
Pizza Pomodoro
Racine
Richoux
Sale e Pepe
San Lorenzo
Signor Sassi
Verbanella
Wagamama
Yo! Sushi
Zuma

Marylebone
Ayoush
Blandford Street
Carluccio's Caffe
Chutney's
Defune
Fairuz
Garbo's
Getti
Giraffe
Great Nepalese
Ibla
Innecto
John Burton-Race
Kandoo
Langan's Bistro
La Porte des Indes
La Rueda
Levant
Locanda Locatelli
Mandalay
Maroush
New Culture Rev.
Odin's
Original Tagine
Orrery
Ozer Rest. & Bar
Patisserie Valerie
Providores/Tapa Rm.
Purple Sage
Ravi Shankar
Reubens
Royal China
Seashell
Six-13
Sofra
Spighetta
Strada
Tootsies
Union Cafe
Wagamama
Yas
Yo! Sushi
Zizzi

Mayfair
Al Hamra
Alloro
Al Sultan
Ask Pizza
Benihana
Bice
Brown's Hotel, 1837
Browns Rest.
Cafe at Sotheby's
Café Grand Prix
Carluccio's Caffe

Location Index

Caviar Kaspia
Cecconi's
Chez Gérard
Chor Bizarre
Condotti
Connaught
Deca
Dorchester, Grill Rm.
Dorchester, Oriental
Embassy
Four Seasons, Lanes
Gordon Ramsay/Claridge's
Greenhouse
Hush
Ikeda
Kai
Langan's Brasserie
Le Boudin Blanc
Le Gavroche
Le Soufflé
Maroush
Masala Zone
Mirabelle
Miyama
Nicole's
Noble Rot
Nobu
Patara
Pescatori
Princess Garden
Rasa
Richoux
Rocket
Saga
Sartoria
Scotts
Shogun
Sofra
Square
Strada
Sumosan
Tamarind
TECA
Truc Vert
Veeraswamy
Windows on the World
Yatra
Zen Central

Piccadilly
Atlantic B&G
Bentley's
Criterion Grill
Diverso
Ed's Easy Diner
Fakhreldine
Gaucho Grill
Hard Rock Cafe
Momo
Planet Hollywood
Rainforest Cafe
Richoux
Terrace
Waterstones Red Rm.
Yoshino
Zinc B&G

Soho
Alastair Little
Andrew Edmunds
Aperitivo
Aroma Chinese
Balans
Bertorelli
Busaba Eathai
Café Boheme
Cafe Fish
Cafe Lazeez
Cafe Med
Cafe Rouge
Chiang Mai
Circus
Crivelli's Garden
Ed's Easy Diner
French House
Gay Hussar
Getti
Gopal's of Soho
Hi Sushi
Il Forno
Incognico
Joy King Lau
Kettners
Kulu Kulu Sushi
La Trouvaille
L'Escargot
Little Italy
Mela
Melati
Mezzo
Mezzonine
Mildreds
Ophim
Patisserie Valerie
Pizza Express
Portrait
Quo Vadis
Randall & Aubin
Red Cube B&G
Red Fort

Location Index

Richard Corrigan/Lindsay
Saigon
Satsuma
Signor Zilli
Soho Spice
Souk
Spiga
Sri Siam
Sugar Club
Sugar Reef
Teatro
Thai Pavilion
Vasco & Piero's
Wagamama
Yo! Sushi
Zilli Fish
Zizzi

St. James's
Al Duca
Avenue
Brasserie Roux
Che
China House
Fortnum's Fountain
Getti
Greens
Just St. James's
Le Caprice
L'Oranger
Matsuri
Mitsukoshi
Pétrus
Quaglino's
Quilon
Quod
Ritz
Rowley's
Suntory
Texas Embassy Cantina
Thai Square
Wagamama
Wheeler's, St. James's
Wilton's

Victoria
Ask Pizza
Bank Westminster/Zander
Boisdale
Christopher's
Goring Dining Rm.
Mango Tree
Noura
Olivo
Simply Nico

Westminster
Cinnamon Club
Shepherd's
Tate Gallery Rest.

EAST/SOUTH EAST LONDON

Blackfriars/City
Alba
Arkansas Cafe
Aurora
Aykoku-Kaku
Baltic
Ben's Thai
Boisdale
Browns Rest.
Cafe Spice Namaste
Caravaggio
Chamberlain's
Chez Gérard
City Miyama
City Rhodes
Coq d'Argent
Don, The
Fishmarket
Gaucho Grill
George Bar
Gladwins
Imperial City
Just the Bridge
Lahore Kebab Hse.
Les Trois Garcons
Little Bay
Livebait
Moshi Moshi Sushi
Noto
1 Lombard St.
1 Lombard St. Brass.
Pacific Oriental
Pizza Express
Pizza Pomodoro
Place Below
Poons in the City
Prism
QC
Ravi Shankar
Searcy's/Barbican
Silks & Spice
Singapura
Sri Siam City
Sri Thai
Sweetings
Tatsuso
Terminus
Thai Square

Location Index

Wagamama
Ye Olde Cheshire Cheese
Zuccato

Canary Wharf/Docklands
Browns Rest.
Fish!
Four Seasons, Quadrato
Gaucho Grill
Moshi Moshi Sushi
Royal China
Smollensky's/Strand
Tabla
Ubon
Wapping Food
Yellow River Cafe

Clerkenwell/Smithfield
Bierodrome
Bleeding Heart
Cafe Lazeez
Carluccio's Caffe
Cellar Gascon
Chez Gérard
Cicada
Clerkenwell Din. Rm./Bar
Club Gascon
Dibbens
Eagle
East One
Gaudí
Le Café du Marché
Maison Novelli
Moro
Mustards Smithfield
Peasant
Potemkin
Quality Chop Hse.
Rudland Stubbs
Smiths of Smithfield - Din.
Smiths of Smithfield-Top
St. John
Strada

Stream, Bubble & Shell
Yo! Sushi

Greenwich/Blackheath
Fish!

Shoreditch/Spitalfields
Cantaloupe
Eyre Brothers
Great Eastern Dining Rm.
Real Greek
Viet Hoa

South Bank
Bankside
Cafe, Level Seven
Cantina Vinopolis
Fina Estampa
Fish!
Honest Cabbage
Oxo Tower
Oxo Tower Brasserie
Simply Nico

Tower Bridge
Arancia
Bengal Clipper
Blue Print Cafe
Butlers Wharf Chop Hse.
Cantina del Ponte
Champor-Champor
Le Pont de la Tour
Tentazioni

Waterloo
Chez Gérard
County Hall
Fish!
Four Regions
Livebait
Meson Don Felipe
People's Palace
Rebato's
R.S.J.
Tas
Waterloo Fire Station

NORTH/NORTH WEST LONDON

Camden Town/Chalk Farm/Kentish Town
Ask Pizza
Belgo Noord
Camden Brasserie
Daphne
Engineer
Feng Shang Floating Rest.
Julono

Lansdowne
Lemonia
New Culture Rev.
Odette's
Silks & Spice
Vegia Zena
Vine
Wagamama
Zamoyski

186   www.zagat.com

Location Index

Golders Green/Finchley
Ben's Thai
Bloom's
Bradley's
Cafe Japan
Ed's Easy Diner
Globe
Kaifeng
Laurent
Smollensky's/Strand
Solly's
Two Brothers Fish
Yo! Sushi
Zuccato

Hampstead/Kilburn
Artigiano
Black Truffle
Byron's
Calzone
China Dream
Cucina
Gate
Gaucho Grill
Giraffe
Good Earth
Green Cottage
Gung-Ho
Halepi
Hi Sushi
House/Rosslyn Hill
Jin Kichi
La Cage Imaginaire
Little Bay
Maxwell's
Nautilus Fish
Rani
Salusbury Pub
Singapore Garden
Toast
Tootsies
ZeNW3

Highgate/Muswell Hill
Florians
Jim Thompson's Wok
Parsee
Vrisaki

Islington
Almeida
Bierodrome
Browns Rest.
Cafe Med
Calzone
Casale Franco
Duke of Cambridge
Frederick's
Gallipoli
Giraffe
Granita
Independence
Iznik
La Piragua
La Porchetta Pizzeria
Le Mercury
Lola's
Metrogusto
New Culture Rev.
Pasha
Santa Fe
Strada
Tartuf
Tiger Lil's
Tuk Tuk Thai
Yellow River Cafe
Yo! Sushi

St. John's Wood
Benihana
Ben's Thai
Cafe Med
Cafe Rouge
Greek Valley
Green Olive
Jason's
L'Aventure
Oslo Court
Otto Dining Lounge
Red Pepper
Richoux
Rosmarino
Royal China
Salt House
Vale
Zizzi

Stoke Newington
La Porchetta Pizzeria
LMNT
Mesclun
Rasa
Yum Yum Thai

SOUTH/SOUTH WEST LONDON

Barnes
Browns Rest.
MVH

Riva
Sonny's

Location Index

Battersea
Cafe Rouge
Cantinetta Venegazzu
Chelsea Bun
Giraffe
Glaister's Garden
Lan Na Thai
Metrogusto
Osteria Antica Bologna
Pizza Express
Pizza Metro
Ransome's Dock
Stepping Stone
Zizzi

Brixton/Clapham
Bierodrome
Bombay Bicycle Club
Bug-Bar, Rest. & Lounge
Buona Sera
Cafe Spice Namaste
Cinnamon Cay
Eco
Kennington Lane
La Rueda
Lobster Pot
Pepper Tree
Pizzeria Castello
Polygon B&G
Sand Bar
Spago
Strada
Tartuf
Thyme
Tiger Lil's
Tootsies
Tsunami

Chelsea
Admiral Codrington
Ask Pizza
Aubergine
Benihana
Big Easy
Bluebird
Brinkley's
Builders Arms
Buona Sera at the Jam
Busabong Too
Calzone
Caraffini
Carpaccio
Chelsea Bun
Chives
Chutney Mary
Creelers
Dan's
Daphne's
Ed's Easy Diner
El Blason
El Gaucho
Elistano
English Garden
Enterprise
Formula Veneta
Friends
Gaucho Grill
Glaister's Garden
Gordon Ramsay/68 Royal
itsu
La Famiglia
Le Colombier
Le Suquet
Lomo
Made in Italy
Mao Tai
Monkeys
New Culture Rev.
Oriel
Painted Heron
Pellicano
Pizza Express
PJ's Bar & Grill
Poissonnerie de l'Avenue
Pucci Pizza
Randall & Aubin
Riccardo's
Sabbia
Sambuca
Scalini
Simply Nico
Sophie's Steakhse.
Spiga
Tandoori of Chelsea
Thai on the River
Thierry's
Toto's
Vama
Vingt-Quatre
Wok Wok
Zaika Bazaar
Zen Chelsea
Ziani

Dulwich
Belair House
Strada

Earl's Court
Cambio de Tercio
Catch

Location Index

Chez Max
El Gaucho
Ifield
Langan's Coq d'Or
Lou Pescadou
Mr. Wing
Nam Long Le Shaker
Nikita's
Troubadour

Fulham
Bierodrome
Blue Elephant
De Cecco
Jim Thompson's Wok
La Perla B&G
La Rueda
Mao Tai
Montana
Pizza Express
Salisbury Tavern
Strada
Sugar Hut
Tootsies

Pimlico
Blue Jade
Como Lario
Grumbles
Hunan
La Fontana
La Poule au Pot
L'Incontro
Pomegranates
Rhodes in the Square
Roussillon

Putney/Richmond
Ask Pizza
Bayee House
Canyon
Del Buongustaio
Enoteca Turi
Glasshouse
Jim Thompson's Wok
Ma Goa
Memories of India
Naked Turtle
Phoenix B&G
Pope's Eye

Putney Bridge
Redmonds
Wok Wok

South Kensington
Al Bustan
Ask Pizza
Babylon
Bangkok
Bibendum
Bibendum Oyster Bar
Bistrot 190
Blakes Hotel
Bombay Brasserie
Cactus Blue
Cafe Lazeez
Collection
Crescent
Daquise
Il Falconiere
Joe's
Khan's of Kensington
Kulu Kulu Sushi
La Bouchée
La Brasserie
Lundum's
Memories of India
Noor Jahan
190, Downstairs
Pasha
Patara
Pizza Organic
Sandrini
San Frediano
Spago
Star of India
Tootsies

Wandsworth/Balham
Bayee House
Chez Bruce
Jim Thompson's Wok
Kastoori
Light House
Livebait
San Lorenzo Fuoriporta
Sarkhel's
Strada
Tootsies

WEST LONDON

Bayswater
Alounak
Al San Vincenzo
Al Waha
Fairuz

Fakhreldine Express
Four Seasons Chinese
Ginger
Halepi
Harry's Social Club

Location Index

I-Thai
Kalamaras Taverna
Khan's
L'Accento Italiano
Mandarin Kitchen
Mandola
Poons
Rodizio Rico
Royal China
T.G.I. Friday's
Tiger Lil's

Chiswick

Ask Pizza
Cafe Med
Cafe Rouge
Chiswick, The
Clock
Dumela
Fish Hoek
La Trompette
Monsieur Max
Parade
Pizza Organic
Pug
Silks & Spice
Tootsies
Yellow River Cafe

Hammersmith

Cafe Rouge
Carluccio's Caffe
Cotto
Gate
Glaister's Garden
Maquis
River Cafe
Smollensky's/Strand
Tootsies

Kensington

Abingdon
Ark
Ask Pizza
Balans
Belvedere
Black & Blue
Churchill Arms
Clarke's
ffiona's
Kensington Place
Koi
Launceston Place
Maggie Jones's
Memories of China
Phoenicia
Pizza Express
Sticky Fingers
Stratford's
Sushi Wong
Tenth
Terrace
Timo
Wagamama
Wòdka
Wok Wok
Zaika

Notting Hill Gate

Alastair Little/Lancaster Rd.
Ask Pizza
Assaggi
Belgo Zuid
Books for Cooks
Cafe Med
Cafe Rouge
Calzone
Chez Moi
Costa's Grill
Cow, The
Dakota
E&O
Electric Brasserie
First Floor
Galicia
Geale's Fish
Il Posto
Julie's
Lee Fook
Livebait
Lucky Seven
Malabar
Manor
Mediterraneo
New Culture Rev.
Notting Grill
Notting Hill Brasserie
Oak, The
192
Orsino
Osteria Basilico
Pharmacy
Pizza Express
Prince Bonaparte
Tom's Deli
Tootsies
Westbourne
Zilli
Zucca

Olympia

Alounak
Cibo
Havelock Tavern

Location Index

Pope's Eye
Yas

Shepherd's Bush
Anglesea Arms
Blah! Blah! Blah!
Brackenbury

Bush Bar & Grill
Cafe Rouge
Chinon
Esarn Kheaw
Snows on the Green
Zizzi

IN THE COUNTRY

Cliveden, Waldo's
Fat Duck
French Horn
Gravetye Manor
Hartwell House

Le Manoir/Quat'Saisons
Sir Charles Napier
Vineyard/Stockcross
Waterside Inn

Special Feature Index

SPECIAL FEATURES

All-Day Dining
Al Hamra (W1)
Alounak (multi. loc.)
Al Sultan (W1)
Al Waha (W2)
Aperitivo (W1)
Ask Pizza (multi. loc.)
Balans (multi. loc.)
Belgo Centraal (WC2)
Bibendum Oyster Bar (SW3)
Big Easy (SW3)
Bistrot 190 (SW7)
Bloom's (NW11)
Browns Rest. (multi. loc.)
Cafe Lazeez (multi. loc.)
Cafe, Level Seven (SE1)
Cafe Pacifico (WC2)
Cafe Rouge (multi. loc.)
Calzone (multi. loc.)
Cantina Vinopolis (SE1)
Carluccio's Caffe (multi. loc.)
Casale Franco (N1)
Chelsea Bun (multi. loc.)
Chuen Cheng Ku (W1)
Condotti (W1)
Crivelli's Garden (WC2)
Ed's Easy Diner (multi. loc.)
Efes Kebab (multi. loc.)
Fakhreldine (multi. loc.)
Fifth Floor Cafe (SW1)
Food for Thought (WC2)
Fortnum's Fountain (W1)
Fung Shing (WC2)
George Bar (EC2)
Golden Dragon (W1)
Green Cottage (NW3)
Hi Sushi (W1)
House/Rosslyn Hill (NW3)
Ikkyu (multi. loc.)
Imperial City (EC3)
Indigo (WC2)
Ishbilia (SW1)
itsu (SW3)
Jade Garden (W1)
Jim Thompson's Wok (multi. loc.)
Joe Allen (WC2)
Joe's Rest. Bar (SW1)
Kettners (W1)
La Bouchée (SW7)
La Brasserie (SW3)
Lahore Kebab Hse. (E1)
Langan's Brasserie (W1)
La Piragua (N1)
Lee Fook (W2)
Lee Ho Fook (W1)
Le Metro (SW3)
Little Bay (NW6)
Little Italy (W1)
Lucky Seven (W2)
Mandarin Kitchen (W2)
Maroush (multi. loc.)
Maxwell's (multi. loc.)
Melati (W1)
Memories of India (SW7)
Mildreds (W1)
Mustards Smithfield (EC1)
New Culture Rev. (multi. loc.)
New World (W1)
Noura (SW1)
Oriel (SW1)
Orsino (W11)
Orso (WC2)
Patisserie Valerie (multi. loc.)
Pepper Tree (SW4)
Phoenicia (W8)
Pizza Express (multi. loc.)
Pizza on the Park (SW1)
Pizza Pomodoro (multi. loc.)
Pizzeria Castello (SE1)
PJ's Bar & Grill (SW3)
Planet Hollywood (W1)
Porters (WC2)
Portrait (WC2)
Pucci Pizza (SW3)
Rainforest Cafe (W1)
Randall & Aubin (multi. loc.)
Richoux (multi. loc.)
Royal China (multi. loc.)
Rules (WC2)
Seashell (NW1)
Singapura (multi. loc.)
Sofra (multi. loc.)
Soho Spice (W1)
Solly's (NW11)
Sticky Fingers (W8)
Terminus (EC2)
Texas Embassy Cantina (SW1)
T.G.I. Friday's (multi. loc.)
Tokyo Diner (WC2)
Tom's Deli (W11)
Tootsies (multi. loc.)
Truc Vert (W1)
Tuttons Brasserie (WC2)
Vingt-Quatre (SW10)
Wagamama (multi. loc.)
Wong Kei (W1)
Yellow River Cafe (multi. loc.)
Ye Olde Cheshire Cheese (EC4)

Special Feature Index

Yo! Sushi (multi. loc.)
Zilli Fish (W1)
Zinc B&G (W1)

Breakfast/Brunch
(See also Hotel Dining;
BR=breakfast; B=brunch)
Abingdon (W8) (B)
Admiral Codrington (SW3) (B)
Admiralty (WC2) (B)
Avenue (SW1) (B)
Balans (multi. loc.) (BR,B)
Bank Aldwych (WC2) (BR,B)
Bank Westminster/Zander (SW1) (BR,B)
Belvedere (W8) (B)
Bistrot 190 (SW7) (BR,B)
Bluebird (SW3) (B)
Blue Elephant (SW6) (B)
Books for Cooks (W11) (BR)
Browns Rest. (multi. loc.) (B)
Bush Bar & Grill (W12) (B)
Butlers Wharf (SE1) (B)
Cactus Blue (SW3) (B)
Cafe at Sotheby's (W1) (BR)
Cafe, Level Seven (SE1) (BR)
Camden Brasserie (NW1) (B)
Cantaloupe (EC2) (B)
Canyon (Richmond) (B)
Carluccio's Caffe (W1) (BR,B)
Chelsea Bun (multi. loc.) (BR,B)
Christopher's (WC2) (B)
Chutney Mary (SW10) (B)
Cinnamon Club (SW1) (BR)
Clarke's (W8) (B)
Coq d'Argent (EC2) (BR,B)
Dakota (W11) (B)
Emporio Armani (SW3) (BR)
Engineer (NW1) (BR,B)
Fifth Floor Cafe (SW1) (BR,B)
Fortnum's Fountain (W1) (BR)
Giraffe (multi. loc.) (BR,B)
Honest Cabbage (SE1) (B)
Joe Allen (WC2) (B)
Joe's (SW3) (BR,B)
Joe's Rest. Bar (SW1) (BR,B)
La Brasserie (SW3) (BR,B)
Langan's Coq d'Or (SW5) (B)
La Porte des Indes (W1) (B)
Le Caprice (SW1) (B)
Le Metro (SW3) (BR)
Lola's (N1) (B)
Lucky Seven (W2) (BR)
Lundum's (SW7) (B)
Manor (W11) (B)
Mash (W1) (BR,B)
Montana (SW6) (BR,B)
Motcomb's (SW1) (B)
Nicole's (W1) (BR,B)
Oriel (SW1) (BR)
Osteria Ant. Bologna (SW11) (B)
Patisserie Val. (multi. loc.) (BR,B)
PJ's Bar & Grill (SW3) (B)
Polygon B&G (SW4) (B)
Providores/Tapa Rm. (W1) (B)
Quaglino's (SW1) (B)
Ransome's Dock (SW11) (B)
Richoux (multi. loc.) (BR,B)
Salusbury Pub (NW6) (B)
Simpson's/Strand/Grand (WC2) (BR)
Smiths of Smithfield-Top (EC1) (B)
Tom's Deli (W11) (BR,B)
Troubadour (SW5) (BR,B)
Truc Vert (W1) (BR,B)
Vale (W9) (B)
Villandry (W1) (B)
Vingt-Quatre (SW10) (BR,B)

Business Dining
Alba (EC1)
Al Duca (SW1)
Alloro (W1)
Almeida (N1)
Aurora (EC2)
Avenue (SW1)
Axis (WC2)
Bank Aldwych (WC2)
Bank Westminster/Zander (SW1)
Belvedere (W8)
Bentley's (W1)
Bibendum (SW3)
Bice (W1)
Blakes Hotel (SW7)
Blandford Street (W1)
Bleeding Heart (EC1)
Blue Print Cafe (SE1)
Brown's Hotel, 1837 (W1)
Capital (SW3)
Caravaggio (EC3)
Caviar Kaspia (W1)
Cecconi's (W1)
Chez Gérard (multi. loc.)
Christopher's (multi. loc.)
Cibo (W14)
Cinnamon Club (SW1)
Circus (W1)
City Rhodes (EC4)
Clarke's (W8)
Club Gascon (EC1)
Connaught (W1)
Criterion Grill (W1)
Dorchester, Grill Rm. (W1)
Dorchester, Oriental (W1)

www.zagat.com 193

Special Feature Index

Drones (SW1)
Elena's l'Etoile (W1)
Embassy (W1)
Fakhreldine (multi. loc.)
Fifth Floor (SW1)
Floriana (SW3)
Foliage (SW1)
Four Seasons, Lanes (W1)
Four Seasons, Quadrato (E14)
Glasshouse (Kew)
Gordon Ramsay/Claridge's (W1)
Gordon Ramsay/68 Royal (SW3)
Goring Dining Rm. (SW1)
Gravetye Manor (W. Sus)
Greenhouse (W1)
Greens (SW1)
Grissini (SW1)
Hartwell House (Bucks)
Il Convivio (SW1)
Il Forno (W1)
Imperial City (EC3)
Incognico (WC2)
Indigo (WC2)
I-Thai (W2)
Ivy (WC2)
John Burton-Race (NW1)
J. Sheekey (WC2)
Just St. James's (SW1)
Kai (W1)
La Brasserie (SW3)
Lanesborough (SW1)
Langan's Bistro (W1)
Langan's Brasserie (W1)
La Tante Claire (SW1)
La Trompette (W4)
Launceston Place (W8)
Le Café du Marché (EC1)
Le Caprice (SW1)
Le Gavroche (W1)
Le Manoir/Quat'Saisons (Oxon)
Le Pont de la Tour (SE1)
L'Escargot (W1)
Le Soufflé (W1)
L'Incontro (SW1)
Locanda Locatelli (W1)
L'Oranger (SW1)
Manzi's (WC2)
Memories of China (multi. loc.)
Mirabelle (W1)
Mitsukoshi (SW1)
Miyama (W1)
Mju (SW1)
Nahm (SW1)
Neal Street (WC2)
Nobu (W1)
Odin's (W1)
One-O-One (SW1)
One-Seven-Nine (WC2)
Orrery (W1)
Oxo Tower (SE1)
Pétrus (SW1)
Pied à Terre (W1)
Poissonnerie de l'Avenue (SW3)
Princess Garden (W1)
Providores/Tapa Rm. (W1)
QC (WC1)
Quaglino's (SW1)
Quo Vadis (W1)
Rasa (multi. loc.)
Red Fort (W1)
Rib Room/Oyster Bar (SW1)
Ritz (W1)
River Cafe (W6)
Rules (WC2)
Sandrini (SW3)
Santini (SW1)
Savoy Grill (WC2)
Savoy River (WC2)
Scotts (W1)
Shepherd's (SW1)
Shogun (W1)
Smiths of Smithfield - Din. (EC1)
Smiths of Smithfield-Top (EC1)
Square (W1)
Suntory (SW1)
Tamarind (W1)
Tatsuso (EC1)
Terminus (EC2)
Ubon (E14)
Vong (SW1)
Waterside Inn (Berks)
West Street (WC2)
Wheeler's, St. James's (SW1)
Wilton's (SW1)
Windows on the World (W1)
Zafferano (SW1)
Zaika (W8)
Zen Central (W1)
Zen Chelsea (SW3)
ZeNW3 (NW3)

BYO

Alounak (multi. loc.)
Blah! Blah! Blah! (W12)
Books for Cooks (W11)
Chelsea Bun (multi. loc.)
Chez Max (SW10)
Eco (SW9)
El Gaucho (SW3)
Food for Thought (WC2)
Gallipoli (N1)
Kalamaras Taverna (W2)
Kandoo (W2)
Lahore Kebab Hse. (E1)

Special Feature Index

Mandola (W11)
Monsieur Max (Hampton Hill)
Tom's Deli (W11)

Celebrity Chefs
Belvedere (W8),
  Marco Pierre White
Brasserie Roux (SW1),
  Albert Roux
Cafe Spice Namaste (multi. loc.),
  Cyrus Todiwala
Capital (SW3), *Eric Chavot*
Chez Bruce (SW17), *Bruce Poole*
City Rhodes (EC4), *Gary Rhodes*
Clarke's (W8), *Sally Clarke*
Club Gascon (EC1),
  Pascal Aussignac
Connaught, The (W1),
  Gordon Ramsay
Criterion Grill (W1),
  Marco Pierre White
Deca (W1), *Nico Ladenis*
Drones (SW1),
  Marco Pierre White
Fat Duck (Berks),
  Heston Blumenthal
Gordon Ramsay/Claridge's (W1),
  Gordon Ramsay
Gordon Ramsay/68 Royal (SW3),
  Gordon Ramsay
Greenhouse (W1), *Paul Merrett*
Ifield (SW10), *Ed Baines*
Incognico (WC2), *Nico Ladenis*
Ivy (WC2), *Mark Hix*
John Burton-Race (NW1),
  John Burton-Race
J. Sheekey (WC2), *Mark Hix*
Kensington Place (W8),
  Rowley Leigh
La Tante Claire (SW1),
  Pierre Koffman
Le Caprice (SW1), *Mark Hix*
Le Gavroche (W1), *Michel Roux*
Le Manoir/Quat'Saisons (Oxon),
  Raymond Blanc
Locanda Locatelli (W1),
  Giorgio Locatelli
Maison Novelli (EC1),
  Jean-Christophe Novelli
Monte's (SW1X), *Jamie Oliver*
Moro (EC1), *Sam & Sam Clark*
Mosimann's (SW1),
  Anton Mosimann
Nahm (SW1), *David Thompson*
Neal Street (WC2),
  Antonio Carluccio
Nobu (W1), *Nobu Matsuhisa, Mark Edwards*
Notting Grill (W11),
  Antony Worrall Thompson
Orrery (W1), *Chris Galvin*
Parisienne Chophse. (SW3),
  Marco Pierre White
Pétrus (SW1), *Marcus Wareing*
Providores/Tapa Rm. (W1),
  Peter Gordon
Racine (SW3), *Henry Harris*
Randall & Aubin (multi. loc.),
  Ed Baines
Real Greek (N1),
  Theodore Kyriakou
Rhodes in the Square (SW1),
  Gary Rhodes
Richard Corrigan/Lindsay (W1),
  Richard Corrigan
River Cafe (W6), *Rose Gray, Ruth Rodgers*
Savoy Grill (WC2), *Anton Edelman*
Smiths of Smithfield - Din. (EC1),
  John Torode
Smiths of Smithfield-Top (EC1),
  John Torode
Spoon+ at Sanderson (W1),
  Alain Ducasse
Square (W1), *Philip Howard*
Tamarind (W1), *Cyrus Todiwala*
Vong (SW1),
  Jean-Georges Vongerichten
Waterside Inn (Berks),
  Michel Roux
West Street (WC2), *Rowley Leigh*
Yellow River Cafe (multi. loc.),
  Ken Hom
Zaika (W8), *Vineet Bhatia*
Zaika Bazaar (SW3),
  Vineet Bhatia
Zilli (W11), *Aldo Zilli*
Zilli Fish (multi. loc.), *Aldo Zilli*

Cheeseboards
Alba (EC1)
Aubergine (SW10)
Aurora (EC2)
Bibendum (SW3)
Bleeding Heart (EC1)
Brown's Hotel, 1837 (W1)
Cecconi's (W1)
Chez Bruce (SW17)
Chez Moi (W11)
Chinon (W14)
Christopher's (WC2)
Cliveden, Waldo's (Berks)

Special Feature Index

Dorchester, Grill Rm. (W1)
Elena's l'Etoile (W1)
Fat Duck (Berks)
French Horn (Berks)
Glasshouse (Kew)
Gordon Ramsay/Claridge's (W1)
Gordon Ramsay/68 Royal (SW3)
Goring Dining Rm. (SW1)
Gravetye Manor (W. Sus)
Greens (SW1)
Hartwell House (Bucks)
John Burton-Race (NW1)
Lanesborough (SW1)
La Tante Claire (SW1)
La Trompette (W4)
Le Gavroche (W1)
Le Manoir/Quat'Saisons (Oxon)
Le Soufflé (W1)
Monsieur Max (Hampton Hill)
One-Seven-Nine (WC2)
Orrery (W1)
Pétrus (SW1)
Pied à Terre (W1)
Putney Bridge (SW15)
Richard Corrigan/Lindsay (W1)
Ritz (W1)
Riva (SW13)
Roussillon (SW1)
Savoy Grill (WC2)
Savoy River (WC2)
Sir Charles Napier (Oxon)
Smiths of Smithfield-Top (EC1)
Square (W1)
Vale (W9)
Waterside Inn (Berks)
Windows on the World (W1)

Child-Friendly

(Besides the normal fast-food places; *children's menu available)
Abingdon (W8)*
Al Hamra (W1)*
Aperitivo (W1)
Ask Pizza (multi. loc.)
Balans (W8)
Bank Aldwych (WC2)*
Bank Westminster/Zander (SW1)*
Belair House (SE21)
Belgo Centraal (WC2)*
Belgo Noord (NW1)
Belgo Zuid (W10)*
Benihana (multi. loc.)*
Big Easy (SW3)*
Bloom's (NW11)*
Bluebird (SW3)*
Blue Elephant (SW6)
Bombay Bicycle Club (SW12)
Bombay Brasserie (SW7)*
Buona Sera (SW11)*
Cafe Fish (W1)*
Cafe, Level Seven (SE1)
Cafe Med (multi. loc.)*
Cafe Pacifico (WC2)*
Cafe Spice Namaste (E1)
Calzone (multi. loc.)*
Cantina del Ponte (SE1)*
Canyon (Richmond)*
Carluccio's Caffe (W1)*
Casale Franco (N1)
Chelsea Bun (multi. loc.)
China House (W1)
Chiswick, The (W4)
Christopher's (multi. loc.)*
Chuen Cheng Ku (W1)
Chutney Mary (SW10)
Clock (W7)*
Como Lario (SW1)
Dakota (W11)*
Del Buongustaio (SW15)*
Dorchester, Grill Rm. (W1)*
Eagle (EC1)
Ed's Easy Diner (multi. loc.)*
Fifth Floor Cafe (SW1)
Fish! (multi. loc.)*
Florians (N8)
Fortnum's Fountain (W1)*
Frederick's (N1)*
Garbo's (W1)*
Gaucho Grill (NW3)*
Giraffe (multi. loc.)*
Glaister's Garden (SW13)*
Hakkasan (W1)
Hard Rock Cafe (W1)*
itsu (multi. loc.)
Jim Thompson's (multi. loc.)*
Joe Allen (WC2)
Julie's (W11)*
Kensington Place (W8)
Kettners (W1)
La Famiglia (SW10)
Lanesborough (SW1)*
La Porte des Indes (W1)
Little Bay (NW6)*
Livebait (multi. loc.)*
Locanda Locatelli (W1)
Lou Pescadou (SW5)*
Made in Italy (SW3)
Masala Zone (W1)*
Matsuri (SW1)
Maxwell's (multi. loc.)*
Metrogusto (N1)
Mitsukoshi (SW1)*
Montana (SW6)*

Special Feature Index

Moshi Moshi Sushi (multi. loc.)
Naked Turtle (SW14)*
New Culture Rev. (multi. loc.)
Noura (SW1)
Oliveto (SW1)
Oxo Tower Brasserie (SE1)
Palm Court (WC2)*
People's Palace (SE1)*
Phoenix B&G (SW15)*
Pizza Express (multi. loc.)
Pizza Metro (SW11)
Pizza on the Park (SW1)
Pizza Organic (multi. loc.)*
PJ's Bar & Grill (SW3)
PJ's Grill (WC2)*
Planet Hollywood (W1)*
Porters (WC2)*
Quaglino's (SW1)*
Rainforest Cafe (W1)*
Ransome's Dock (SW11)
Redmonds (SW14)*
Red Pepper (W9)
Riccardo's (SW3)
Richoux (multi. loc.)*
River Cafe (W6)
RK Stanley's (W1)*
Royal China (multi. loc.)
Santa Fe (N1)*
Sarkhel's (SW18)*
Seashell (NW1)*
Smollensky's/Strand (multi. loc.)*
Sonny's (SW13)*
Spiga (multi. loc.)
Spighetta (W1)*
Sticky Fingers (W8)*
Texas Embassy Cantina (SW1)*
T.G.I. Friday's (multi. loc.)*
Tiger Lil's (multi. loc.)*
Timo (W8)
Tootsies (multi. loc.)*
Veeraswamy (W1)*
Vingt-Quatre (SW10)
Wagamama (multi. loc.)
Wok Wok (multi. loc.)*
Yellow River Cafe (multi. loc.)*
Yo! Sushi (multi. loc.)*
Zafferano (SW1)

Critic-Proof
(Get lots of business despite so-so food)
Ask Pizza (multi. loc.)
Atlantic B&G (W1)
Balans (multi. loc.)
Bierodrome (multi. loc.)
Big Easy (SW3)
Cactus Blue (SW3)
Cafe Rouge (multi. loc.)
Collection (SW3)
Ed's Easy Diner (multi. loc.)
Hard Rock Cafe (W1)
Kettners (W1)
Mash (W1)
Oriel (SW1)
Planet Hollywood (W1)
Rainforest Cafe (W1)
Richoux (multi. loc.)
Smollensky's/Strand (multi. loc.)
Sticky Fingers (W8)
Texas Embassy Cantina (SW1)
T.G.I. Friday's (multi. loc.)
Tootsies (multi. loc.)
Wok Wok (multi. loc.)
Wong Kei (W1)

Dancing/Entertainment
(D=dancing; call for days and times of performances)
Adam Street (WC2) (D/piano)
Avenue (SW1) (piano)
Ayoush (W1) (belly dancer/DJ)
Baltic (SE1) (jazz)
Bankside (SE1) (D/jazz)
Big Easy (SW3) (rock)
Bluebird (SW3) (piano)
Boisdale (SW1) (jazz)
Bombay Brasserie (SW7) (piano)
Café Boheme (W1) (jazz)
Cafe Lazeez (SW7) (jazz)
Chutney Mary (SW10) (jazz)
Circus (W1) (D/DJ)
Coq d'Argent (EC2) (jazz)
County Hall (SE1) (jazz)
Efes Kebab (W1) (belly dancer)
Goring Dining Rm. (SW1) (piano)
Greek Valley (NW8) (accordion)
Ishbilia (SW1) (Arabic dancers)
Joe Allen (WC2) (piano)
Julono (NW3) (belly dancer)
Just St. James's (SW1) (D/jazz)
Kai (W1) (harp)
Lanesborough (SW1) (D/jazz)
Langan's Brasserie (W1) (jazz)
La Rueda (multi. loc.) (D/bands/guitar)
Le Cafe du Jardin (WC2) (piano)
Le Café du Marché (EC1) (jazz)
Le Pont de la Tour (SE1) (piano)
Le Soufflé (W1) (D/piano)
Levant (W1) (belly dancer)
Ma Goa (SW15) (Goan music)
Maroush (W2) (D/Lebanese)
Meson Don Felipe (SE1) (guitar)
Mezzo (W1) (D/bands)

Special Feature Index

Mezzonine (W1) (D/DJ)
Montana (SW6) (piano)
Mr. Wing (SW5) (piano/singer)
Naked Turtle (SW14) (jazz/magic)
Nikita's (SW10) (accordion/guitar)
Noble Rot (W1) (jazz)
Notting Hill Brass. (W11) (jazz)
190, Downstairs (SW7) (D)
Oxo Tower Brasserie (SE1) (jazz)
Palm Court (WC2) (D/band/harp)
Pharmacy (W11) (D/DJ)
Pizza on Park (SW1) (cabaret/jazz)
PJ's Grill (WC2) (jazz)
Potemkin (EC1) (singer)
Princess Garden (W1) (piano)
Quaglino's (SW1) (jazz/piano)
Rebato's (SW8) (piano/singer)
Red Cube B&G (WC2) (DJ)
Rib Room/Oyster Bar (SW1) (piano/singer)
Ritz (W1) (D/band)
Rodizio Rico (W2) (D)
Sartoria (W1) (piano)
Savoy River (WC2) (D/band)
Simpson's/Strand/Simply (WC2) (piano/singer)
Smiths/Smithfield - Din. (EC1) (DJ)
Smollensky's/Strand (multi. loc.) (D/varies)
Soho Spice (W1) (DJ)
Souk (WC2) (D/belly dancer)
Sugar Reef (W1) (D/DJ)
Tenth (W8) (D/jazz)
Windows on the World (W1) (D/band)
Yatra (W1) (D/varies)
Zamoyski (NW3) (guitar/singer)

Delivery/Takeaway
(D=delivery, T=takeaway)
Al Hamra (W1) (D,T)
Alounak (multi. loc.) (D,T)
Al Sultan (W1) (D,T)
Al Waha (W2) (T)
Arkansas Cafe (E1) (T)
Aroma Chinese (multi. loc.) (T)
Ask Pizza (multi. loc.) (T)
Aykoku-Kaku (EC4) (T)
Ayoush (W1) (T)
Bangkok (SW7) (T)
Bayee House (multi. loc.) (T)
Beiteddine (SW1) (D,T)
Bengal Clipper (SE1) (T)
Benihana (multi. loc.) (T)
Ben's Thai (multi. loc.) (T)

Big Easy (SW3) (T)
Bloom's (NW11) (D,T)
Blue Elephant (SW6) (T)
Blue Jade (SW1) (T)
Busabong Too (SW10) (T)
Cafe Lazeez (multi. loc.) (D,T)
Cafe Spice Namaste (multi. loc.) (D,T)
Calzone (multi. loc.) (T)
Cantina del Ponte (SE1) (T)
Carluccio's Caffe (multi. loc.) (D,T)
Chelsea Bun (SW11) (T)
China Dream (NW3) (D,T)
Chor Bizarre (W1) (D,T)
Chutney Mary (SW10) (T)
Chutney's (NW1) (T)
Condotti (W1) (T)
Defune (W1) (T)
ECapital (W1) (D,T)
Ed's Easy Diner (multi. loc.) (D,T)
Esarn Kheaw (W12) (T)
Fairuz (W1) (D,T)
Fakhreldine Exp. (multi. loc.) (D,T)
Friends (SW10) (T)
Garbo's (W1) (T)
Gaucho Grill (multi. loc.) (T)
Geale's Fish (W8) (T)
Giraffe (multi. loc.) (D,T)
Good Earth (multi. loc.) (D,T)
Greek Valley (NW8) (T)
Gung-Ho (NW6) (T)
Halepi (multi. loc.) (T)
Hard Rock Cafe (W1) (T)
Ikeda (W1) (T)
Ishbilia (SW1) (D,T)
itsu (multi. loc.) (D,T)
Kaifeng (NW4) (D,T)
Kulu Kulu Sushi (multi. loc.) (T)
Lahore Kebab Hse. (E1) (D,T)
La Porte des Indes (W1) (T)
Lee Ho Fook (W1) (T)
Lobster Pot (SE11) (D)
Lucky Seven (W2) (T)
Made in Italy (SW3) (T)
Mango Tree (SW1) (T)
Mao Tai (multi. loc.) (T)
Maroush (multi. loc.) (D,T)
Masala Zone (W1) (D,T)
Matsuri (SW1) (D,T)
Mela (WC2) (T)
Memories of China (multi. loc.) (D,T)
Moshi Moshi Sushi (multi. loc.) (D,T)
New Culture Rev. (multi. loc.) (D,T)

Special Feature Index

Noor Jahan (SW5) (T)
Noura (SW1) (D,T)
Oak, The (W2) (T)
Oliveto (SW1) (T)
Osteria Basilico (W11) (T)
Ozer Rest. & Bar (W1) (T)
Painted Heron (SW10) (D,T)
Parsee (N19) (T)
Patara (multi. loc.) (T)
Pepper Tree (SW4) (T)
Phoenicia (W8) (D,T)
Pizza Express (multi. loc.) (T)
Pizza Metro (SW11) (T)
Planet Hollywood (W1) (T)
Poons (multi. loc.) (T)
Randall & Aubin (W1) (T)
Rani (N3) (T)
Rasa (multi. loc.) (T)
Red Pepper (W9) (T)
Riccardo's (SW3) (D,T)
Richoux (multi. loc.) (T)
Royal China (multi. loc.) (T)
Saga (W1) (T)
Salloos (SW1) (D,T)
Sarkhel's (SW18) (T)
Satsuma (W1) (T)
Seashell (NW1) (T)
Silks & Spice (multi. loc.) (T)
Singapore Garden (NW6) (D,T)
Singapura (EC4) (T)
Soho Spice (W1) (T)
Solly's (NW11) (T)
Sushi Wong (W8) (D,T)
Tamarind (W1) (D,T)
Tartuf (SW4) (T)
Tas (SE1) (T)
T.G.I. Friday's (multi. loc.) (T)
Tom's Deli (W11) (T)
Truc Vert (W1) (D,T)
Two Brothers Fish (N3) (T)
Vama (SW10) (D,T)
Veeraswamy (W1) (T)
Viet Hoa (E2) (T)
Villandry (W1) (T)
Wagamama (multi. loc.) (T)
Wok Wok (multi. loc.) (T)
Yellow River Cafe (multi. loc.) (D,T)
Yo! Sushi (multi. loc.) (D,T)
Yum Yum Thai (N16) (T)
Zaika Bazaar (SW3) (D,T)
Zen Central (W1) (D,T)
Zen Chelsea (SW3) (D,T)
ZeNW3 (NW3) (D,T)

Dining Alone
(Other than hotels and places with counter service)
Bibendum Oyster Bar (SW3)
Books for Cooks (W11)
Cafe at Sotheby's (W1)
Cafe, Level Seven (SE1)
Cafe Rouge (multi. loc.)
Carluccio's Caffe (multi. loc.)
China House (W1)
Chuen Cheng Ku (W1)
Ed's Easy Diner (SW3)
Emporio Armani Caffe (SW3)
Fifth Floor Cafe (SW1)
Fortnum's Fountain (W1)
Joe's Rest. Bar (SW1)
Le Colombier (SW3)
Le Metro (SW3)
Matsuri (SW1)
Mezzonine (W1)
Mildreds (W1)
Mitsukoshi (SW1)
Mon Plaisir (WC2)
New Culture Rev. (NW1)
Nicole's (W1)
Oriel (SW1)
Patisserie Valerie (SW3)
Porters (WC2)
Portrait (WC2)
Providores/Tapa Rm. (W1)
Randall & Aubin (multi. loc.)
Richoux (multi. loc.)
Terminus (EC2)
Tom's Deli (W11)
Truc Vert (W1)
Villandry (W1)
Wagamama (W1)
Wok Wok (multi. loc.)
Yellow River Cafe (multi. loc.)

Fireplaces
Admiral Codrington (SW3)
Anglesea Arms (W6)
Bam-Bou (W1)
Belair House (SE21)
Bistrot 190 (SW7)
Bleeding Heart (multi. loc.)
Brasserie Roux (SW1)
Brown's Hotel, 1837 (W1)
Cambio de Tercio (SW5)
Caviar Kaspia (W1)
Cicada (EC1)
Clerkenwell Din. Rm./Bar (EC1)
Cliveden, Waldo's (Berks)
Daphne's (SW3)
Fat Duck (Berks)
French Horn (Berks)

Special Feature Index

Ginger (W2)
Glaister's Garden (SW11)
Gravetye Manor (W. Sus)
Grenadier (SW1)
Havelock Tavern (W14)
I-Thai (W2)
Julie's (W11)
Lansdowne (NW1)
La Poule au Pot (SW1)
Le Manoir/Quat'Saisons (Oxon)
L'Escargot (W1)
LMNT (E8)
Mediterraneo (W11)
Naked Turtle (SW14)
Notting Grill (W11)
Parade (W5)
Prince Bonaparte (W2)
Richard Corrigan/Lindsay (W1)
Rules (WC2)
Salt House (NW8)
Santa Fe (N1)
Sir Charles Napier (Oxon)
Sonny's (SW13)
Waterside Inn (Berks)
Westbourne (W2)

Game in Season

Adam Street (WC2)
Alastair Little (W1)
Andrew Edmunds (W1)
Archipelago (W1)
Arkansas Cafe (E1)
Assaggi (W2)
Aubergine (SW10)
Aurora (EC2)
Axis (WC2)
Bibendum (SW3)
Blandford Street (W1)
Bluebird (SW3)
Brackenbury (W6)
Brown's Hotel, 1837 (W1)
Butlers Wharf Chop Hse. (SE1)
Caraffini (SW1)
Caravaggio (EC3)
Carpaccio (SW3)
Cecconi's (W1)
Chez Moi (W11)
Chinon (W14)
Chiswick, The (W4)
Chives (SW10)
Chutney Mary (SW10)
Cibo (W14)
Cinnamon Club (SW1)
Cliveden, Waldo's (Berks)
Club Gascon (EC1)
Creelers (SW3)
Dorchester, Grill Rm. (W1)

Embassy (W1)
English Garden (SW3)
Enoteca Turi (SW15)
Fat Duck (Berks)
ffiona's (W8)
French Horn (Berks)
Gaudí (EC1)
Glasshouse (Kew)
Goring Dining Rm. (SW1)
Gravetye Manor (W. Sus)
Greenhouse (W1)
Green Olive (W9)
Greens (SW1)
Grenadier (SW1)
Hartwell House (Bucks)
Havelock Tavern (W14)
John Burton-Race (NW1)
Kensington Place (W8)
La Famiglia (SW10)
La Fontana (SW1)
La Poule au Pot (SW1)
La Tante Claire (SW1)
La Trompette (W4)
La Trouvaille (W1)
Le Gavroche (W1)
Le Manoir/Quat'Saisons (Oxon)
Le Soufflé (W1)
L'Incontro (SW1)
L'Oranger (SW1)
Lundum's (SW7)
Maquis (W6)
Mirabelle (W1)
Monkeys (SW3)
Monsieur Max (Hampton Hill)
Monza (SW3)
Moro (EC1)
Motcomb's (SW1)
MVH (SW13)
Noble Rot (W1)
Notting Grill (W11)
Odette's (NW1)
Olivo (SW1)
1 Lombard St. (EC3)
192 (W11)
One-Seven-Nine (WC2)
Orrery (W1)
Osteria Antica Bologna (SW11)
Palm Court (WC2)
Parade (W5)
Parisienne Chophse. (SW3)
Passione (W1)
Pied à Terre (W1)
Polygon B&G (SW4)
Prism (EC3)
Providores/Tapa Rm. (W1)
Putney Bridge (SW15)
QC (WC1)

200   www.zagat.com

Special Feature Index

Randall & Aubin (W1)
Ransome's Dock (SW11)
Rhodes in the Square (SW1)
Richard Corrigan/Lindsay (W1)
Ritz (W1)
Riva (SW13)
River Cafe (W6)
Roussillon (SW1)
Rules (WC2)
Sabbia (SW3)
Santini (SW1)
Sartoria (W1)
Savoy Grill (WC2)
Savoy River (WC2)
Scalini (SW3)
Simpson's/Strand/Grand (WC2)
Sir Charles Napier (Oxon)
Smiths of Smithfield - Din. (EC1)
Smiths of Smithfield-Top (EC1)
Square (W1)
St. John (EC1)
Toto's (SW3)
Vale (W9)
Verbanella (SW3)
Villandry (W1)
Waterside Inn (Berks)
Wilton's (SW1)
Wòdka (W8)
Zafferano (SW1)
Ziani (SW3)

Historic Places

(Year opened; *building)
1598 Gravetye Manor (W. Sus)
1662 Bleeding Heart (EC1)*
1667 Ye Olde Cheshire Cheese (EC4)
1700's Admiralty (WC2)*
1742 Grenadier (SW1)
1742 Wilton's (SW1)
1798 Rules (WC2)
1828 Simpson's/Strand/Grand (WC2)
1828 Simpson's/Strand/Simply (WC2)
1889 Sweetings (EC4)
1897 Connaught (W1)
1906 Ritz (W1)

Hotel Dining

Berkeley Hotel
    La Tante Claire (SW1)
    Vong (SW1)
Blakes Hotel
    Blakes Hotel (SW7)
Brown's Hotel
    Brown's Hotel, 1837 (W1)
Capital, The
    Capital (SW3)
Carlton Tower
    Grissini (SW1)
    Rib Room/Oyster Bar (SW1)
Churchill Inter-Continental
    Locanda Locatelli (W1)
Claridge's Hotel
    Gordon Ramsay/Claridge's (W1)
Cliveden Hotel, The
    Cliveden, Waldo's (Berks)
Connaught Hotel
    Connaught (W1)
Crowne Plaza London St. James
    Quilon (SW1)
Dolphin Square Hotel
    Rhodes in the Square (SW1)
Dorchester, The
    Dorchester, Grill Rm. (W1)
    Dorchester, Oriental (W1)
Four Seasons Canary Wharf
    Four Seasons, Quadrato (E14)
Four Seasons Hotel
    Four Seasons, Lanes (W1)
French Horn Hotel
    French Horn (Berks)
Gore Hotel
    190, Downstairs (SW7)
    Bistrot 190 (SW7)
Goring Hotel, The
    Goring Dining Rm. (SW1)
Gravetye Manor Hotel
    Gravetye Manor (W. Sus)
Great Eastern Hotel
    Aurora (EC2)
    Fishmarket (EC2)
    George Bar (EC2)
    Terminus (EC2)
Halkin Hotel
    Nahm (SW1)
Hartwell House
    Hartwell House (Bucks)
Hempel Hotel
    I-Thai (W2)
Hilton Park Lane
    Windows on the World (W1)
Hotel Inter-Continental
    Le Soufflé (W1)
Landmark London
    John Burton-Race (NW1)
Lanesborough, The
    Lanesborough (SW1)
Le Manoir aux Quat'Saisons
    Le Manoir/Quat'Saisons (Oxon)
Le Meridien Piccadilly
    Terrace (W1)

Special Feature Index

Le Meridien Waldorf
  Palm Court (WC2)
L'Hotel
  Le Metro (SW3)
London Bridge Hotel
  Simply Nico (SE1)
London Marriott County Hall
  County Hall (SE1)
Mandarin Oriental Hyde Park
  Foliage (SW1)
Metropolitan Hotel
  Nobu (W1)
Millennium Knightsbridge Hotel
  Mju (SW1)
Millennium Mayfair Hotel
  Shogun (W1)
Montcalm Nikko Hotel
  Crescent (W1)
One Aldwych Hotel
  Axis (WC2)
  Indigo (WC2)
Renaissance-Chancery Court
  QC (WC1)
Ritz Hotel
  Ritz (W1)
Royal Garden Hotel
  Tenth (W8)
Royal National Hotel
  Poons (WC1)
Sanderson Hotel
  Spoon+ at Sanderson (W1)
Savoy Hotel
  Savoy Grill (WC2)
  Savoy River (WC2)
  Upstairs/Savoy (WC2)
Sheraton Park Tower
  One-O-One (SW1)
St. Martin's Lane Hotel
  Asia de Cuba (WC2)
  Tuscan Steak (WC2)
Thistle Victoria Hotel
  Christopher's (SW1)
Vineyard at Stockcross
  Vineyard/Stockcross (Berks)
Waterside Inn
  Waterside Inn (Berks)

"In" Places

Admiral Codrington (SW3)
Aperitivo (W1)
Assaggi (W2)
Avenue (SW1)
Axis (WC2)
Baltic (SE1)
Bam-Bou (W1)
Belgo Centraal (WC2)
Belgo Noord (NW1)
Belgo Zuid (W10)
Belvedere (W8)
Bibendum (SW3)
Bibendum Oyster Bar (SW3)
Bierodrome (multi. loc.)
Blakes Hotel (SW7)
Bush Bar & Grill (W12)
Cafe at Sotheby's (W1)
Cafe Lazeez (SW7)
Canyon (Richmond)
Carluccio's Caffe (multi. loc.)
Catch (SW5)
Cecconi's (W1)
Cellar Gascon (EC1)
Chez Bruce (SW17)
Chez Max (SW10)
Christopher's (multi. loc.)
Cinnamon Club (SW1)
Circus (W1)
City Rhodes (EC4)
Clarke's (W8)
Club Gascon (EC1)
Criterion Grill (W1)
Daphne's (SW3)
Drones (SW1)
E&O (W11)
ECapital (W1)
Electric Brasserie (W11)
Emporio Armani Caffe (SW3)
Fifth Floor (SW1)
Fifth Floor Cafe (SW1)
Fish! (multi. loc.)
Glasshouse (Kew)
Gordon Ramsay/Claridge's (W1)
Gordon Ramsay/68 Royal (SW3)
Hakkasan (W1)
Harry's Social Club (W2)
Hush (W1)
Incognico (WC2)
itsu (SW3)
Ivy (WC2)
Joe's (SW3)
Joe's Rest. Bar (SW1)
J. Sheekey (WC2)
Kensington Place (W8)
Langan's Brasserie (W1)
La Trompette (W4)
Le Caprice (SW1)
Les Trois Garcons (E1)
Livebait (multi. loc.)
Locanda Locatelli (W1)
Lola's (N1)
Maison Novelli (EC1)
Maquis (W6)
Masala Zone (W1)
Mirabelle (W1)
Momo (W1)

Special Feature Index

Monsieur Max (Hampton Hill)
Montana (SW6)
Nahm (SW1)
Nam Long Le Shaker (SW5)
Nicole's (W1)
Nobu (W1)
Oliveto (SW1)
Olivo (SW1)
Orrery (W1)
Orsino (W11)
Orso (WC2)
Oxo Tower (SE1)
Parisienne Chophse. (SW3)
Pasha (SW7)
Pétrus (SW1)
Pharmacy (W11)
Pizza Metro (SW11)
PJ's Bar & Grill (SW3)
Providores/Tapa Rm. (W1)
Putney Bridge (SW15)
Quo Vadis (W1)
Racine (SW3)
Randall & Aubin (multi. loc.)
Real Greek (N1)
Richard Corrigan/Lindsay (W1)
River Cafe (W6)
Rosmarino (NW8)
San Lorenzo (SW3)
Smiths of Smithfield - Din. (EC1)
Spiga (multi. loc.)
Spighetta (W1)
Spoon+ at Sanderson (W1)
Square (W1)
St. John (EC1)
Sugar Club (W1)
Timo (W8)
Tom's Deli (W11)
Tsunami (SW4)
Vingt-Quatre (SW10)
Vong (SW1)
Wagamama (multi. loc.)
Wapping Food (E1)
West Street (WC2)
Yo! Sushi (multi. loc.)
Zafferano (SW1)
Zaika (W8)
Zaika Bazaar (SW3)
Ziani (SW3)
Zilli Fish (multi. loc.)
Zuma (SW7)

Late Dining
(Weekday closing hour;
*check locations)
Balans (W1) (3 AM)
Café Boheme (W1) (midnight)
Cafe Lazeez (multi. loc.) (1 AM)
Efes Kebab (W1) (2 AM)
Fakhreldine (W2) (1 AM)
Jen Hong Kong (W1) (3 AM)
Joe Allen (WC2) (2.45 AM)
Lee Ho Fook (W1) (midnight)
Le Mercury (N1) (1 AM)
Little Italy (W1) (4 AM)
Maroush (multi. loc.)*
Mezzonine (W1) (1 AM)
Mr. Kong (WC2) (2.45 AM)
Noble Rot (W1) (3 AM)
Pizza Pomodoro (SW3) (1 AM)
Soho Spice (W1) (midnight)
Souk (WC2) (1 AM)
Vingt-Quatre (SW10) (24 hrs.)
Yas (W14) (5 AM)

No Smoking Sections
Admiralty (WC2)
Archipelago (W1)
Arkansas Cafe (E1)
Ask Pizza (multi. loc.)
Bankside (SE1)
Big Easy (SW3)
Black & Blue (W8)
Blandford Street (W1)
Bombay Brasserie (SW7)
Brasserie Roux (SW1)
Brasserie St. Quentin (SW3)
Brown's Hotel, 1837 (W1)
Cafe Fish (W1)
Cafe Japan (NW11)
Cantina Vinopolis (SE1)
Canyon (Richmond)
Carluccio's Caffe (W1)
Casale Franco (N1)
Caviar Kaspia (W1)
Chamberlain's (EC3)
Chez Bruce (SW17)
Chez Gérard (multi. loc.)
China House (W1)
Chiswick, The (W4)
Chuen Cheng Ku (W1)
Chutney Mary (SW10)
Clerkenwell Din. Rm./Bar (EC1)
Creelers (SW3)
Daquise (SW7)
Duke of Cambridge (N1)
Enoteca Turi (SW15)
Eyre Brothers (EC2)
Fakhreldine (W1)
Fifth Floor Cafe (SW1)
Fish Hoek (W4)
Fortnum's Fountain (W1)
Four Seasons, Lanes (W1)
Four Seasons, Quadrato (E14)
Frederick's (N1)

Special Feature Index

Gordon Ramsay/Claridge's (W1)
Hard Rock Cafe (W1)
Hi Sushi (W1)
Joe Allen (WC2)
Kettners (W1)
Khan's (W2)
Kulu Kulu Sushi (multi. loc.)
Le Soufflé (W1)
Light House (SW19)
Livebait (multi. loc.)
Lucky Seven (W2)
Mango Tree (SW1)
Manor (W11)
Mao Tai (multi. loc.)
Maquis (W6)
Mimmo d'Ischia (SW1)
Mitsukoshi (SW1)
Montana (SW6)
Moshi Moshi Sushi (multi. loc.)
Motcomb's (SW1)
Myna Bird (WC1)
Naked Turtle (SW14)
New Culture Rev. (multi. loc.)
Nicole's (W1)
Nobu (W1)
Noura (SW1)
Orsino (W11)
Orso (WC2)
Otto Dining Lounge (W9)
Ozer Rest. & Bar (W1)
Pacific Oriental (EC2)
Painted Heron (SW10)
Palm Court (WC2)
Parsee (N19)
Patara (multi. loc.)
Patisserie Valerie (multi. loc.)
People's Palace (SE1)
Pepper Tree (SW4)
Pescatori (multi. loc.)
Philip Owens' (WC2)
Phoenix B&G (SW15)
Pizza Express (multi. loc.)
Pizza on the Park (SW1)
Pizza Organic (multi. loc.)
Pizza Pomodoro (EC2)
Planet Hollywood (W1)
QC (WC1)
Quality Chop Hse. (EC1)
Quilon (SW1)
Racine (SW3)
Rasa (W1)
Red Fort (W1)
Richoux (multi. loc.)
RK Stanley's (W1)
Rocket (W1)
Saga (W1)
Santa Fe (N1)
Sarkhel's (SW18)
Savoy River (WC2)
Scotts (W1)
Seashell (NW1)
Shepherd's (SW1)
Six-13 (W1)
Solly's (NW11)
Spighetta (W1)
Stepping Stone (SW8)
Strada (multi. loc.)
Sugar Club (W1)
Tabla (E14)
Tandoori of Chelsea (SW3)
Tas (SE1)
Tate Gallery Rest. (SW1)
Tenth (W8)
Terminus (EC2)
Terrace (W1)
T.G.I. Friday's (multi. loc.)
Thierry's (SW3)
Two Brothers Fish (N3)
Union Cafe (W1)
Vale (W9)
Vineyard/Stockcross (Berks)
Vong (SW1)
Windows on the World (W1)
Yoshino (W1)
Zamoyski (NW3)
Zuma (SW7)

Noteworthy Newcomers

Adam Street (WC2)
Al Bustan (SW7)
Almeida (N1)
Babylon (W8)
Blandford Street (W1)
Brasserie Roux (SW1)
Brasserie/Sans Culottes (WC2)
Café Grand Prix (W1)
Carpaccio (SW3)
Chamberlain's (EC3)
China Dream (NW3)
Clerkenwell Din. Rm./Bar (EC1)
Connaught (W1)
Deca (W1)
Dumela (W4)
E&O (W11)
ECapital (W1)
Electric Brasserie (W11)
Embassy (W1)
Eyre Brothers (EC2)
Fish Hoek (W4)
Harry's Social Club (W2)
Il Posto (W11)
Independence (N1)
Innecto (W1)
Just the Bridge (EC4)

Special Feature Index

Lan Na Thai (SW11)
La Trouvaille (W1)
Le Deuxieme (WC2)
Locanda Locatelli (W1)
Lucky Seven (W2)
Mango Tree (SW1)
Maquis (W6)
MVH (SW13)
Myna Bird (WC1)
Notting Grill (W11)
Oak, The (W2)
Ophim (W1)
Painted Heron (SW10)
Perseverance (WC1)
Philip Owens' (WC2)
Providores/Tapa Rm. (W1)
QC (WC1)
Quod (SW1)
Racine (SW3)
Sabbia (SW3)
Salisbury Tavern (SW6)
Sand Bar (SW4)
Sophie's Steakhse. (SW10)
Sugar Hut (SW6)
Sumosan (W1)
Thyme (SW4)
Timo (W8)
Tsunami (SW4)
West Street (WC2)
Wheeler's, St. James's (SW1)
Zuma (SW7)

Offbeat

Alounak (multi. loc.)
Aperitivo (W1)
Archipelago (W1)
Arkansas Cafe (E1)
Asia de Cuba (WC2)
Belgo Centraal (WC2)
Belgo Noord (NW1)
Belgo Zuid (W10)
Bierodrome (multi. loc.)
Blah! Blah! Blah! (W12)
Bloom's (NW11)
Blue Elephant (SW6)
Boisdale (multi. loc.)
Books for Cooks (W11)
Cambio de Tercio (SW5)
Cellar Gascon (EC1)
Chinon (W14)
Chor Bizarre (W1)
Club Gascon (EC1)
Costa's Grill (W8)
Daquise (SW7)
Feng Shang Floating Rest. (NW1)
ffiona's (W8)
Food for Thought (WC2)

itsu (multi. loc.)
Jason's (W9)
Jim Thompson's Wok (multi. loc.)
Kaifeng (NW4)
Kulu Kulu Sushi (multi. loc.)
La Porte des Indes (W1)
Les Trois Garcons (E1)
Levant (W1)
LMNT (E8)
Lola's (N1)
Lucky Seven (W2)
Maggie Jones's (W8)
Mju (SW1)
Momo (W1)
Moro (EC1)
Moshi Moshi Sushi (EC2)
MVH (SW13)
Nahm (SW1)
Nautilus Fish (NW6)
Ozer Rest. & Bar (W1)
Pharmacy (W11)
Pizza Metro (SW11)
Place Below (EC2)
Polygon B&G (SW4)
Providores/Tapa Rm. (W1)
Quality Chop Hse. (EC1)
Rainforest Cafe (W1)
Randall & Aubin (W1)
Ransome's Dock (SW11)
Richard Corrigan/Lindsay (W1)
Sale e Pepe (SW1)
Solly's (NW11)
Souk (WC2)
Spoon+ at Sanderson (W1)
St. John (EC1)
Sugar Club (W1)
Tate Gallery Rest. (SW1)
Tom's Deli (W11)
Troubadour (SW5)
Truc Vert (W1)
Tsunami (SW4)
Wagamama (multi. loc.)
Wapping Food (E1)
Yo! Sushi (multi. loc.)
Zaika Bazaar (SW3)

Outdoor Dining

(G=garden; P=patio;
PV=pavement; T=terrace;
W=waterside)
Admiral Codrington (SW3) (P)
Al Hamra (W1) (P)
Archipelago (W1) (P)
Ark (W8) (T)
Artigiano (NW3) (PV)
Bam-Bou (W1) (T)

Special Feature Index

Bank Westminster/Zander (SW1) (T)
Belair House (SE21) (T,W)
Belvedere (W8) (T)
Bibendum Oyster Bar (SW3) (P)
Black Truffle (NW1) (G)
Blandford Street (W1) (PV)
Boisdale (SW1) (G)
Brackenbury (W6) (P)
Brinkley's (SW10) (G,PV)
Builders Arms (SW3) (PV)
Bush Bar & Grill (W12) (P)
Butlers Wharf (SE1) (T)
Cantina del Ponte (SE1) (T,W)
Cantinetta Venegazzu (SW11) (P)
Canyon (Richmond) (P,T)
Caraffini (SW1) (PV)
Casale Franco (N1) (P)
Chamberlain's (EC3) (PV)
Chiswick, The (W4) (PV)
Chives (SW10) (G)
Cigala (WC1) (P)
Clerkenwell Din. Rm. (EC1) (PV)
Coq d'Argent (EC2) (G,T)
Costa's Grill (W8) (G)
Cotto (W14) (PV)
Dakota (W11) (T)
Dan's (SW3) (G)
Daphne's (SW3) (G)
El Gaucho (SW3) (T)
Elistano (SW3) (PV)
Enterprise (SW3) (PV)
Fifth Floor Cafe (SW1) (T)
Four Seasons, Quadrato (E14) (T)
Gaudí (EC1) (T)
Giraffe (SW11) (T)
Hard Rock Cafe (W1) (T)
Havelock Tavern (W14) (G,PV)
House/Rosslyn Hill (NW3) (T)
Hush (W1) (P)
Ishbilia (SW1) (PV)
Jason's (W9) (T,W)
Joe's (SW3) (PV)
Julie's (W11) (P,PV)
Just the Bridge (EC4) (T)
La Famiglia (SW10) (G)
Langan's Coq d'Or (SW5) (T)
La Poule au Pot (SW1) (PV)
La Trompette (W4) (P)
La Trouvaille (W1) (PV)
Le Boudin Blanc (W1) (T)
Le Colombier (SW3) (T)
Le Pont de la Tour (SE1) (T,W)
L'Oranger (SW1) (P)
Lundum's (SW7) (P)
Made in Italy (SW3) (T)
Maquis (W6) (P)
Mediterraneo (W11) (P)
Mirabelle (W1) (P,G)
Monza (SW3) (PV)
Moro (EC1) (PV)
Motcomb's (SW1) (PV)
MVH (SW13) (P,T)
Oak, The (W2) (PV)
Odette's (NW1) (G,PV)
Oriel (SW1) (PV)
Orrery (W1) (T)
Osteria Basilico (W11) (P)
Oxo Tower (SE1) (T,W)
Oxo Tower Brasserie (SE1) (T,W)
Painted Heron (SW10) (T)
Passione (W1) (P)
Pellicano (SW3) (PV)
Phoenix B&G (SW15) (T)
Pizza Metro (SW11) (PV)
Pizza on the Park (SW1) (PV)
PJ's Bar & Grill (SW3) (PV)
PJ's Grill (WC2) (PV)
Place Below (EC2) (G)
Pucci Pizza (SW3) (PV)
Ransome's Dock (SW11) (T,W)
Real Greek (N1) (PV)
Riccardo's (SW3) (P)
Ritz (W1) (G)
River Cafe (W6) (P)
Rocket (W1) (PV)
Rosmarino (NW8) (T)
Salisbury Tavern (SW6) (P)
Smiths/Smithfield-Top (EC1) (T)
Spiga (SW3) (PV)
Spoon+ at Sanderson (W1) (G)
Stratford's (W8) (PV)
Sweetings (EC4) (PV)
Thai on the River (SW10) (P,W)
Tom's Deli (W11) (G)
Toto's (SW3) (G)
Vama (SW10) (P)
Vine (NW5) (G)
Vingt-Quatre (SW10) (PV)
Wapping Food (E1) (P)
Zilli Fish (WC2) (PV)

People-Watching

Admiral Codrington (SW3)
Avenue (SW1)
Bam-Bou (W1)
Bangkok (SW7)
Belvedere (W8)
Bibendum (SW3)
Bibendum Oyster Bar (SW3)
Blakes Hotel (SW7)
Bluebird (SW3)
Cafe at Sotheby's (W1)
Caraffini (SW1)

Special Feature Index

Cecconi's (W1)
Christopher's (WC2)
Circus (W1)
Club Gascon (EC1)
Dakota (W11)
Daphne's (SW3)
Drones (SW1)
E&O (W11)
Emporio Armani Caffe (SW3)
Fifth Floor (SW1)
Fifth Floor Cafe (SW1)
Glasshouse (Kew)
Gordon Ramsay/Claridge's (W1)
Gordon Ramsay/68 Royal (SW3)
Hakkasan (W1)
Hush (W1)
Ivy (WC2)
Joe's (SW3)
J. Sheekey (WC2)
Kensington Place (W8)
La Famiglia (SW10)
Langan's Bistro (W1)
Langan's Brasserie (W1)
La Trompette (W4)
Le Caprice (SW1)
Le Gavroche (W1)
Locanda Locatelli (W1)
Manor (W11)
Mirabelle (W1)
Momo (W1)
Nicole's (W1)
Nobu (W1)
Orso (WC2)
Parisienne Chophse. (SW3)
Pasha (SW7)
Pétrus (SW1)
Pharmacy (W11)
PJ's Bar & Grill (SW3)
Providores/Tapa Rm. (W1)
Quaglino's (SW1)
Quo Vadis (W1)
River Cafe (W6)
San Lorenzo (SW3)
Santini (SW1)
Savoy Grill (WC2)
Savoy River (WC2)
Smiths of Smithfield - Din. (EC1)
Spoon+ at Sanderson (W1)
Sugar Club (W1)
Teatro (W1)
Timo (W8)
Tom's Deli (W11)
Tsunami (SW4)
Tuscan Steak (WC2)
Vong (SW1)
Waterside Inn (Berks)
West Street (WC2)
Zafferano (SW1)
Zaika (W8)
Zilli Fish (W1)
Zinc B&G (W1)

Power Scenes
Aurora (EC2)
Avenue (SW1)
Bank Aldwych (WC2)
Belvedere (W8)
Blue Print Cafe (SE1)
Caravaggio (EC3)
Cecconi's (W1)
City Rhodes (EC4)
Club Gascon (EC1)
Daphne's (SW3)
Dorchester, Grill Rm. (W1)
Drones (SW1)
Four Seasons, Lanes (W1)
Gordon Ramsay/Claridge's (W1)
Gordon Ramsay/68 Royal (SW3)
Goring Dining Rm. (SW1)
Greenhouse (W1)
Greens (SW1)
Ivy (WC2)
J. Sheekey (WC2)
Langan's Brasserie (W1)
Launceston Place (W8)
Le Caprice (SW1)
Le Gavroche (W1)
Le Manoir/Quat'Saisons (Oxon)
Le Soufflé (W1)
L'Incontro (SW1)
Mirabelle (W1)
Neal Street (WC2)
Nobu (W1)
Odin's (W1)
1 Lombard St. (EC3)
Pétrus (SW1)
Prism (EC3)
Ritz (W1)
San Lorenzo (SW3)
Savoy Grill (WC2)
Savoy River (WC2)
Shepherd's (SW1)
Spoon+ at Sanderson (W1)
Square (W1)
West Street (WC2)
Wilton's (SW1)
Zafferano (SW1)

Pre-Theatre Menus
(Call for prices and times)
Almeida (N1)
Archipelago (W1)
Aroma Chinese (multi. loc.)
Asia de Cuba (WC2)

Special Feature Index

Atlantic B&G (W1)
Avenue (SW1)
Axis (WC2)
Bank Aldwych (WC2)
Belgo Zuid (W10)
Benihana (multi. loc.)
Bentley's (W1)
Bice (W1)
Bistrot 190 (SW7)
Bluebird (SW3)
Brasserie St. Quentin (SW3)
Bush Bar & Grill (W12)
Café des Amis du Vin (WC2)
Cafe Fish (W1)
Cantina del Ponte (SE1)
Che (SW1)
Chez Gérard (multi. loc.)
Chor Bizarre (W1)
Christopher's (multi. loc.)
Chutney Mary (SW10)
Cinnamon Club (SW1)
Circus (W1)
Clerkenwell Din. Rm./Bar (EC1)
County Hall (SE1)
Criterion Grill (W1)
Dorchester, Grill Rm. (W1)
East One (EC1)
Food for Thought (WC2)
Frederick's (N1)
Goring Dining Rm. (SW1)
Greens (SW1)
House/Rosslyn Hill (NW3)
Incognico (WC2)
Indigo (WC2)
Joe Allen (WC2)
La Bouchée (SW7)
Lanesborough (SW1)
Le Cafe du Jardin (WC2)
Le Caprice (SW1)
Le Deuxieme (WC2)
L'Escargot (W1)
L'Estaminet (WC2)
Livebait (multi. loc.)
Lola's (N1)
L'Oranger (SW1)
Manzi's (WC2)
Matsuri (SW1)
Mela (WC2)
Mezzo (W1)
Mezzonine (W1)
Mitsukoshi (SW1)
Mon Plaisir (WC2)
Monsieur Max (Hampton Hill)
One-Seven-Nine (WC2)
Orsino (W11)
Orso (WC2)
Oxo Tower Brasserie (SE1)

People's Palace (SE1)
Phoenicia (W8)
Planet Hollywood (W1)
Polygon B&G (SW4)
Porters (WC2)
Prospect Grill (WC2)
Purple Sage (W1)
QC (WC1)
Quaglino's (SW1)
Quo Vadis (W1)
Real Greek (N1)
Red Fort (W1)
Richard Corrigan/Lindsay (W1)
Richoux (multi. loc.)
Ritz (W1)
Rowley's (SW1)
R.S.J. (SE1)
Rules (WC2)
Savoy River (WC2)
Searcy's/Barbican (EC2)
Simpson's/Strand/Grand (WC2)
Simpson's/Strand/Simply (WC2)
Smollensky's/Strand (WC2)
Sofra (multi. loc.)
Soho Spice (W1)
Stratford's (W8)
Sugar Reef (W1)
Tamarind (W1)
Teatro (W1)
Tenth (W8)
Thai Pavilion (W1)
Upstairs/Savoy (WC2)
Vama (SW10)
Vasco & Piero's (W1)
Veeraswamy (W1)
Villandry (W1)
Vong (SW1)
Waterloo Fire Station (SE1)
Zen Chelsea (SW3)
Zilli Fish (multi. loc.)

Private Rooms

Adam Street (WC2)
Admiralty (WC2)
Alastair Little (W1)
Alloro (W1)
Almeida (N1)
Aperitivo (W1)
Arkansas Cafe (E1)
Atlantic B&G (W1)
Axis (WC2)
Baltic (SE1)
Bam-Bou (W1)
Belgo Centraal (WC2)
Belvedere (W8)
Blakes Hotel (SW7)
Bluebird (SW3)

Special Feature Index

Bombay Bicycle Club (SW12)
Brasserie Roux (SW1)
Brown's Hotel, 1837 (W1)
Cactus Blue (SW3)
Café Grand Prix (W1)
Cantina Vinopolis (SE1)
Capital (SW3)
Caviar Kaspia (W1)
Chez Bruce (SW17)
Christopher's (WC2)
Chuen Cheng Ku (W1)
Chutney Mary (SW10)
Cinnamon Club (SW1)
Circus (W1)
City Rhodes (EC4)
Connaught (W1)
Creelers (SW3)
Dakota (W11)
Dan's (SW3)
Daphne's (SW3)
Deca (W1)
Dorchester, Oriental (W1)
Drones (SW1)
E&O (W11)
Elena's l'Etoile (W1)
English Garden (SW3)
Fairuz (W1)
Floriana (SW3)
Garbo's (W1)
Gordon Ramsay/Claridge's (W1)
Goring Dining Rm. (SW1)
Gravetye Manor (W. Sus)
Great Eastern Dining Rm. (EC2)
Greens (SW1)
Grissini (SW1)
Hard Rock Cafe (W1)
Hartwell House (Bucks)
Hush (W1)
Il Convivio (SW1)
I-Thai (W2)
Ivy (WC2)
Jason's (W9)
John Burton-Race (NW1)
Julie's (W11)
Just St. James's (SW1)
Kai (W1)
Kensington Place (W8)
La Famiglia (SW10)
Lanesborough (SW1)
La Porte des Indes (W1)
La Poule au Pot (SW1)
La Tante Claire (SW1)
La Trouvaille (W1)
Launceston Place (W8)
Le Colombier (SW3)
Le Gavroche (W1)
Le Manoir/Quat'Saisons (Oxon)
Lemonia (NW1)
Le Pont de la Tour (SE1)
L'Escargot (W1)
Les Trois Garcons (E1)
Le Suquet (SW3)
L'Incontro (SW1)
Lola's (N1)
L'Oranger (SW1)
Maison Novelli (EC1)
Manor (W11)
Mao Tai (SW6)
Maquis (W6)
Mimmo d'Ischia (SW1)
Mirabelle (W1)
Mitsukoshi (SW1)
Momo (W1)
Moro (EC1)
Motcomb's (SW1)
Mr. Chow (SW1)
MVH (SW13)
Neal Street (WC2)
Nicole's (W1)
Nobu (W1)
Notting Grill (W11)
1 Lombard St. (EC3)
1 Lombard St. Brass. (EC3)
One-Seven-Nine (WC2)
Orsino (W11)
Parade (W5)
Pasha (SW7)
Passione (W1)
People's Palace (SE1)
Perseverance (WC1)
Philip Owens' (WC2)
Pied à Terre (W1)
Planet Hollywood (W1)
Poissonnerie de l'Avenue (SW3)
Prism (EC3)
Prospect Grill (WC2)
Quaglino's (SW1)
Quo Vadis (W1)
Racine (SW3)
Rainforest Cafe (W1)
Red Fort (W1)
Rib Room/Oyster Bar (SW1)
Richard Corrigan/Lindsay (W1)
Ritz (W1)
Rocket (W1)
Roussillon (SW1)
Royal China (multi. loc.)
Rules (WC2)
Salt House (NW8)
San Lorenzo Fuoriporta (SW19)
Santa Fe (N1)
Sartoria (SW1)
Scotts (W1)
Sir Charles Napier (Oxon)

Special Feature Index

Six-13 (W1)
Smiths of Smithfield - Din. (EC1)
Smiths of Smithfield-Top (EC1)
Souk (WC2)
Spoon+ at Sanderson (W1)
Square (W1)
St. John (EC1)
Sugar Club (W1)
Suntory (SW1)
Tatsuso (EC1)
Tentazioni (SE1)
Texas Embassy Cantina (SW1)
Thai Square (SW1)
Thierry's (SW3)
Timo (W8)
Vale (W9)
Vasco & Piero's (W1)
Veeraswamy (W1)
Vineyard/Stockcross (Berks)
Waterside Inn (Berks)
West Street (WC2)
Wheeler's, St. James's (SW1)
Wilton's (SW1)
Ye Olde Cheshire Cheese (EC4)
Yoshino (W1)

Pubs/Microbreweries

Admiral Codrington (SW3)
Anglesea Arms (W6)
Builders Arms (SW3)
Chiswick, The (W4)
Churchill Arms (W8)
Cow, The (W2)
Duke of Cambridge (N1)
Eagle (EC1)
Engineer (NW1)
Enterprise (SW3)
George Bar (EC2)
Grenadier (SW1)
Havelock Tavern (W14)
Honest Cabbage (SE1)
Independence (N1)
Lansdowne (NW1)
Mash (W1)
Oak, The (W2)
Peasant (EC1)
Perseverance (WC1)
Prince Bonaparte (W2)
Salisbury Tavern (SW6)
Salt House (NW8)
Salusbury Pub (NW6)
Vine (NW5)
Westbourne (W2)
Ye Olde Cheshire Cheese (EC4)

Pudding Specialists

Alastair Little (W1)
Almeida (N1)
Asia de Cuba (WC2)
Aubergine (SW10)
Aurora (EC2)
Belvedere (W8)
Bibendum (SW3)
Blakes Hotel (SW7)
Brown's Hotel, 1837 (W1)
Capital (SW3)
City Rhodes (EC4)
Clarke's (W8)
Club Gascon (EC1)
Embassy (W1)
Fat Duck (Berks)
Fifth Floor (SW1)
Foliage (SW1)
Fortnum's Fountain (W1)
Four Seasons, Lanes (W1)
Glasshouse (Kew)
Gordon Ramsay/Claridge's (W1)
Gordon Ramsay/68 Royal (SW3)
Greenhouse (W1)
Lanesborough (SW1)
La Tante Claire (SW1)
La Trompette (W4)
Le Cabanon (W1)
Le Gavroche (W1)
Le Manoir/Quat'Saisons (Oxon)
Le Soufflé (W1)
Locanda Locatelli (W1)
L'Oranger (SW1)
Maison Novelli (EC1)
Mirabelle (W1)
Monkeys (SW3)
Nobu (W1)
Orrery (W1)
Patisserie Valerie (multi. loc.)
Pétrus (SW1)
Providores/Tapa Rm. (W1)
Richard Corrigan/Lindsay (W1)
Richoux (multi. loc.)
Ritz (W1)
River Cafe (W6)
Spoon+ at Sanderson (W1)
Square (W1)
Vong (SW1)
Waterside Inn (Berks)

Quiet Conversation

Al Sultan (W1)
Aubergine (SW10)
Aurora (EC2)
Axis (WC2)
Belair House (SE21)
Bengal Clipper (SE1)
Bentley's (W1)
Bice (W1)
Blakes Hotel (SW7)

Special Feature Index

Brown's Hotel, 1837 (W1)
Capital (SW3)
Chives (SW10)
Creelers (SW3)
Dan's (SW3)
Dorchester, Oriental (W1)
Embassy (W1)
English Garden (SW3)
Foliage (SW1)
Four Seasons, Lanes (W1)
Four Seasons, Quadrato (E14)
Gordon Ramsay/Claridge's (W1)
Goring Dining Rm. (SW1)
Greens (SW1)
Hartwell House (Bucks)
Il Convivio (SW1)
Indigo (WC2)
Just St. James's (SW1)
Lanesborough (SW1)
La Tante Claire (SW1)
Launceston Place (W8)
Le Gavroche (W1)
Le Manoir/Quat'Saisons (Oxon)
L'Oranger (SW1)
Lundum's (SW7)
Mitsukoshi (SW1)
Mju (SW1)
Monkeys (SW3)
Odin's (W1)
One-O-One (SW1)
Orrery (W1)
Pétrus (SW1)
Ritz (W1)
Roussillon (SW1)
Salloos (SW1)
Savoy River (WC2)
Scotts (W1)
Stratford's (W8)
Waterside Inn (Berks)
Wilton's (SW1)
Windows on the World (W1)

Romantic Places
Andrew Edmunds (W1)
Aurora (EC2)
Belvedere (W8)
Blakes Hotel (SW7)
Blue Elephant (SW6)
Capital (SW3)
Caviar Kaspia (W1)
Chez Moi (W11)
Clarke's (W8)
Club Gascon (EC1)
Criterion Grill (W1)
Daphne's (SW3)
Drones (SW1)
Frederick's (N1)

French Horn (Berks)
Gordon Ramsay/Claridge's (W1)
Gordon Ramsay/68 Royal (SW3)
Gravetye Manor (W. Sus)
Hakkasan (W1)
Hartwell House (Bucks)
Julie's (W11)
Lanesborough (SW1)
La Poule au Pot (SW1)
Launceston Place (W8)
L'Aventure (NW8)
Le Café du Marché (EC1)
Le Caprice (SW1)
Le Gavroche (W1)
Le Manoir/Quat'Saisons (Oxon)
Le Pont de la Tour (SE1)
Les Trois Garcons (E1)
Locanda Locatelli (W1)
L'Oranger (SW1)
Lundum's (SW7)
Maggie Jones's (W8)
Mirabelle (W1)
Momo (W1)
Monkeys (SW3)
Nobu (W1)
Odette's (NW1)
Odin's (W1)
Orrery (W1)
Pétrus (SW1)
Pomegranates (SW1)
Prism (EC3)
Richard Corrigan/Lindsay (W1)
Ritz (W1)
River Cafe (W6)
Roussillon (SW1)
San Lorenzo (SW3)
Savoy River (WC2)
Snows on the Green (W6)
Square (W1)
Toto's (SW3)
Waterside Inn (Berks)
Windows on the World (W1)
Zafferano (SW1)

Senior Appeal
Al Duca (SW1)
Belair House (SE21)
Belvedere (W8)
Bentley's (W1)
Bloom's (NW11)
Brasserie St. Quentin (SW3)
Cafe at Sotheby's (W1)
Capital (SW3)
Caviar Kaspia (W1)
Cecconi's (W1)
Dan's (SW3)
Deca (W1)

www.zagat.com 211

Special Feature Index

Dorchester, Grill Rm. (W1)
Dorchester, Oriental (W1)
Drones (SW1)
Elena's l'Etoile (W1)
English Garden (SW3)
Floriana (SW3)
Foliage (SW1)
Fortnum's Fountain (W1)
Four Seasons, Lanes (W1)
Four Seasons, Quadrato (E14)
Glasshouse (Kew)
Gordon Ramsay/Claridge's (W1)
Gordon Ramsay/68 Royal (SW3)
Goring Dining Rm. (SW1)
Gravetye Manor (W. Sus)
Greenhouse (W1)
Greens (SW1)
Hartwell House (Bucks)
Ivy (WC2)
Jason's (W9)
John Burton-Race (NW1)
J. Sheekey (WC2)
Kai (W1)
Lanesborough (SW1)
Langan's Bistro (W1)
La Poule au Pot (SW1)
La Tante Claire (SW1)
Launceston Place (W8)
Le Caprice (SW1)
Le Gavroche (W1)
Le Manoir/Quat'Saisons (Oxon)
Le Soufflé (W1)
L'Incontro (SW1)
L'Oranger (SW1)
Lundum's (SW7)
Manzi's (WC2)
Mimmo d'Ischia (SW1)
Mirabelle (W1)
Monkeys (SW3)
Montpeliano (SW7)
Motcomb's (SW1)
Neal Street (WC2)
Noura (SW1)
Odin's (W1)
One-O-One (SW1)
Orrery (W1)
Parade (W5)
Patisserie Valerie (SW3)
Pétrus (SW1)
Poissonnerie de l'Avenue (SW3)
Racine (SW3)
Red Fort (W1)
Reubens (W1)
Rib Room/Oyster Bar (SW1)
Richoux (NW8)
Ritz (W1)
Riva (SW13)
Rosmarino (NW8)
Rowley's (SW1)
Rules (WC2)
Sartoria (W1)
Savoy Grill (WC2)
Savoy River (WC2)
Scalini (SW3)
Scotts (W1)
Shepherd's (SW1)
Simpson's/Strand/Grand (WC2)
Simpson's/Strand/Simply (WC2)
Square (W1)
Stratford's (W8)
Tate Gallery Rest. (SW1)
Toto's (SW3)
Upstairs/Savoy (WC2)
Waterside Inn (Berks)
Waterstones Red Rm. (W1)
Wilton's (SW1)
Zen Central (W1)
Zen Chelsea (SW3)

Set-Price Menus
(Call for prices and times)
Alastair Little (W1)
Alastair Little/Lancaster Rd. (W11)
Al Duca (SW1)
Alloro (W1)
Almeida (N1)
Archipelago (W1)
Aubergine (SW10)
Avenue (SW1)
Bibendum (SW3)
Blue Elephant (SW6)
Brasserie St. Quentin (SW3)
Brown's Hotel, 1837 (W1)
Butlers Wharf Chop Hse. (SE1)
Cantinetta Venegazzu (SW11)
Capital (SW3)
Caravaggio (EC3)
Caviar Kaspia (W1)
Chez Bruce (SW17)
Chez Gérard (multi. loc.)
Chiswick, The (W4)
Chor Bizarre (W1)
Christopher's (multi. loc.)
Chutney Mary (SW10)
Cinnamon Club (SW1)
Circus (W1)
City Miyama (EC4)
Clarke's (W8)
Clerkenwell Din. Rm./Bar (EC1)
Club Gascon (EC1)
Dan's (SW3)
Deca (W1)
Del Buongustaio (SW15)
Dorchester, Grill Rm. (W1)

Special Feature Index

Dorchester, Oriental (W1)
Drones (SW1)
Embassy (W1)
English Garden (SW3)
Foliage (SW1)
Four Seasons, Lanes (W1)
Four Seasons, Quadrato (E14)
Glasshouse (Kew)
Gordon Ramsay/Claridge's (W1)
Gordon Ramsay/68 Royal (SW3)
Goring Dining Rm. (SW1)
Il Convivio (SW1)
Ivy (WC2)
Jason's (W9)
John Burton-Race (NW1)
J. Sheekey (WC2)
Julie's (W11)
Lanesborough (SW1)
La Porte des Indes (W1)
La Poule au Pot (SW1)
La Tante Claire (SW1)
La Trompette (W4)
Launceston Place (W8)
Le Caprice (SW1)
Le Colombier (SW3)
Le Deuxieme (WC2)
Le Gavroche (W1)
Le Pont de la Tour (SE1)
L'Escargot (W1)
Le Soufflé (W1)
L'Incontro (SW1)
Lola's (N1)
L'Oranger (SW1)
Lundum's (SW7)
Mao Tai (multi. loc.)
Mela (WC2)
Mezzo (W1)
Mitsukoshi (SW1)
Miyama (W1)
Momo (W1)
Monsieur Max (Hampton Hill)
Motcomb's (SW1)
Nahm (SW1)
Nobu (W1)
Odin's (W1)
1 Lombard St. (EC3)
Orrery (W1)
Oslo Court (NW8)
Oxo Tower (SE1)
People's Palace (SE1)
Pharmacy (W11)
Phoenicia (W8)
Pied à Terre (W1)
Poissonnerie de l'Avenue (SW3)
Pomegranates (SW1)
Princess Garden (W1)
Putney Bridge (SW15)
Quaglino's (SW1)
Quo Vadis (W1)
Racine (SW3)
Real Greek (N1)
Rib Room/Oyster Bar (SW1)
Richard Corrigan/Lindsay (W1)
Ritz (W1)
Rosmarino (NW8)
Roussillon (SW1)
Sarkhel's (SW18)
Sartoria (W1)
Savoy Grill (WC2)
Savoy River (WC2)
Searcy's/Barbican (EC2)
Shogun (W1)
Six-13 (W1)
Snows on the Green (W6)
Sonny's (SW13)
Square (W1)
Suntory (SW1)
Tabla (E14)
Tamarind (W1)
Tate Gallery Rest. (SW1)
Tatsuso (EC1)
Teatro (W1)
Tentazioni (SE1)
Tenth (W8)
Thai on the River (SW10)
Thai Pavilion (W1)
Thierry's (SW3)
Ubon (E14)
Upstairs/Savoy (WC2)
Vale (W9)
Vama (SW10)
Veeraswamy (W1)
Zafferano (SW1)

Singles Scenes

Admiral Codrington (SW3)
Asia de Cuba (WC2)
Atlantic B&G (W1)
Avenue (SW1)
Balans (multi. loc.)
Bank Aldwych (WC2)
Bank Westminster/Zander (SW1)
Belgo Centraal (WC2)
Belgo Noord (NW1)
Belgo Zuid (W10)
Bierodrome (multi. loc.)
Big Easy (SW3)
Bistrot 190 (SW7)
Bluebird (SW3)
Brinkley's (SW10)
Browns Rest. (multi. loc.)
Buona Sera at the Jam (SW3)
Cactus Blue (SW3)
Cafe Pacifico (WC2)

Special Feature Index

Cantaloupe (EC2)
Cecconi's (W1)
Cellar Gascon (EC1)
Che (SW1)
Christopher's (multi. loc.)
Circus (W1)
Collection (SW3)
E&O (W11)
Ebury Wine Bar (SW1)
Engineer (NW1)
Enterprise (SW3)
Fifth Floor Cafe (SW1)
First Floor (W11)
George Bar (EC2)
Hakkasan (W1)
Hush (W1)
Just St. James's (SW1)
Kettners (W1)
La Perla B&G (multi. loc.)
La Rueda (multi. loc.)
Manor (W11)
Maroush (multi. loc.)
Mezzo (W1)
Mezzonine (W1)
Momo (W1)
Moro (EC1)
Motcomb's (SW1)
Nam Long Le Shaker (SW5)
Noble Rot (W1)
Nobu (W1)
Oriel (SW1)
Oxo Tower (SE1)
Oxo Tower Brasserie (SE1)
Pharmacy (W11)
Pizza on the Park (SW1)
PJ's Bar & Grill (SW3)
PJ's Grill (WC2)
Putney Bridge (SW15)
Quaglino's (SW1)
Red Cube B&G (WC2)
Smiths of Smithfield - Din. (EC1)
Spiga (multi. loc.)
Spighetta (W1)
Spoon+ at Sanderson (W1)
Sticky Fingers (W8)
Stream, Bubble & Shell (EC1)
Sugar Reef (W1)
Sumosan (W1)
Teatro (W1)
Terminus (EC2)
Texas Embassy Cantina (SW1)
Waterloo Fire Station (SE1)
West Street (WC2)
Zinc B&G (W1)
Zuma (SW7)

Sleepers
(Good to excellent food, but little known)
Al San Vincenzo (W2)
Arancia (SE16)
Blue Jade (SW1)
Byron's (NW3)
Champor-Champor (SE1)
Chinon (W14)
Cinnamon Cay (SW11)
Creelers (SW3)
Diverso (W1)
Esarn Kheaw (W12)
Fina Estampa (SE1)
Galicia (W10)
Gladwins (EC3)
Ikeda (W1)
Ishbilia (SW1)
Kandoo (W2)
Kastoori (SW17)
L'Accento Italiano (W2)
Lee Fook (W2)
Lobster Pot (SE11)
Manor (W11)
Mesclun (N16)
Metrogusto (multi. loc.)
Nautilus Fish (NW6)
Original Tagine (W1)
Parade (W5)
Parsee (N19)
Pizzeria Castello (SE1)
Quilon (SW1)
Rani (N3)
Redmonds (SW14)
Saga (W1)
Stepping Stone (SW8)
Stratford's (W8)
Tabla (E14)
Tenth (W8)
Terrace (W8)
Tsunami (SW4)
Vrisaki (N22)
Yoshino (W1)
Yum Yum Thai (N16)
Zamoyski (NW3)

Smoking Prohibited
(May be permissable at bar)
Books for Cooks (W11)
Busaba Eathai (W1)
Cafe at Sotheby's (W1)
Cafe, Level Seven (SE1)
Chutney's (NW1)
Clarke's (W8)
Crescent (W1)
Food for Thought (WC2)
Giraffe (multi. loc.)

Special Feature Index

Gravetye Manor (W. Sus)
Hartwell House (Bucks)
itsu (W1)
Kaifeng (NW4)
Le Manoir/Quat'Saisons (Oxon)
Mandalay (W2)
Masala Zone (W1)
Mildreds (W1)
Mju (SW1)
Moshi Moshi Sushi (EC2)
Place Below (EC2)
Portrait (WC2)
Providores/Tapa Rm. (W1)
Rainforest Cafe (W1)
Rasa (multi. loc.)
Satsuma (W1)
Sir Charles Napier (Oxon)
Spighetta (W1)
T.G.I. Friday's (multi. loc.)
Tom's Deli (W11)
Truc Vert (W1)
Villandry (W1)
Wagamama (multi. loc.)
Yo! Sushi (multi. loc.)

Special Occasions

Almeida (N1)
Asia de Cuba (WC2)
Aubergine (SW10)
Avenue (SW1)
Belvedere (W8)
Bibendum (SW3)
Blakes Hotel (SW7)
Blue Elephant (SW6)
Brown's Hotel, 1837 (W1)
Capital (SW3)
Cecconi's (W1)
Chez Bruce (SW17)
Cinnamon Club (SW1)
Clarke's (W8)
Club Gascon (EC1)
Connaught (W1)
Criterion Grill (W1)
Daphne's (SW3)
Dorchester, Grill Rm. (W1)
Dorchester, Oriental (W1)
Drones (SW1)
Foliage (SW1)
French Horn (Berks)
Glasshouse (Kew)
Gordon Ramsay/Claridge's (W1)
Gordon Ramsay/68 Royal (SW3)
Goring Dining Rm. (SW1)
Gravetye Manor (W. Sus)
Greenhouse (W1)
Hartwell House (Bucks)
I-Thai (W2)

Ivy (WC2)
John Burton-Race (NW1)
J. Sheekey (WC2)
Lanesborough (SW1)
La Tante Claire (SW1)
La Trompette (W4)
Launceston Place (W8)
Le Caprice (SW1)
Le Gavroche (W1)
Le Manoir/Quat'Saisons (Oxon)
Le Pont de la Tour (SE1)
Le Soufflé (W1)
Locanda Locatelli (W1)
L'Oranger (SW1)
Lundum's (SW7)
Mirabelle (W1)
Mju (SW1)
Momo (W1)
Nahm (W1)
Neal Street (WC2)
Nobu (W1)
Orrery (W1)
Pétrus (SW1)
Pied à Terre (W1)
Providores/Tapa Rm. (W1)
QC (WC1)
Quaglino's (SW1)
Quo Vadis (W1)
Richard Corrigan/Lindsay (W1)
Ritz (W1)
River Cafe (W6)
San Lorenzo (SW3)
Sartoria (W1)
Savoy River (WC2)
Smiths of Smithfield - Din. (EC1)
Smiths of Smithfield-Top (EC1)
Spoon+ at Sanderson (W1)
Square (W1)
Sumosan (W1)
Toto's (SW3)
Ubon (E14)
Vong (SW1)
Waterside Inn (Berks)
West Street (WC2)
Wilton's (SW1)
Windows on the World (W1)
Zafferano (SW1)
Zaika (W8)
Zuma (SW7)

Sunday Dining

(B=brunch; L=lunch;
D=dinner; plus all hotels
and most Asians)
Abingdon (W8) (B,L,D)
Admiral Codrington (SW3) (B,L,D)
Admiralty (WC2) (L,D)

Special Feature Index

Al Duca (SW1) (L,D)
Al Hamra (W1) (L,D)
Al Sultan (W1) (L,D)
Anglesea Arms (W6) (L,D)
Arkansas Cafe (E1) (L)
Asia de Cuba (WC2) (D)
Avenue (SW1) (B,L,D)
Bank Aldwych (WC2) (B,D)
Belair House (SE21) (L,D)
Belgo Centraal (WC2) (L,D)
Belgo Noord (NW1) (L,D)
Belgo Zuid (W10) (L,D)
Belvedere (W8) (L,D)
Bengal Clipper (SE1) (L,D)
Bentley's (W1) (L,D)
Bibendum (SW3) (L,D)
Bibendum Oyster Bar (SW3) (L,D)
Big Easy (SW3) (L,D)
Bistrot 190 (SW7) (B,D)
Black Truffle (NW1) (D)
Bloom's (NW11) (L,D)
Bluebird (SW3) (B,D)
Blue Elephant (SW6) (L,D)
Blue Print Cafe (SE1) (L,D)
Brackenbury (W6) (L,D)
Builders Arms (SW3) (L,D)
Busaba Eathai (W1) (L,D)
Butlers Wharf (SE1) (B,L)
Cactus Blue (SW3) (B,L,D)
Cafe Lazeez (multi. loc.) (L,D)
Cafe, Level Seven (SE1) (L)
Cafe Pacifico (WC2) (L,D)
Cantaloupe (EC2) (B)
Cantina del Ponte (SE1) (L,D)
Cantina Vinopolis (SE1) (B,L)
Cantinetta Venegazzu (SW11) (L,D)
Canyon (Richmond) (B,D)
Casale Franco (N1) (L,D)
Chez Bruce (SW17) (L)
Chez Max (SW10) (L,D)
Chiswick, The (W4) (B,L)
Christopher's (WC2) (B)
Chutney Mary (SW10) (B)
Coq d'Argent (EC2) (D)
Creelers (SW3) (B,L,D)
Crescent (W1) (B,L,D)
Criterion Grill (W1) (D)
Crivelli's Garden (WC2) (L)
Dakota (W11) (B,L,D)
Daphne's (SW3) (B,L,D)
Del Buongustaio (SW15) (L,D)
Drones (SW1) (L,D)
Eagle (EC1) (B,L)
Electric Brasserie (W11) (B)
El Gaucho (SW3) (L,D)
English Garden (SW3) (L,D)
Enterprise (SW3) (L,D)

Fairuz (W1) (L,D)
Fakhreldine Exp. (multi. loc.) (L,D)
ffiona's (W8) (B,D)
Fifth Floor (SW1) (L)
Fifth Floor Cafe (SW1) (L)
French Horn (Berks) (L)
Glasshouse (Kew) (L)
Gopal's of Soho (W1) (L,D)
Greens (SW1) (L,D)
Grenadier (SW1) (L,D)
Hakkasan (W1) (L,D)
Hard Rock Cafe (W1) (L,D)
House/Rosslyn Hill (NW3) (L,D)
Ifield (SW10) (L,D)
itsu (multi. loc.) (L,D)
Ivy (WC2) (L,D)
Jason's (W9) (B,L)
Joe Allen (WC2) (B,L,D)
Joe's (SW3) (B,L)
J. Sheekey (WC2) (L,D)
Julie's (W11) (L,D)
Kai (W1) (L,D)
Kensington Place (W8) (B,L,D)
La Brasserie (SW3) (B,L,D)
La Famiglia (SW10) (L,D)
La Fontana (SW1) (L,D)
Langan's Coq d'Or (SW5) (B,L,D)
La Porte des Indes (W1) (B,D)
La Poule au Pot (SW1) (L,D)
La Trompette (W4) (L,D)
Launceston Place (W8) (L,D)
L'Aventure (NW8) (L,D)
Le Caprice (SW1) (B,L,D)
Le Colombier (SW3) (L,D)
Lemonia (NW1) (L)
Le Pont de la Tour (SE1) (D)
Le Suquet (SW3) (L,D)
Levant (W1) (L,D)
L'Incontro (SW1) (D)
Livebait (multi. loc.) (L,D)
Lola's (N1) (B,L,D)
Lomo (SW10) (L,D)
Lundum's (SW7) (B)
Made in Italy (SW3) (L,D)
Maroush (multi. loc.) (L,D)
Masala Zone (W1) (L,D)
Mediterraneo (W11) (L,D)
Mela (WC2) (L,D)
Mezzo (W1) (L,D)
Mirabelle (W1) (L,D)
Monsieur Max (Hampton Hill) (L)
Montana (SW6) (B,D)
Montpeliano (SW7) (L,D)
Motcomb's (SW1) (B,L)
Nahm (SW1) (D)
Nobu (W1) (D)
Odette's (NW1) (L)

216   www.zagat.com

Special Feature Index

Oliveto (SW1) (L,D)
Olivo (SW1) (D)
One-O-One (SW1) (L,D)
Oriel (SW1) (L,D)
Original Tagine (W1) (D)
Orrery (W1) (L,D)
Orsino (W11) (L,D)
Orso (WC2) (L,D)
Osteria Basilico (W11) (L,D)
Oxo Tower (SE1) (L,D)
Oxo Tower Brasserie (SE1) (L,D)
Ozer Rest. & Bar (W1) (D)
Parade (W5) (L,D)
Parisienne Chophse. (SW3) (L,D)
Parsee (N19) (L,D)
Patara (multi. loc.) (L,D)
People's Palace (SE1) (L,D)
Pharmacy (W11) (B,L,D)
Phoenicia (W8) (L,D)
Phoenix B&G (SW15) (B,L,D)
Pizza Express (multi. loc.) (L,D)
Pizza Metro (SW11) (L,D)
Pizza on the Park (SW1) (L,D)
PJ's Bar & Grill (SW3) (B,L,D)
PJ's Grill (WC2) (B,L,D)
Planet Hollywood (W1) (L,D)
Porters (WC2) (L,D)
Portrait (WC2) (L)
Putney Bridge (SW15) (L)
Quaglino's (SW1) (L,D)
Quality Chop Hse. (EC1) (B,L,D)
Rainforest Cafe (W1) (L,D)
Ransome's Dock (SW11) (B)
Redmonds (SW14) (B,L)
Red Pepper (W9) (L,D)
Rib Room/Oyster Bar (SW1) (L,D)
Riccardo's (SW3) (L,D)
Richoux (multi. loc.) (B,L,D)
Riva (SW13) (L,D)
River Cafe (W6) (L)
Rodizio Rico (W2) (L,D)
Rosmarino (NW8) (L,D)
Rowley's (SW1) (L,D)
Royal China (multi. loc.) (L,D)
Rules (WC2) (L,D)
Salusbury Pub (NW6) (B,L,D)
Sandrini (SW3) (L,D)
San Lorenzo Fuoriporta (SW19) (L,D)
Santa Fe (N1) (L,D)
Santini (SW1) (D)
Sarkhel's (SW18) (L,D)
Sartoria (W1) (D)
Scalini (SW3) (L,D)
Searcy's/Barbican (EC2) (L,D)
Shogun (W1) (D)
Simpson's/Strand/Grand (WC2) (L,D)
Smiths/Smithfield-Top (EC1) (B,L,D)
Sofra (multi. loc.) (L,D)
Solly's (NW11) (L,D)
Sonny's (SW13) (L)
Souk (WC2) (L,D)
Spiga (multi. loc.) (L,D)
Spighetta (W1) (D)
Spoon+/Sanderson (W1) (B,L,D)
Square (W1) (D)
Sticky Fingers (W8) (L,D)
Stratford's (W8) (L,D)
Sugar Club (W1) (L,D)
Suntory (SW1) (D)
Tamarind (W1) (L,D)
Tandoori of Chelsea (SW3) (L,D)
Tate Gallery Rest. (SW1) (L)
Terminus (EC2) (L,D)
Texas Embassy (SW1) (L,D)
T.G.I. Friday's (multi. loc.) (B,L,D)
Thierry's (SW3) (L,D)
Tom's Deli (W11) (B)
Tootsies (multi. loc.) (B,L,D)
Toto's (SW3) (L,D)
Tuttons Brasserie (WC2) (L,D)
Vale (W9) (B,L)
Vama (SW10) (L,D)
Veeraswamy (W1) (L,D)
Villandry (W1) (B,L)
Vingt-Quatre (SW10) (B,L,D)
Vong (SW1) (L,D)
Wilton's (SW1) (L,D)
Windows on the World (W1) (B)
Zafferano (SW1) (L,D)
Zaika (W8) (L,D)
Ziani (SW3) (L,D)

Tea Service

(See also Hotel Dining)
Berkeley Hotel (SW1)
Blakes Hotel (SW7)
Brown's Hotel (W1)
Cafe at Sotheby's (W1)
Cafe, Level Seven (SE1)
Capital (SW3)
Claridge's Hotel (W1)
Connaught (W1)
Criterion Grill (W1)
Dorchester, The (W1)
Emporio Armani Caffe (SW3)
Four Seasons Hotel (W1)
Goring Dining Rm. (SW1)
Hartwell House (Bucks)
Landmark London (NW1)
Lanesborough (SW1)
Mandarin Oriental Hyde Pk. (SW1)

Special Feature Index

Nicole's (W1)
One Aldwych (WC2)
Palm Court (WC2)
Patisserie Valerie (multi. loc.)
Portrait (WC2)
Richoux (multi. loc.)
Ritz Hotel (W1)
Savoy Hotel (WC2)
St. Martin's Ln. Hotel (WC2)
Tuscan Steak (WC2)
Waterstones Red Rm. (W1)

Visitors on Expense Account

Almeida (N1)
Asia de Cuba (WC2)
Aurora (EC2)
Bank Aldwych (WC2)
Bank Westminster/Zander (SW1)
Belair House (SE21)
Belvedere (W8)
Bentley's (W1)
Bibendum (SW3)
Bice (W1)
Blakes Hotel (SW7)
Brown's Hotel, 1837 (W1)
Capital (SW3)
Caravaggio (EC3)
Caviar Kaspia (W1)
Cecconi's (W1)
Christopher's (multi. loc.)
City Rhodes (EC4)
Clarke's (W8)
Club Gascon (EC1)
Connaught (W1)
Coq d'Argent (EC2)
Criterion Grill (W1)
Daphne's (SW3)
Dorchester, Grill Rm. (W1)
Drones (SW1)
Elena's l'Etoile (W1)
Embassy (W1)
English Garden (SW3)
Fifth Floor (SW1)
Floriana (SW3)
Foliage (SW1)
Four Seasons, Lanes (W1)
Glasshouse (Kew)
Gordon Ramsay/Claridge's (W1)
Gordon Ramsay/68 Royal (SW3)
Gravetye Manor (W. Sus)
Greenhouse (W1)
Greens (SW1)
Incognico (WC2)
I-Thai (W2)
Ivy (WC2)
John Burton-Race (NW1)
J. Sheekey (WC2)
Kai (W1)
Lanesborough (SW1)
Langan's Brasserie (W1)
La Tante Claire (SW1)
Launceston Place (W8)
Le Caprice (SW1)
Le Gavroche (W1)
Le Manoir/Quat'Saisons (Oxon)
Le Pont de la Tour (SE1)
L'Incontro (SW1)
Locanda Locatelli (W1)
L'Oranger (SW1)
Maison Novelli (EC1)
Matsuri (SW1)
Mirabelle (W1)
Mitsukoshi (SW1)
Mju (SW1)
Nahm (SW1)
Neal Street (WC2)
Nobu (W1)
Odin's (W1)
One-O-One (SW1)
Orrery (W1)
Oxo Tower (SE1)
Pétrus (SW1)
Pied à Terre (W1)
Poissonnerie de l'Avenue (SW3)
Providores/Tapa Rm. (W1)
Quaglino's (SW1)
Red Fort (W1)
Rhodes in the Square (SW1)
Ritz (W1)
Riva (SW13)
River Cafe (W6)
San Lorenzo (SW3)
Santini (SW1)
Sartoria (W1)
Savoy Grill (WC2)
Savoy River (WC2)
Shogun (W1)
Smiths of Smithfield-Top (EC1)
Spoon+ at Sanderson (W1)
Square (W1)
Sumosan (W1)
Suntory (SW1)
Tamarind (W1)
Tatsuso (EC1)
Tuscan Steak (WC2)
Ubon (E14)
Vong (SW1)
Waterside Inn (Berks)
Wilton's (SW1)
Windows on the World (W1)
Zafferano (SW1)

Special Feature Index

Zaika (W8)
Zen Central (W1)
Zuma (SW7)

Water Views
Blue Print Cafe (SE1)
Butlers Wharf Chop Hse. (SE1)
Cantina del Ponte (SE1)
Canyon (Richmond)
County Hall (SE1)
Feng Shang Floating Rest. (NW1)
Fish! (E14)
Four Regions (SE1)
Four Seasons, Quadrato (E14)
French Horn (Berks)
Jason's (W9)
Just the Bridge (EC4)
Le Pont de la Tour (SE1)
Oxo Tower (SE1)
Oxo Tower Brasserie (SE1)
People's Palace (SE1)
Putney Bridge (SW15)
Ransome's Dock (SW11)
River Cafe (W6)
Savoy River (WC2)
Thai on the River (SW10)
Ubon (E14)
Waterside Inn (Berks)

Winning Wine Lists
Aubergine (SW10)
Belvedere (W8)
Bibendum (SW3)
Boisdale (multi. loc.)
Brown's Hotel, 1837 (W1)
Cafe at Sotheby's (W1)
Cantina Vinopolis (SE1)
Cantinetta Venegazzu (SW11)
Capital (SW3)
Caravaggio (EC3)
Cecconi's (W1)
Cellar Gascon (EC1)
Che (SW1)
Chez Bruce (SW17)
Christopher's (WC2)
Clarke's (W8)
Club Gascon (EC1)
Criterion Grill (W1)
Dorchester, Grill Rm. (W1)
Drones (SW1)
Ebury Wine Bar (SW1)
Embassy (W1)
Enoteca Turi (SW15)
Fifth Floor (SW1)
Foliage (SW1)
Four Seasons, Lanes (W1)
Glasshouse (Kew)
Gordon Ramsay/Claridge's (W1)
Gordon Ramsay/68 Royal (SW3)
Gravetye Manor (W. Sus)
Il Convivio (SW1)
Isola (SW1)
John Burton-Race (NW1)
Lanesborough (SW1)
Langan's Bistro (W1)
La Tante Claire (SW1)
La Trompette (W4)
Le Gavroche (W1)
Le Manoir/Quat'Saisons (Oxon)
Le Metro (SW3)
Le Pont de la Tour (SE1)
L'Escargot (W1)
Le Soufflé (W1)
L'Incontro (SW1)
Locanda Locatelli (W1)
L'Oranger (SW1)
Mirabelle (W1)
Monkeys (SW3)
Odette's (NW1)
Orrery (W1)
Pétrus (SW1)
Pied à Terre (W1)
Prism (EC3)
Ransome's Dock (SW11)
Rib Room/Oyster Bar (SW1)
Richard Corrigan/Lindsay (W1)
Ritz (W1)
R.S.J. (SE1)
Sartoria (W1)
Savoy Grill (WC2)
Savoy River (WC2)
Square (W1)
Tate Gallery Rest. (SW1)
TECA (W1)
Vineyard/Stockcross (Berks)
Waterside Inn (Berks)
Wilton's (SW1)
Windows on the World (W1)
Zafferano (SW1)

Wine Vintage Chart 1985–2000

This chart is designed to help you select wine to go with your meal. It is based on the same 0 to 30 scale used throughout this *Survey*. The ratings (prepared by our friend **Howard Stravitz**, a law professor at the University of South Carolina) reflect both the quality of the vintage and the wine's readiness for present consumption. Thus, if a wine is not fully mature or is over the hill, its rating has been reduced. We do not include 1987, 1991–1993 vintages because they are not especially recommended for most areas.

	'85	'86	'88	'89	'90	'94	'95	'96	'97	'98	'99	'00
WHITES												
French:												
Alsace	24	18	22	28	28	26	25	23	23	25	23	25
Burgundy	24	24	18	26	21	22	27	28	25	24	25	–
Loire Valley	–	–	–	26	25	22	24	26	23	22	24	–
Champagne	28	25	24	26	29	–	24	27	24	24	–	–
Sauternes	22	28	29	25	27	–	22	23	24	24	–	20
California:												
Chardonnay	–	–	–	–	–	21	26	22	25	24	25	–
REDS												
French:												
Bordeaux	26	27	25	28	29	24	26	25	23	24	22	25
Burgundy	23	–	22	26	29	20	26	27	25	23	26	–
Rhône	25	19	26	29	28	23	25	22	24	28	26	–
Beaujolais	–	–	–	–	–	–	22	20	24	22	24	–
California:												
Cab./Merlot	26	26	–	21	28	27	26	24	28	23	26	–
Zinfandel	–	–	–	–	–	26	24	25	23	24	25	–
Italian:												
Tuscany	26	–	24	–	26	23	25	19	28	24	25	–
Piedmont	25	–	25	28	28	–	24	26	28	26	25	–

Finally...dinner AND *a movie!*

ZAGATSURVEY

MOVIE GUIDE

Watch it on

E

Enjoy the Show.

After 20+ years of helping choose the right restaurant, Zagat Survey is now helping you with the rest of the evening's entertainment by introducing the Zagat Survey Movie Guide, covering the top 1,000 films of all time. Ratings and reviews are by avid moviegoers, i.e., people like you.

So, where are you going *after* dinner?

ZAGATSURVEY

LONDON NIGHTLIFE

Check out the new Zagat Survey London Nightlife guide, available in December. Hundreds of pubs, lounges and clubs rated by thousands of night-crawlin' Londoners.